ELITE PREDATORS
FROM JIMMY SAVILE AND LORD MOUNTBATTEN TO JEFFREY EPSTEIN AND GHISLAINE MAXWELL

WAR ON DRUGS BOOK 6
SHAUN ATTWOOD

First published in Great Britain by Gadfly Press in 2022

Copyright © Shaun Attwood 2022

The right of Shaun Attwood to be identified as the author of this work has been asserted by him in accordance with the Copyright, Designs and Patents Act 1988. All rights reserved

No part of this book may be reproduced, stored in a retrieval system or transmitted in any form or by any means (electronic, mechanical, photocopying, recording or otherwise) without the prior written permission of the author, except in cases of brief quotations embodied in reviews or articles. It may not be edited, amended, lent, resold, hired out, distributed or otherwise circulated without the publisher's written permission

Permission can be obtained from gadflypress@outlook.com

This book is a work of non-fiction based on research by the author

A catalogue record of this book is available from the British Library

Typeset and cover design by Jane Dixon-Smith

ISBN 978-1-912885-24-4

SPELLING DIFFERENCES: UK V USA

This book was written in UK English, so USA readers may notice some spelling differences with American English: e.g. color = colour, meter = metre and pedophile = paedophile

DEDICATION

This book is dedicated to all of the brave survivors who helped to bring some of these monsters to justice including Juliette Bryant, Maria and Annie Farmer and Virginia Giuffre

SHAUN'S BOOKS

English Shaun Trilogy
Party Time
Hard Time
Prison Time

War on Drugs Series
Pablo Escobar: Beyond Narcos
American Made: Who Killed Barry Seal?
Pablo Escobar or George HW Bush
The Cali Cartel: Beyond Narcos
Clinton Bush and CIA Conspiracies:
From the Boys on the Tracks to Jeffrey Epstein
Who Killed Epstein? Prince Andrew or Bill Clinton

Un-Making a Murderer:
The Framing of Steven Avery and Brendan Dassey
The Mafia Philosopher: Two Tonys
Life Lessons

Pablo Escobar's Story (3-book series)

SOCIAL-MEDIA LINKS

Email: attwood.shaun@hotmail.co.uk
YouTube: Shaun Attwood
Blog: Jon's Jail Journal
Website: shaunattwood.com
Instagram: @shaunattwood
Twitter: @shaunattwood
LinkedIn: Shaun Attwood
Goodreads: Shaun Attwood
Facebook: Shaun Attwood, Jon's Jail Journal,
T-Bone Appreciation Society

Shaun welcomes feedback on any of his books and YouTube videos. Thank you for the Amazon and Goodreads reviews and to all of the people who have subscribed to Shaun's YouTube channel!

CONTENTS

Chapter 1: Ghislaine Maxwell's Monstrous Father	1
Chapter 2: Prince Andrew aka Randy Andy	32
Chapter 3: Lord Mountbatten's Lust For Boys	54
Chapter 4: Global Human Trafficking	73
Chapter 5: Billionaire Predator Peter Nygård	91
Chapter 6: Ghislaine Maxwell Meets Epstein	121
Chapter 7: My Two Years with Epstein and Maxwell - Juliette Bryant	143
Chapter 8: Ghislaine Maxwell's Trial	153
Chapter 9: Jimmy Savile's Abuse Begins	187
Chapter 10: Untouchable Jimmy Savile	208
Who Killed Epstein? Prince Andrew or Bill Clinton	246
Other Books by Gadfly Press	252
Hard Time by Shaun Attwood	264
Prison Time by Shaun Attwood	271
About the Author	276

CHAPTER 1

GHISLAINE MAXWELL'S MONSTROUS FATHER

Epstein survivor, Maria Farmer, described how Ghislaine could flip in an instant from charming and breezy, the life of the party, to stone-cold evil. Maria was referring to occasions in New York when, fresh from her latest shopping trip, Ghislaine would be giddy with happiness at her acquisitions then, with the flip of a switch, her whole manner and expression would change as she said, "I'm going out to get the nubiles." She was referring to her trips, scouring the streets of New York for high-school girls, some as young as thirteen, whom she would offer up to her paedophile partner, Jeffrey Epstein, on the pretence that they would be auditioning for positions as Victoria's Secret models.

Maria described Ghislaine, a woman who phoned her over a period of years to issue death threats down the phone, as a psychopath, a Jekyll-and-Hyde character and, "the most terrifying person I've ever met in my life." But how did the apparently happy-go-lucky rich kid of the press spotlight develop such a dark side to her personality? How did Ghislaine go from spoilt socialite to paedophile's procurer? The answer lies, as it so often does, in her past.

Born on Christmas Day, 1961, the eighth child of Robert and Elisabeth Maxwell, Ghislaine had been wished for by both parents as a way to partly assuage the loss of their other baby girl, Karine, who died at age three from leukaemia, just four years earlier. But instead of providing relief, Ghislaine's birth only heralded further tragedy. Two days later, on a car journey home from a Christmas dance at a friend's house in Oxfordshire, Robert and Betty's oldest son, Michael, was involved in a car crash. The sixteen-year-old boy – his father's favourite – was left in a coma, which would last another seven years before he was ultimately declared brain-dead and allowed to die.

According to Betty Maxwell in her memoir, *A Mind of my Own*, the whole family was so torn apart by grief that new-born Ghislaine was hardly spared a glance. This lack of attention affected the young toddler so badly that she became afflicted with a kind of anorexia, refusing to eat her food at meal times. Betty recounted how, "One day, aged three, she planted herself in front of me and said simply, 'Mummy, I exist.'" It was a devastating blow and a shocking admission, but what happened next might have played just as important a part in the formation of Ghislaine's character as the early neglect. Wracked with guilt, the whole family started showering Ghislaine with attention from then on. Everyone fussed over her so much that, according to Betty, "She became spoiled, the only one of my children I can truly say that about."

Perhaps this is one of the reasons Ghislaine became her father's favourite. The media tycoon, owner of the Mirror Group Newspapers, named his super-yacht, the Lady Ghislaine, after her, and even staff at his various companies noticed the favouritism with which he treated his youngest child. Roy Greenslade, editor of *The Daily Mirror* under Maxwell, told investigative journalist, John Sweeney, how it was clear he doted on her and that she was daddy's girl. Greenslade noted the marked difference between the way Maxwell treated Ghislaine and her older siblings, Ian and Kevin, whom he was sharp with, even in public.

Sweeney, whom I interviewed for my Epstein podcast, tells how former Private Eye editor, Richard Ingrams, believed the relationship between Maxwell and Ghislaine might have stretched the bounds of propriety between father and daughter. Ingrams recounted to Sweeney several reports of Ghislaine sitting on her father's knees, even as an adult, while he caressed her. Ingrams believed Maxwell was sexually attracted to his daughter; however, the accounts are unsubstantiated and there is no evidence of Maxwell being attracted to underage girls.

Another account highlights a distinctly sadistic side to the relationship. Eleanor Berry is an author and daughter of another newspaper magnate, who may have had an affair with Maxwell. In her book, *Robert Maxwell as I Knew Him*, Berry tells the story of how she discovered an uncomfortable secret about Maxwell's relationship with the young Ghislaine. Berry describes how the nine-year-old Ghislaine showed her an array of punitive instruments laid out on a table at the family home in Oxfordshire, including a riding crop, a ruler and a stick. According to Berry, Ghislaine told her that Daddy was nice to her because he allowed her to choose which implement she would be beaten with.

Could the stark polarities in the way Maxwell treated his daughter explain the almost schizophrenic divide in Ghislaine's personality, which Maria Farmer describes? Several observers believe that to truly know Ghislaine, you must first understand the make-up and influence of the larger-than-life figure that cast such a giant shadow over her formative years.

Robert Maxwell's was a rags-to-riches story, if ever there was one. Born in 1923 into a poor Jewish family in the village of Slatinské Doly, in what was then Czechoslovakia, the young Abraham Leib Hoch, as he was named at birth, was one of seven children, two of whom died of pneumonia in early childhood.

Maxwell's childhood was one of cold, hunger and deprivation. He later told how he and his siblings were forced to share a single pair of shoes, which they adjusted to size by stuffing them with paper. Betty Maxwell tells in her memoir how the winters were so harsh in the small village in the foothills of the Carpathian mountains that old men's beards would freeze while they slept and villagers would be forced to burn their own garden fences to keep warm. Growing up, young Leiby, as he was known to the family, lived, ate, studied and slept in a single room of his grandfather Yankel's three-room house, alongside his six siblings and his mother, Hannah and father, Mechel. The cramped conditions were supposed to be a temporary arrangement until Maxwell's young parents found their feet, but the worsening economic situation meant otherwise.

Mechel was the poorest of his brothers, who all worked in the family butcher trade. Mechel had been an apprentice butcher for his father, then went on to work for his elder brother, Lipman. However, when the Great Depression of the 1930s struck, Lipman could no longer afford to employ Mechel as an assistant butcher and the younger brother became a roving cattle buyer, searching for cheap meat to supply the butchery.

Mechel's life was one of itinerant misery, walking the length and breadth of the region from daybreak to sundown each day, to find and bargain for cheap cows. He was paid in animal hides, which he would then have to resell to leather dealers for cash. He sometimes managed to supplement this sparse income by trading the furs of foxes, rabbits and other rodents, as well as taking on casual work chopping and felling trees or haymaking in the summer. Another means of sustenance in the village was smuggling. Maxwell's grandfather, Yankel, had made his modest fortune smuggling cattle over the river and most of the village was involved in some way in contraband food, alcohol and other goods smuggled from across the border in Romania.

While Mechel was away for days on end roaming the mountains, it fell to Maxwell's mother, Hannah, to look after the upbringing of their son and six daughters. Like Mechel, she was a pious Jew, following the Hasidic branch of the faith. However, Hannah also had a strong interest in politics, particularly socialism, and was an active member of the Czech Social Democratic Party. She was also an avid reader and soon became interested in Zionism – the idea of re-establishing a homeland for the Jews in Palestine. Hannah realised early that her son was highly intelligent, with an aptitude for learning, and quickly formulated a dream of him becoming a rabbi, who would help recreate a Palestinian home for their community. Spurred on by her ambitions, she taught the young Leiby to read and write at age four.

Maxwell was a good student but already there were signs of the reckless maverick in him. At age five, and without knowing how to swim, Leiby copied the other boys by jumping off the local bridge into the fast-flowing river Tisa that ran through the town. Remarkably, he survived but got a beating from his father that, according to Betty, he remembered with a shudder, even at the age of sixty. On another occasion, the seven-year-old Maxwell gulped down a cup of alcohol that was lying around in his grandfather's house. He passed out in a gutter and was returned home by local gendarmes at three o'clock in the morning. A similarly memorable thrashing with Mechel's belt followed – the inspiration perhaps for Maxwell's later treatment of his own children. Maxwell had another brush with misadventure when a horse reared up and kicked him in the head, knocking him out and breaking his jaw. His mother rushed him to nearby Berehevo hospital in a hired sleigh, having to sell the family's only goose-feather pillow to pay for the treatment. An emergency operation ensured no lasting damage but Maxwell's jaw was secured with a metal pin for the rest of his life.

At age six, Maxwell started education in the local state primary school, where all lessons were taught in Czech. This meant, from an early age, he picked up the Czech language to add to his family's Yiddish and the other locally spoken languages, Hungarian and Romanian. Maxwell also received a traditional Jewish religious education at the local Jewish primary school, opposite his grandfather's house. These lessons would begin at five in the morning. Maxwell would then join the other students at the Czech primary from eight o'clock until four in the afternoon. After that, he would return to the religious school until half past seven in the evening. It was a long day for a young boy and it was perhaps the source of the work ethic that drove Maxwell throughout his adult life, when he would frequently survive on just five hours' sleep and work from early morning until late into the night.

What little leisure time there was, Maxwell spent swimming in the river with the other local children, wandering into the forest or playing football barefoot with a ball made from rags. Leiby was a particularly aggressive centre forward and his team invariably won the match. Already, the young Maxwell was learning to use his imposing physical presence – and an element of bullying – to get what he wanted.

As a young boy from a poor family expending so much energy, Maxwell was always hungry and dreamed of his family owning a cow. The only times when he and the other local children had their appetites fully satiated was twice yearly, when donations from an American charity of Carpathian-US emigrants called JOINT would arrive. The money, gifts and food would be distributed by the head of the community to the poorest families in the village. Despite the lack of food, on religious festivals and holidays, Hannah would strive to cook the traditional dishes, even if they called for expensive chicken, meat or fish. Somehow, with their mother's excellent cooking and their father's resourcefulness, the children always ate well on these special occasions. Such was the case on the day of Maxwell's circumcision, when Mechel threw an improvised explosive device into the river and came home with enough fish to feed all the friends and relatives attending the party.

As Maxwell grew, he followed his mother's habit of reading voraciously. He also took up her political leanings, joining a local paramilitary Zionist youth organisation. Increasingly aware of their son's precocious intellect, Mechel and Hannah resolved to send him to the local yeshiva or Jewish religious secondary school. First, he had to brush up on his Hebrew, so he was sent to stay with a family in nearby Churst, to join the son's Hebrew classes. By the age of twelve, Maxwell was ready for the yeshiva and moved to the nearby village of Sighet to study there. In Sighet, he stayed with his aunt Myriam, where, for the first time in his life, he experienced the luxury of having his own bedroom.

Maxwell's teacher was so impressed with his young student, he advised Mechel and Hannah to send the boy to the large yeshiva in Bratislava, a renowned centre of Jewish learning across all of

Europe. Hannah was delighted and made all the necessary preparations for her thirteen-year-old son to make the 500km trip to Bratislava. Maxwell would live as a boarder at the school, with his bed and breakfast provided. But, as his family could afford no more, his other meals depended on the charity of seven or eight local families, which took it in turns to feed the poorer students. It was a necessary but humiliating experience for the proud young Maxwell, having to depend on others' charity to eat and may have been one of the contributing factors to his life-long habit of gorging himself on the most expensive food and champagne.

Maxwell worked hard at the yeshiva in Bratislava, studying from 6am to 11pm most days. His phenomenal capacity for retaining information, which people would comment on throughout his life, now came to the fore. On one trip home, the local rabbi tested Maxwell on his knowledge and claimed he knew the Torah and Talmud by heart. Maxwell kept up his religious studies for the best part of two years but, in the spring term of 1938, he became disaffected with the narrowness of his education, which was restricted to the Torah and Talmud, and reflected none of the political realities that were manifesting around him. In nearby Vienna, the Nazis were already in occupation, after annexing Austria in March of that year. Maxwell began to skip school and soon decided to visit the Czech capital, Prague. He had to beg and sell trinkets to earn enough money to make the journey, but after all the effort to get there, he was refused entry to the city because he had no papers. He was suddenly made painfully aware of the limitations of his traditional Jewish appearance in the current anti-Semitic climate and he cut off his side locks and discarded his traditional Hasidic clothes and hat. Returning to Bratislava, he quit the yeshiva and began socialising with a group of similar disaffected youngsters, who met regularly to discuss the worsening political situation.

Maxwell and some of his new friends tried to join the Czech army to fight the Nazis, only to be brushed off by one of the officers, who said, "Go home, boys, we'll call you if we need you." When

Maxwell returned home for the summer holidays, his mother was so shocked and disappointed by his new appearance and manners that she banished him from the home. Maxwell was sent packing back to Bratislava, this time accompanied by his younger cousin, Michael Tabak. Without any money, it took the pair two months to reach the city, sleeping rough and begging as they made their way predominantly on foot. Back in Bratislava, Maxwell survived for a while peddling cheap jewellery, a profession which probably contributed a great deal to his famed bargaining skills later in life.

However, life in Bratislava soon became untenable. Czechoslovakia was being carved up piecemeal and Maxwell's home village was handed back to Hungary. Meanwhile, Slovakia and thus Bratislava had fallen under the protection of Nazi Germany, making it no place for two young Jews to hang around. Maxwell and his cousin began the slow journey home, which this time took a month. Maxwell was now nearly sixteen, tall, slim and strikingly handsome. He yearned to escape the village of his birth and make his way to freedom, to fight the Nazis. After much discussion with his mother, who had now forgiven him, Maxwell and his cousin, Tabak, decided to head for Budapest, where they could find work and ultimately seek passage to Palestine or the West.

It was a 350km walk to Budapest. When they arrived in late 1939, the two cousins found lodging with another of Maxwell's cousins, who had moved to Budapest earlier. Maxwell found a job as a delivery boy and soon made connections with the local underground. Maxwell helped the organisation by aiding Czech refugees arriving in Budapest, finding them shelter in local safe houses. After changing his name to Jan Hoch, he was promoted to helping teams of Czech refugees escape across the border to Yugoslavia, where they would join the French Foreign Legion and make their way via Greece, Turkey and Lebanon to the Legion's base in Algeria.

It was on one of these dangerous missions that Maxwell was caught on the border by Hungarian police and transported back to Budapest, accused of spying. As the leader of the expedition,

Maxwell was sentenced to death. Fortunately, the French authorities intervened and pointed out that, as he was still a minor, he couldn't be given the death penalty. An appeal trial was set for the end of January 1940, but Maxwell was not prepared to take his chances with Hungarian justice. On the way to the court, he hit his guard over the head with his manacles and fled, making his way to the French embassy.

Maxwell now joined one of the escape teams he had previously been leading and made his way across the Yugoslav border to Belgrade. Via Turkey, Syria and Palestine, Maxwell, now calling himself Ludvik Hoch, eventually made it to France by mid-1940, where he transferred from the Foreign Legion to the Free Czech army. Trained as a motorcycle sidecar machine gunner, he was sent to the front line to help hold back the crushing German advance. Tasked with protecting the French army's retreat, Maxwell's regiment was overtaken by the swiftness of the German advance and routed, with many of the officers deserting, leaving the troops to their own devices.

Czech soldiers fighting for the Allies were earmarked for death by the Wehrmacht, so Maxwell and the rest of his regiment fled towards the Mediterranean coast. On his way, Maxwell recounted spending an uncomfortable night in the Roquefort cheese caves. For the rest of his life, he couldn't bear the smell of this particular cheese because of the terrifying memories it brought back. Maxwell and 1,600 fellow Czech survivors eventually made it to Sete on the French Mediterranean coast, just in time to be picked up by the British navy, which transported him to Gibraltar and onward to Liverpool, where he arrived in July 1940, a gangly emaciated teenager who spoke no English, called Ludvik Hoch.

In England, he joined the rest of the free Czech forces near Chester, but he became involved in a rebellion by 500 of the soldiers, who refused to take orders from the officers who had abandoned them in France and had escaped to England before the rest of the troops. He was transferred to a military prison camp in Sutton Coldfield near Birmingham and then discharged from the Czech legion. It was in Sutton Coldfield that he met the woman, Hazel, who would teach him English and with whom he probably had an affair.

Maxwell quickly applied to join the British army and was accepted for the Pioneer Corps, where he spent almost three years alongside other foreign troops doing menial jobs around the country, like quarrying slate or building roads, huts and ammunition dumps. Suffering from pain in his abdomen, he had his appendix removed and was sent to a convalescent hospital near Cambridge. It was here that he met and fell in love with a young nurse. She introduced him to her middle-class family and Maxwell began to learn English manners, to go with his rapidly improving command of the language.

It was in another hospital that Maxwell's English education continued. After breaking a thumb in a fight with another soldier, he ended up convalescing in Bedford, where he met an older woman called Mrs Tillard, who had lost her only son in a bombing raid over Germany. Mrs Tillard mothered the young Maxwell and introduced him to a widow called Sylvia, with whom he fell in love. Through these two women, Maxwell was introduced to higher-class families, whose manners he imitated, trying to present himself as the quintessential English gentleman. His love affair with Sylvia also left a lasting impression on him. He later told Betty, "She was the turning point of my first life. With her, I turned from an adolescent into a man, and with her, I left behind all that was unsettled in me, all my youth."

Sylvia also helped Maxwell transfer to a unit that would enable him to fight the Germans. She introduced him to an infantry commander called Brigadier Carthew-Yorstoun, who agreed to put in a word for the eager young soldier. In October 1943, Maxwell finally got his transfer. He was assigned to the North Staffordshire regiment, stationed near Margate. As a foreigner from a German-occupied country, he had to be given a new name. No stranger to name changes, Maxwell chose the apparently refined-sounding Leslie Ivan du Maurier, based on his favourite brand of cigarettes.

Maxwell got straight into training for the D-Day invasion and, by May 1944, due to being a good shot and almost recklessly brave, he had risen to the position of sniper sergeant. By July, he was in Normandy and soon had his first engagement in a little village near Bayeux. Although he was terrified throughout, he did well enough for his commanding officer to recommend him for a commission to become an officer, but it was turned down because he was not a British national.

His most memorable battle came at a bridge across the River Orne. The British had forced a bridgehead over the river but faced a heavy counterattack by the 11th SS Panzer Division. As panicking soldiers began to flee back across the bridge, Maxwell stood there in the open with his machine gun, threatening to shoot them himself if they didn't hold their positions. His bravery and uncompromising leadership in this action were contrasted by a more compassionate side of his character. Seeing a young combat engineer, shell-shocked and unable to move on the bank of the river, Maxwell ran over to him under heavy shelling, threw him over his shoulder and ran him back to a house, where he could receive medical attention.

After the battle of the Orne, Maxwell was again recommended for a commission, which he this time received. But it had come at a price. The North Staffs had been involved in such heavy fighting in Normandy that they had lost 555 men. They were so badly decimated that the regiment was disbanded and the survivors sent to other units. Maxwell was sent to Arras to become an intelligence officer, where his knowledge of several European languages, including German, would be an asset in interrogating the thousands of Axis troops that had already surrendered or been captured.

After brief sojourns in Arras and Brussels, Maxwell, now self-styled Leslie Jones, obtained seven days' leave in Paris. He headed for the French Welcome Committee, which paired battle-weary Allied officers with local Parisians. At the Welcome Committee office, he spotted across the room a young woman, whom he described as having "the most lovely pair of blue eyes I had ever seen. She had a lovely look of slight childish desperation as she was talked to by so many people at the same time. I loved her dearly there and then. From the minute I saw her, I wanted her for my wife."

Elisabeth Meynard couldn't have been more different from her future husband. Shy and unassuming, cultured, delicate and polite, Betty was born in 1921 in a small village in southeast France, into a protestant Christian family. Her father was a cavalry officer with a distinguished service record in the First World War. Her mother was a frail but courageous woman, who had also won medals for her bravery as a telephone operator in the Great War. Elisabeth had an idyllic childhood in a massive ten-bedroom house near the town of La Grive, where she played, explored the vast grounds and got into various scrapes with her elder sister, Vonnic.

As the daughter of the most important family in the town, who owned the local silk factory, Betty had a privileged upbringing. At school, her and her sister's desks were at the front of the class, separated by an extra row from the rest of the students. Their coat hooks were similarly kept apart, to prevent them from catching lice from the poorer children. Betty's father was one of the first men in France to own a motor car and the family travelled all over the country on long trips, visiting friends and relatives and famous tourist destinations. One of Betty's earliest memories was of getting lost on a beach near Calais and being returned to her family by a kind Englishman – a foreshadowing perhaps of how another Englishman would sweep her off her feet and 'rescue' her from the crowds at the Welcome Committee Office in Paris.

Things changed, however, with the great Crash of 1929 and the subsequent Depression. In 1932, the silk factory went into liquidation and the family were forced to leave their grand mansion in the country for more modest accommodation in Lyon. Betty's mother opened a boarding school. Meanwhile, Betty, aged just ten, was sent to join her sister in a convent school in England.

Betty spent five months with the nuns and learned rudimentary English. She returned again the following year and, when she came back to France, the family move to Lyon was consolidated.

In Lyon, Betty continued her schooling, excelling at French and English, before being sent to a boarding school in Saint Omer, in the north near Calais. She stayed there until 1938, when her parents moved to Paris. Betty joined them and spent her last year of school at a college in the heart of the Jewish quarter. She graduated with a commendation and enrolled to study classics and philosophy at the Sorbonne. Her first term at the university, in the autumn of 1939, coincided with the outbreak of the Second World War. In the spring of 1940, she fell in love with a Czech airman in exile, called Mihalek. Betty was a naïve 19-year-old and the relationship was purely platonic. She exchanged letters with Mihalek until he was sent to England, where he was killed in the early days of the Battle of Britain.

To earn extra money, she found a job looking after girls in a boarding school in the suburbs of Paris. Not long after she got the position, Germany invaded the Netherlands and Belgium and all Parisian children were deported to the country. Betty and her charges found themselves in a summer camp near the resort town of Cabourg in Normandy. The Nazi advance soon reached France and Betty saw thousands of ragged French troops tramping through the lanes of Normandy, fleeing the unstoppable German Blitzkrieg.

Despite the initial signs of conflict, life continued normally for a month with the 600 children in Betty and the other adults' care, studying and going to the beach every day. Then, in June, German planes were seen overhead and, soon afterwards, the entire sky turned black. The children thought it was literally the end of the world but soon discovered that the Luftwaffe had bombed the oil reserves at Le Havre.

The next day, they were evacuated in trucks but, by the afternoon, they were being attacked by German planes. Several times, the children had to leave the vehicles and crouch in a ditch by the road as German planes strafed them with machine-gun fire. Later the same day, the captain in charge of the convoy abandoned them on a country road, after receiving orders to move out. The children were later picked up by a convoy of fleeing Moroccan troops, who gave them a lift as far as the city of Condé-sur-Noireau. Betty and the children holed up in an abandoned factory outside the city for a few days, while the surrounding area was overrun by the invading forces. She met her first occupying German soldiers when she biked into town to help one of the children, who was suffering from appendicitis. The local hospital had been captured and she had to ask the German commander for permission to use one of the ambulances to fetch the sick child. Fortunately, he agreed and the boy was saved by an operation from a German surgeon.

The children stayed in the factory for two months before returning in September to a different Paris to the one they had left. German troops marched in the streets and the children even had to share their school buildings with occupying soldiers. Life carried on as normally as it could for several months and Betty started re-attending classes at the Sorbonne. During this time, Betty managed to attract the attention of a German officer, who relentlessly wooed her, calling her at the school regularly and taking her out on dates that she was too scared to decline. Although Betty grew to like the man and found him attractive, she was glad when his unit was sent away from Paris, as the stigma of being seen out with an occupying German was embarrassing and potentially dangerous. However, Lieutenant Hoffmann probably saved her life on one occasion.

A German officer had been killed by the Resistance earlier that day and the Nazis were rounding up hostages to be shot in reprisal. As the two were walking along in central Paris, a military patrol pulled up and a soldier tried to force Betty into a car. Hoffmann, who was in civilian clothes, managed to intervene, and after several minutes of desperate negotiating, was able to prevent them taking her. This almost certainly prevented her from being shot in reprisal for the Resistance killing. The last Betty heard from the Lieutenant was a call from the Russian front just outside of Moscow. Hoffmann was later captured by the Russians but he survived the war.

After getting poor grades for her course, Betty changed her degree to law, which she studied for two years before trying her hand at becoming a primary teacher. After several months' teaching, she went back to studying law full time. She was studying law in June 1944 when she heard the long-wished-for news: the Allies had landed in Normandy. The Paris uprising began in earnest and, by August 24, when the first Allied units rolled into the city, large parts of the capital were already in French hands. Betty joined thousands of other liberated Parisians in a joyous but solemn congregation around the Arc de Triomphe. The next day, she watched with tens of thousands of others, as Charles de Gaulle, leader of the Free French forces, strode down the Champs Elysée, marking the liberation of Paris.

Determined to do something positive to help the continuing war effort and bored with her law degree, Betty presented herself at the Welcome Committee for Allied Officers and, because of her knowledge of English, was taken on immediately, helping to organise the pairing of Allied officers, stationed or on leave in Paris, with residents who were willing to entertain them. The tiny two-office space on the Place de la Madeleine was constantly inundated with servicemen and the put-upon employees were in the middle of a constant maelstrom of shouting and questions.

It was here, in September 1944, that Maxwell first spotted her with a look of "slight childish desperation" on her face, as she tried to deal with a dozen questions at once. Maxwell fell in love at once and was determined to have her. Betty wasn't aware of him herself until she was called into her boss's office to deal personally with the case of Sergeant Ivan du Maurier, who wanted to be set up with someone who could tell him about the lifestyles and hardships the Parisians had undergone in the last four years. Betty duly arranged for him to meet a local lawyer and said goodbye, but she found herself "disturbed" by the young soldier's personality and found it hard to put him out of her mind. The next day, he was back in the office, watching her from across the room. Eventually, she asked him if something was wrong and he replied that he would like to take her out that evening. Betty made an excuse but, the next day, he was back, staring at her again with those piercing eyes. This time, she felt an extreme physical reaction. "I was rooted to the spot, transfixed. A strange sensation of warmth flooded through my body, then the blood seemed to drain from me, my legs felt like jelly, and I fell with a thud on the chair, my head swimming, the room revolving around me."

In a flash, Maxwell caught the swooning Betty and swept her out of the office, telling her boss that she was hungry and needed to eat immediately. Maxwell half-carried her to the nearby Cancellier Hotel, where they had lunch. They chatted long into the afternoon and Maxwell asked her to meet him again that evening. After watching a film, they had dinner and Maxwell declared his love in a typically brash way. "Whatever might have happened to you before," Betty recounts him saying, "whatever you did or didn't do, whoever you met, whatever you thought, whatever your ambitions were, your successes and your failures, I want you as you are now. Life starts all over again with you."

And so began the love affair that would dominate both their lives. They had a few magical weeks together in Paris and Maxwell proposed. Betty's parents were less than convinced but, after Maxwell presented a letter of recommendation from his military benefactor, Brigadier Carthew-Yorstoun, the couple were able to celebrate their engagement on New Year's Eve, 1944. But by January 6, Maxwell, having received his commission as a lieutenant, had to join his new unit, the Queen's Royal Regiment, on the front line in The Netherlands.

Betty and Maxwell wrote to each other daily during the remaining months of the war, Maxwell addressing his letters to "My Darling Betuska" and at 11.30 each night, they took a moment to think about each other intensely, in order to feel some kind of contact.

Maxwell was in the thick of the fighting. He received the Military Cross for one particular engagement, during an attack on the Dutch city of Paarlo. A strong enemy counter-attack had overrun a platoon on Maxwell's platoon's flank. Maxwell's Major ordered him to retreat but Maxwell asked for permission to attack the position, saying he believed some of the men were still alive and holding out. Despite being threatened with a court martial by his commanding officer, Maxwell gathered his men and stormed the position, killing several Germans and forcing the rest to retreat. Maxwell's bravery was vindicated – the platoon's officer and a few men were holed up in an abandoned farmhouse and Maxwell's counter-attack saved them from capture or death.

The bravery and strong-headedness of the action summed up everything that was good about Maxwell as a soldier. But another incident would reveal a darker side to his nature. Maxwell had persuaded a German town to surrender by threatening to mortar bomb it. Assured by the mayor that no one would fire on his troops, Maxwell's men entered the settlement. However, a German tank disobeyed orders and fired on them and they were forced to retreat. In a letter to Betty, Maxwell recounted: "Luckily, he missed, so I shot the mayor and withdrew." Shooting an unarmed civilian shows there was a level of cold-blooded callousness in Maxwell's personality, even early on, although it would come to the fore more in later life. Maxwell's actions constituted a war crime and records obtained from the Metropolitan Police in 2006 revealed that he was being investigated for the crime just before his death in 1991, a disclosure which added fuel to speculation that he might have killed himself.

Despite the constant fighting, Maxwell managed to marry Betty on March 14, 1945, during a brief leave in Paris, followed by a four-day honeymoon in Versailles. Maxwell wanted Betty to move to England, so she undertook the dangerous journey, leaving the security of her friends and family behind, to live in a small room in London, belonging to Mrs Stratton-Ferrier, an old lady who had previously taken Maxwell under her wing.

Betty stayed there for the rest of the war, while Maxwell moved to Berlin. There, he led the British section of the 'Four Power Victory Parade' on its march through the streets of the captured capital, to mark the ultimate victory of the Allies over the Axis powers.

While in Berlin, Maxwell applied to become an intelligence officer and was soon transferred to a new position, interrogating prisoners of war and high-ranking Nazis, including Hitler's adjutant, Von Below, and Lieutenant Colonel Hermann Giskes, a high-ranking spy chief. In the meantime, he had heard word from his family in Czechoslovakia – two of his sisters had survived the Holocaust and were making their way to Berlin to rejoin their brother. Sylvia, his younger sister, was just fifteen and Brana, his elder sister, had been through terrible ordeals, including two concentration camps. Maxwell – now a captain – made arrangements for Sylvia to join his own family in London (his first son, Michael, had been born on March 11, 1946) whilst Brana preferred to reunite with relatives in the US. Betty arranged for Sylvia to study at a boarding school in Somerset, where she could train to fulfil her ambitions of becoming an actress. Neither of Maxwell's parents nor the rest of his sisters had survived the war.

It's hard to estimate the effect of this on Maxwell because, according to Betty, he gave no overt signs of his grief, but it undoubtedly motivated him throughout his life in almost everything he did, most clearly in his support for Jews around the world and, specifically, the state of Israel. It also spurred Betty to try and recreate the family he had lost with their own little brood of youngsters.

In Berlin, Maxwell soon tired of the army and began looking for civilian careers, first as the censor for the Berlin newspaper, Der Telegraf. He bought shares in a Czech-run import-export firm in London called Low Bell and, shortly after, started his first business under his own name – European Periodicals Publicity and Advertising Company (EPPAC), which was set up to help restart the export of German technical, scientific and medical publications. Maxwell moved back to be with Betty in London and their second child, Anne, was born in December 1947. She was born at a maternity hospital in Paris, run by Betty's sister, Vonnic, in a tradition that would extend to all future Maxwell children, including Ghislaine.

It was through EPPAC that Maxwell came to do business with Springer Verlag, Germany's, and the world's, leading publisher of scientific books and journals. Maxwell met Ferdinand Springer in post-war Berlin and, from 1947, onwards he began exporting his books to England. He also travelled around the world, helping to sell Springer Verlag publications, helping them overcome the post-war travel restrictions placed on German citizens. But Maxwell wasn't just helping Springer; like a sponge, he was sucking up all the knowledge of the scientific publishing industry he could, from the master. When he had learned enough, it was time to set up his own enterprise. Springer already had a joint publishing venture with British publishing firm Butterworth, called Butterworth Springer, but both sides weren't particularly happy with the arrangements. With the financial help of London banker, Sir Charles Hambro, Maxwell bought out the company and, together with Springer's former editor, Paul Rosbaud, set about creating a British scientific publishing house to rival Springer Verlag. Pergamon Press was born.

Maxwell was away from home travelling so much in the early days of Pergamon that his third child Philip's first words were, according to Betty, "Goodbye, Daddy," which he would say regardless of whether Maxwell was setting off or returning. Despite being an absent father, Maxwell clearly cared deeply for his family and children. When Betty gave birth to twins Isabel and Christine, in 1950, the prematurely born infants came down with toxicosis. The twins were unable to keep any fluids down and were in danger of death. Betty's sister told her that there was only one doctor who could save their lives – Professor Lamy at the Children's Hospital in Paris. Maxwell tried to contact the paediatrician but found he was on holiday at his country home. Maxwell managed to locate Lamy and offered to drive him to the hospital, after which he drove Betty and the twins to the clinic through the streets of central Paris at 100 miles an hour, according to Betty, with the police chasing them. Once at the Children's Hospital, Lamy was able to save the twins' lives, but it was Maxwell's actions that had been the real saviour.

And it wasn't just in emergencies that Maxwell proved himself as a father. On the times when he was at the family's new house in Esher, Surrey, he could be immense fun and he would create his own games, such as 'Wolfie' where the house was made completely dark and the children all ran off to hide, while Maxwell, the wolf, prowled the rooms searching for them. Despite the light-heartedness, it's interesting to note that even in these childish games, he played the part of a predator.

Despite the good times, the young family idyll was not to last. By 1953, Maxwell was almost certainly having an affair – probably his first long-term affair – with his personal assistant, Anne Dove. Betty first became aware of the affair on his return from a trip to Moscow in January 1954, where he had acquired the British rights to around 50 Russian scientific publications. Seeing Maxwell and Dove together at the airport on their return from Moscow, Betty sensed "with the unerring instinct of a wife in love" that the two were having an affair. Soon after, Maxwell invited Betty on a business trip to Canada and she used the chance to confront him with her fears. That spelled the end for Dove, who was promptly transferred to a new position in the New York office. But this would be the first in a long list of affairs for Maxwell, often with personal assistants, secretaries and other female workers at his various companies, not to mention his briefer liaisons while travelling abroad, often with prostitutes.

Another hammer blow came with the death of their daughter, Karine, in 1957. Born just three years earlier, the little girl came down with a sudden fever while her parents were on a winter break in Barbados. They rushed home to find Karine had been diagnosed with leukaemia. Maxwell "moved heaven and Earth" to help his daughter, according to Betty, writing to every known specialist around the world. He had just secured her treatment in a clinic in Boston when she died, just a few weeks after her diagnosis. Maxwell was devastated. He wrote to a friend: "I don't think in all my life I have ever suffered a worse blow than to have this beautiful and intelligent girl snatched away at this early innocent age." But Betty records how, after the initial loss, he didn't express his grief openly but carried it inside like a secret wound, as he did with the deaths of his Czech family.

Karine's death seems to have sowed the seeds of a change in Maxwell, which was exacerbated by the next great tragedy in his life. On 27th December 1961, just two days after Ghislaine's birth, Maxwell's first son, sixteen-year-old Michael, was involved in a car accident that left him in a permanent coma. In her book, *A Mind of My Own*, Betty describes the effect on the family:

"Bob was shaken to the core of his being. He could not believe that fate had dealt him such a cruel blow after all he had already endured. Michael's closest brother, Philip, who worshipped his elder brother, suffered deeply and began a prolonged struggle to accept his loss. Anne lost her natural companion and an elder brother she adored. Her security was shattered and it would take her years to come to terms with her grief. The twins clung to each other and allowed no one to penetrate their world. Ian was found endlessly playing with cars, ambulances, little figures in white coats and making blood-spattered drawings."

Although the two youngest children, Kevin and Ghislaine, seemed unaffected, it was Ghislaine's life which, indirectly, was most influenced by the tragedy. She went from being ignored to being spoilt.

What effect must this sudden shift from neglect to over-compensating attention have had on the young Ghislaine's development? Could it explain, at least in part, the severe dichotomy in her character in later life?

Whatever the case, Betty managed to cure Ghislaine's eating

disorder not long after, thanks to a chance conversation with Nobel-prize-winning Italian chemist, Daniel Bovet, at a dinner party. Confiding her worries about Ghislaine to the chemist, Betty was surprised when he offered her a solution based on his experiments with rats, saying she should stop restricting Ghislaine to eating at mealtimes and let her eat whatever and whenever she wanted. Betty tried the advice and stopped laying a place for Ghislaine at mealtimes. Instead, the toddler was allowed to eat whatever she chose. For a whole week, as Betty recoded, Ghislaine would stuff herself with chocolate or eat so many peaches that Betty feared she would make herself ill. However, after the novelty wore off, Ghislaine began picking pieces of food off the others' plates at dinner time. Finally, she asked why she wasn't included in mealtimes, to which Betty replied that it wasn't possible because she didn't eat like the rest of the family. Feeling left out, Ghislaine demanded to be fed meals like the rest of them and the problem was permanently cured.

By this point, the family were living in Headington Hill Hall in Oxfordshire. The 50-room Victorian mansion, standing in 15 acres of wooded parkland overlooking Oxford, was owned by Oxford City Council, who were looking for a tenant for the dilapidated property which, in 1960, when the Maxwells moved in, had been derelict for 15 years. Growing up at Headington must have been a wonderful but slightly confusing mix of family and business life for young Ghislaine. Once the property had been renovated and the children moved in, Maxwell began the process of relocating Pergamon Press's headquarters to the mansion, where the staff worked in Nissen huts, built during the war for the Red Cross, and the old stable block before a new office building was constructed in the grounds.

Inevitably, the family's life became intimately tied to the business. Betty records having to become an agony aunt for the personal, social and work problems of the staff, and the children were often found inside the Pergamon offices, making friends with the employees. The close family ties to the business must have made it all the harder when, in 1969, Maxwell was unceremoniously kicked off the board of Pergamon. An American company interested in buying a Pergamon subsidiary had looked at the accounts and found that Maxwell had maximised Pergamon's share price by borrowing money via his other companies, a practice he was to engage in throughout his business life. A later inquiry by the Department of Trade and Industry found that "notwithstanding Mr Maxwell's acknowledged abilities and energy, he is not in our opinion a person who can be relied on to exercise proper stewardship of a publicly quoted company."

The effect on Headington was brutal. To keep Maxwell away from the offices, barbed wire-tipped fences were installed on the grounds and an iron gate erected in the cellar, which the Pergamon HQ shared with the main house. From having the run of the grounds, the children were suddenly hemmed in, like prisoners in a concentration camp. One can only imagine the psychological effect this must have had on seven-year-old Ghislaine and her siblings. "They were dark times," Ian Maxwell told John Preston, author of a Maxwell biography. "There seemed to be a fear in the air: a fear that we would be ostracised."

It took five years of exhausting legal battles before Maxwell wrested control back from the board. On the day he won the battle, Maxwell stormed into Pergamon's previously out-of-bounds HQ and told the board: "Right, we're taking over now. You can all go." The same day, the barricades were torn down.

But the stress of the legal wranglings and the damage to his reputation, combined with the spectre of Michael lying in a coma, had snapped something in Maxwell. He became more aggressive, controlling and abusive. This manifested most obviously at Sunday lunches, which were a family tradition throughout Maxwell's life. Increasingly, it became the only time he was home, especially when he became a Labour MP for Buckingham in 1964. It seemed to Betty that all the highs and lows of Maxwell's political and business careers were taken out on the children in those increasingly tense mealtimes. Maxwell, understandably concerned that they receive the education he never got, would fire questions at the children until one of them tripped up. He would then interrogate the unfortunate child, perhaps in the manner he had learned with army intelligence in Berlin, until the poor boy or girl would break down in tears.

"I soon realised that somehow Bob needed to create a sense of drama around him," said Betty. "He would shout and threaten and rant at the children until they were reduced to pulp. Then would come the reconciliation scene when he would eventually forgive them, tears would be dried and smiles returned to their faces." As the scenes grew gradually worse, the children began to dread what Betty termed the weekly "Maxwellian Drama" and would flee the dinner table as fast as possible, avoiding Maxwell until it was time to go back to school.

There was always the threat of physical punishment too, especially when the children received a bad school report. Maxwell was not shy of turning to the cane and, if Eleanor Berry's account is true, a whole armoury of other devices, including sticks and riding crops. The effect on the children of living under the shadow of the constant threat of mental or physical abuse must have been telling. Once or twice, the siblings tried standing up to their father but it was an impossible task. Betty records one incident when, on a yachting holiday in the Mediterranean, Maxwell forced seven-year-old Kevin to eat French beans, which he hated. Kevin refused and Maxwell had him locked in his cabin until he relented. Kevin held out for two whole days until Maxwell threatened to lash him with a rope. Betty remembers Kevin finally capitulating, "his words interrupted by convulsive sobs, saying to Bob, 'I give in, but only because you are bigger and stronger than me, and for no other reason.'"

The family stress affected Ghislaine's school performance and behaviour, so much so that her headmistress advised that she should be removed from the school and seek psychiatric help. A psychiatrist advised a complete change of environment for the eight-year-old girl and Betty transferred her to a boarding school in Somerset, where her behaviour improved. It is interesting to note that it was complete physical removal from the family house that ultimately helped the young Ghislaine.

After the worst family arguments, Betty would try and stick up for the children and get Maxwell to see things from their perspective, but he only accused her of taking sides and trying to turn the family against him. She too was the butt of his constant critical scrutiny, to the extent where she felt she could never live up to the idealised version of a wife he had created in his mind. The feeling of guilt at not measuring up to Maxwell's expectations became so intense that Betty was prepared to give up even her own personality, her own mind, to his all-consuming ego. In a telling letter from the late sixties, she wrote to Maxwell:

"You will only need to say what you want and it will be done, or to express a desire and I will satisfy it. Perhaps you will discover that the half-flayed creature you have stripped naked still deserves to be loved."

Yet no amount of self-abnegation was good enough for Maxwell. Always, there was some tiny detail missing in the service he felt she owed him.

"He would constantly revert to the same old theme – that I did not look after his material needs to a standard he considered acceptable and was therefore incapable of ensuring his happiness. Sometimes there would be a button missing on a shirt or I would forget his evening shirt studs or black tie when I packed his bag. He would complain that his cupboards were not impeccably tidy or that I hadn't got his summer clothes out early enough. The right item would be in the wrong place or something would be missing from his case when he was travelling abroad."

It is hard not to conclude from this that Maxwell expected from his wife the same treatment a young child receives from its mother, the mother he had lost while he was still a young man.

In another frank admission, Betty wrote:

"There is no doubt that Bob had an idealized picture of me and that I fell short of his dream. He also had a rather Oriental view of women: he wanted me to love him, be loyal to him and unconditionally surrender my whole being to him, but whilst he valued my opinion on most things, he found it almost impossible to accept that I should have a life of my own."

It wasn't just Betty from whom Maxwell demanded this unwavering loyalty and selfless devotion, it was all the women in his life, even those he worked with. To succeed with Maxwell, they had to become almost soulless automatons, mere extensions of his own all-consuming ego. "I can't get on with men," he said in an interview with *The Times,* shortly after becoming an MP. "I tried having male assistants at first, but it didn't work. They tend to be too independent. Men like to have individuality. Women can become an extension of the boss."

Just how scared Ghislaine was of disappointing her father is illustrated by a story from my interview with John Sweeney. He recounted how, when researching for his podcast, Hunting Ghislaine, he received a phone call from an old friend at *The Mirror*. The friend told him about a time when he had gone out drinking with Ghislaine and some other *Mirror* staff, after a Labour Party conference. Ghislaine had been so worried about getting up on time the next morning, Sweeny's friend told her to get the hotel to give her an alarm call. Ghislaine was still worried so the friend offered to give her his alarm clock, which he always carried with him. Even this didn't assuage Ghislaine's nerves so he offered to call her himself at 7.30am. Intrigued as to what was so important that she needed three methods of wake-up reminder, Sweeney's friend was shocked to hear the response: "I'm having breakfast with my father."

Who knows what this pressure to achieve did to Ghislaine on a psychological level but perhaps it had something to do with the fact that she never had a successful career and all her self-started businesses failed.

Of course, Ghislaine wasn't the only child to suffer from the unbearable censoriousness of her father and possibly, as his favourite, she was the one who got away the lightest. Ian certainly didn't get away lightly when, as an inexperienced 23-year-old expected to head both Paris and Frankfurt Pergamon operations, he failed to meet his father at Charles de Gaulle airport in Paris, as they had arranged. Maxwell promptly fired his son, saying that if he couldn't keep small commitments, he would never keep big ones. To compound the humiliation, Maxwell told the story publicly in several press conferences.

Kevin suffered a similar fate when Maxwell discovered he had breached an impossibly strict embargo set by his father. Maxwell wasn't keen on Kevin's burgeoning relationship with his girlfriend Pandora, which he thought was interfering with Kevin's business training, so he sent him to America for two years. However, Pandora visited Kevin in the States, which Maxwell regarded as a breach of trust. Kevin was immediately relieved of all his duties in the US.

But perhaps Maxwell's harshest treatment was reserved for Anne, who had become a professional actor. Maxwell was unimpressed with Anne's less-than-meteoric rise to fame, despite her appearing in a film with Sean Connery. Maxwell summed up his feelings with the witty but devastating line: "What have Anne and Pope John got in common? They're both ugly and they're both failed actors."

Even when the children were adults, the Sunday "Maxwellian dramas" continued. All the children were expected to attend or they were accused of disloyalty. Although the beatings had stopped, Betty describes in her memoir the excruciating atmosphere that pervaded these family meetings:

"They [the children] wanted to come but dreaded it at the same time: it was so emotionally draining for us all. We almost never had a conversation that was a real exchange of views: none of us was allowed to hold an opinion that differed significantly from his. I became almost paralyzed when he asked me questions, because as I tried to answer, he would quickly become impatient and interrupt me, saying, "I can't understand what you're trying to say." If I carried on talking, it would not be long before he butted in again with, "What you're really trying to say is…" Or if I asked a question, he would rephrase it completely and preface it with "What you meant to ask was…" and "Why on earth can't you put your questions in a normal way?" Such criticism would finally make me loath to ask or answer any more questions, whereupon I would promptly be accused of sulking. It was endless. Whenever any of us was enthusiastically trying to recount something exciting that had happened, he would repeatedly interrupt, insisting on careful rephrasing until all the joy had gone out of the telling."

Maxwell's arrogance and bullying wasn't just confined to the family. His work staff felt it too, as well as anyone in what Maxwell considered an inferior position. Roy Greenslade, Maxwell's editor at *The Mirror*, recounts several stories of Maxwell's arrogant behaviour, such as at a dinner at a London casino in the 80s. Greenslade said: "He behaved atrociously, sweeping all the cutlery and crockery from the table, saying it was badly laid out." Greenslade recalled another occasion at a charity performance, with Maxwell going on stage to lecture a prima ballerina about a movement. "That was the nature of the beast," he said. "What you have here is a kind of sociopathic, possibly borderline psychopathic, character."

His belief that he always knew better sometimes went beyond patronising, however, and became downright dangerous. Such was the case in another episode told to John Sweeney by Roy Greenslade, who recounted how they were taking the helicopter back from the Labour Party conference when Maxwell, unhappy at the slow progress, actually grabbed the controls from the pilot and tried to take over flying the aircraft. It was only on being shouted at by Betty that Maxell relinquished the controls.

His contempt for those he believed lower than himself was adequately expressed by his habit of urinating off the helipad atop *The Mirror* headquarters in central London, joking that the people below didn't know he was pissing on them. On other occasions, he would leave the door open while in the toilet so that the people waiting for him could hear the sounds of him defecating. And he would regularly wipe his bottom with white towels, which he would throw on the floor for his Filipino maids to pick up.

Maxwell was clearly a monstrous bully and mere contempt could often turn into sadistic pleasure at making others suffer. An interviewee for the Hunting Ghislaine podcast told John Sweeney the story of how Maxwell sacked the interviewee's father, just before Christmas in 1953. The young publisher was invited by his boss, Maxwell, to a dinner at the Savoy. Being newly married, he asked if he could bring along his wife. The man's son recounted to Sweeny how, "During a very pleasant lunch, the boss turns to his young bride and says, 'I've been waiting to tell something to your husband.' What could that be, they thought, could it be a promotion, a Christmas bonus? At which stage the boss turns to the husband and looks him in the eye and points him the finger and says, 'You're fired.'"

As the guest went on to explain, sacking an employee is bad enough, but the added humiliation of the occasion, the deliberately misleading build up and doing it in front of his wife, show a disturbing enjoyment at causing, and watching, another's suffering.

Yet Maxwell's mistreatment of staff could go even further, putting their lives in jeopardy. Mike Molloy, Maxwell's Mirror Group editor-in-chief throughout the 80s, recounted how Maxwell once sent him to represent him on a trip to Kenya, where Maxwell had newspapers. Only later did Molloy find out why – the foreign editor, Nick Davies, had received a call from Mossad, warning him of a possible assassination attempt on Maxwell in Nairobi. Rather than risking it himself, Maxwell sent Molloy to get assassinated in his stead. Peter Jay, Maxwell's top aide in the 80s, said about Maxwell: "There was something not so much amoral about him as pre-moral. As if he was … wholly unaware of things like good and evil."

It seems from what we know of Ghislaine's character and conduct that she inherited many of the flaws of her narcissistic, possibly psychopathic father. Her arrogance and the disdainful treatment of those she considered inferior were common knowledge amongst her father's Mirror Group staff. She was infamously rude to them and would often demand a cigarette before wandering off with the entire packet. Maxwell biographer, Tom Bower, said of her: "She was like her father and he encouraged her to adopt his worst characteristics — arrogance and rudeness, tempered by an ability to charm when required."

She showed both of these sides in an incident recounted by Bower when she was stopped by a London policeman for speeding. Instead of being contrite, she congratulated the officer for recognising her, and got away without a penalty. A social acquaintance of Ghislaine, the writer and journalist Anna Pasternak, told John Sweeney that Ghislaine was the type of person who, "would say hello to you while looking over your shoulder for somebody more interesting, more influential, more powerful." Pasternak described Ghislaine as "brittle" and went on to explain, "I think she was quite emotionally detached and I think that would explain why she's able to behave in the way she went on to behave and does today."

Of course, nobody is purely bad and Ghislaine had her good side. She could be charming and funny and she also had a caring side, even according to some of her victims. Epstein survivor, Virginia Giuffre recorded in her memoirs how, when she was due to leave for Thailand for six months to attend a massage course, Ghislaine put a great deal of effort into making sure everything was planned correctly and she provided Virginia with meticulous notes on staying safe and what to do in any kind of trouble or emergency. Virginia also records how, on several occasions, she and Ghislaine would fall about laughing in genuine mirth over some shared joke.

This brings us back to the question posed at the beginning of the chapter about the apparent schizophrenic split in Ghislaine's personality. It is almost certainly too simplistic to attribute the bad side of her character to her father and the good side to her mother, but there is probably a good deal of truth in the idea that Betty's gentle caring side managed to temper somewhat the rough excesses of Captain Bob. Psychologist Wendy Behary told John Sweeney that she thought Ghislaine suffered from being what she termed the "hostage princess in the palace." She went on to explain:

"Imagine that for people like Ghislaine Maxwell or Ivanka Trump or others in these very high status positions, very exposed celebrity-like positions, that the only attention, the only attachment you can have in the world is through these kind of brutal relationships where there's great demands placed on your appearance and your showmanship and the way you align with your daddy. Then you're going to take it as a child because it's a survival mechanism and you get a lot of goodies that come with that...
... So you will commit yourself, not that you want to be a victim but it's just the only way to be able to have that much needed sense of attachment. And you get kind of addicted to having all the privileges that come along with that. You become addicted to daddy, to the approval that you get from daddy and so daddy becomes the object of that approval and that sense of worth and that sense of value and that sense of having some meaning in the world – if I do this, I have value and I matter."

But what happens when a hostage princess loses their captor/protector? Behary explains:

"Then you find somebody new who's quite a lot like daddy...
.... It's like a creature of habit, it's the familiarity – it feels like, sounds like, smells like, looks like, and it's a mirror. Daddy dies. I've lost my mirror. I've lost my capacity to see my reflection of who I am and how I matter and what my position is and so, seeking that same or similar position of power becomes very relevant."

Ghislaine did lose her father after his infamous death aboard his super-yacht, the aptly-named Lady Ghislaine. Almost immediately afterwards, Ghislaine attached herself to another charming psychopath, Jeffrey Epstein. The hostage princess had exchanged one form of captivity for another, and the world she would soon become part of was, if possible, even darker than the one she had been temporarily freed from.

CHAPTER 2

PRINCE ANDREW AKA RANDY ANDY

The first indication that the relationship between Prince Andrew and Jeffrey Epstein might be less savoury than just friends came in December 2010, when pictures were released of them walking together in New York's Central Park. That the royal family member was seen chatting with a convicted paedophile was bad enough, but other photos emerged of the prince waving coyly goodbye to a young brown-haired woman from behind the door of Epstein's Manhattan mansion. It was revealed that Andrew had attended a dinner party at Epstein's mansion to celebrate the release of the paedophile from his Palm Beach prison sentence. Worse than that, the prince had slept at Epstein's house for four nights during his stay in New York. He had even been seen by one witness receiving a foot massage alongside Epstein, performed by two young Russian women.

Despite the ensuing press storm, the scandal would soon have been forgotten. But then, in 2011, the now-infamous photo of Prince Andrew with his arm around 17-year-old Virginia Roberts was published by the press. *The Daily Mail* soon revealed the story behind the picture – the teenage Roberts had been recruited as Epstein's sex slave and hired out to perform sexual massages on various friends, one of whom was Prince Andrew. As Roberts – now known by her married name, Giuffre – went on to testify in court, she had three encounters with Andrew; one in Ghislaine Maxwell's London townhouse where the picture was taken, where she alleged to have had sex with Andrew, another in Epstein's

Manhattan mansion, and a third occasion on Epstein's island, where she alleged to have been part of an orgy with Epstein, Andrew and eight other girls.

These allegations became formal in 2015 when Giuffre, taking part in a legal case against the US government for entering into a plea deal with Epstein, repeated them under oath. Andrew denied the claims and the judge later struck them from the record as being unnecessary to the case. But if Andrew thought he was off the hook, he was wrong. Following Epstein's arrest for sex trafficking in July 2019, new legal documents appeared in which another Epstein survivor, Johanna Sjoberg, alleged that she had also been sexually assaulted by the prince, corroborating Giuffre's account of her second meeting with Andrew in Manhattan where, both girls claimed, the Prince had groped their breasts with a Spitting Image puppet of himself.

With the press storm raging, Buckingham Palace remained stoically silent until Andrew made the fateful decision to conduct a 'no holds barred' interview with BBC's Newsnight in November. But rather than dousing the flames, the car-crash interview with BBC journalist, Emily Maitlis, only fanned them. In the conversation, Andrew's alibis appeared inconsistent, illogical and sometimes downright weird. He countered the claim that he had danced and sweated at Tramp nightclub in London with the assertion that he was unable to sweat following an overload of adrenalin during the Falklands War. His reason for 'remembering' that he had not left the palace that night was that he had visited a Pizza Express in Woking earlier in the day, for the birthday party of one of Princess Beatrice's friends. The bizarre excuses were interwoven with a distinct absence of sympathy or condolence for the many victims of Epstein's crimes.

The interview was quickly dubbed a PR nightmare and, just four days later, the prince was forced to step down from all royal duties. Among the many reactions to his conduct were that he appeared arrogant, above everyone, dismissive of the justice system and downright stupid. The prince, who had once been a war hero and the darling of a nation, was now a pariah.

But which was the real face of Andrew? Was he really so arrogant, boorish, imprudent and downright thick? What had led to his association with Epstein and how deep did it run? Was Giuffre his only sexual misdemeanour or was there evidence of similar transgressions in his past? As we shall see, hints of what Andrew would become were present right from the beginning.

Born on 19 February 1960, Prince Andrew was the third child of Queen Elizabeth II and Prince Philip, their second son after the heir to the throne, Prince Charles. Andrew was named after his grandfather, Philip's father, Prince Andrew of Greece and Denmark. Andrew's namesake had been twice exiled from his native Greece and had numerous family ties with the Nazis. He was an inveterate gambler and had spent most of his later life cruising around the Caribbean with his mistress, before dying in a hotel room in Monaco. As a choice of namesake, it was perhaps a sign of things to come.

Andrew himself received many nicknames throughout his life, some from friends and family, others from the press, not all of which were flattering. Amongst the first bestowed on him, according to the biography, *Prince Andrew*, by Nigel Cawthorne, were 'Baby Grumpling' from his first nanny, Mabel Anderson, who looked after him in the royal nursery of Buckingham Palace. Anderson struggled to control Andrew's early temper tantrums and to teach him basic manners. Philip, however, took to the boy quickly, recognising a characteristic of himself in his headstrong independent streak, and nicknamed him "the Boss."

From his earliest memories, Andrew was surrounded by opulence and privilege. Accompanied always by his own personal protection officer, he travelled on the royal train or yacht or by Rolls Royce to the various nurseries of the four palaces where he did his growing up – Buckingham Palace, Windsor, Sandringham and Balmoral. There were endless parades, banquets and receptions for visiting dignitaries, and footmen to attend his every need. Even his nanny had two footmen and maids to wait on her.

Originally, Andrew's regime was strictly controlled by the

nanny who had brought up his elder siblings, Charles and Anne. Helen, or Nanny Lightbody, severely restricted parental access to the children, including Andrew, to the extent that the queen didn't even attend his first three birthdays. Everything changed, however, after Lightbody's rule was deemed too despotic and she was replaced by Mabel Anderson. Now, the queen had a much greater hand in the young Andrew's upbringing, letting him play in her study while official visitors were entertained, teaching him to ride his first pony and even bathing him on his nanny's days off. The routine was different to Charles's upbringing and seems to have hugely benefitted Andrew and Elizabeth's relationship. Andrew was seen as the queen's favourite to the extent that, according to Princess Diana's former butler, Paul Burrell, "He has never done anything wrong in her eyes." Andrew and his mother had their own private ritual whenever he was alone at Buckingham Palace. The queen sent a hand-written note to Andrew and he changed into a suit to visit her in her private apartments. Andrew greeted his mother with a bow and kissed her on the hand and both cheeks, in a ritual that the queen adored, according to palace aides.

The early change in upbringing appears to have helped Andrew's already growing sense of confidence. Whereas Charles had been a timid and sweet-natured child, Andrew was a whirlwind of energy and mischievous pranks. According to Cawthorne, the young prince tied sentries' shoelaces together, hid cutlery as footmen were laying the table, dismantled his nanny's radio and even sprinkled itching powder in the queen's bed. On one occasion, he gave Prince Philip a black eye during a playful sparring match and, on another, he used a silver dining tray to toboggan down the palace staircase. His high spirits could sometimes spill over into arrogance and haughtiness, however. On one occasion, while watching Coronation Street with his parents, he exclaimed, "Oh God, look at all those common people!"

Unlike Charles, Andrew was undoubtedly spoilt by his parents, as the queen admitted in private correspondence. The connection with Ghislaine Maxwell's childhood can't go unmentioned here – both Andrew and Ghislaine were consciously spoilt as children, following their parents' feelings of guilt about possible neglect in the past.

Andrew's first school was Heatherdown in Ascot. He quickly gained a reputation as a boisterous prankster, organising midnight feasts and jumbling everyone's shoes up. However, he couldn't be disciplined like all the other boys; instead, a special procedure had to be invoked, which involved the headmaster. His sporting education was equally elitist. He received cricket training at Lords, tennis coaching at Wimbledon and sailing at Cowes.

Yet the privilege was tempered with paranoia and fear. Andrew's youth coincided with an intense period of IRA terrorism and the young prince was considered a prime target and had to be accompanied by a personal protection officer at all times. On one occasion, when Andrew was at Heatherdown, security forces surrounded the building, in response to intelligence concerning a threat to the prince's life. The young Andrew was actually shown how to fire a gun by a police officer during the lockdown. The looming threat of death or violence must have had a huge impact on the young boy's developing psyche, especially as it claimed the lives of others in his family. This intense period of 'the troubles' culminated in the IRA assassination of Andrew's great-uncle and Charles's mentor, Lord Mountbatten. The aging earl was on his fishing boat with six of his family and friends off the northwest coast of Ireland, when the IRA detonated a pre-planted bomb consisting of 50 pounds of gelignite. Mountbatten, a friend, his grandson, the mother of his son-in-law and another friend were all killed and the others suffered serious injuries.

It has been alleged that Mountbatten's abuse of boys contributed to his early demise. In 2019, an FBI dossier on Mountbatten, released to author Andrew Lownie under the Freedom of Information Act, described Mountbatten and his wife as "persons of extremely low morals". USA intelligence officers commenced collecting information on Mountbatten in 1944, after he became the Supreme Allied Commander of Southeast Asia. The FBI file alleged that Mountbatten was a paedophile with "a perversion for young boys." If this were true and known in royal circles, what kind of warped value system was signalled to Andrew by his great uncle?

To continue his education, Andrew was sent to Gordonstoun, a remote Scottish boarding school, where both Philip and Charles had received spartan educations, designed to turn them into mature and selfless leaders. However, Andrew didn't shine at Gordonstoun like his father had. According to Cawthorne, other students thought he was 'boastful' and 'big-headed' and he received the nickname 'the Sniggerer' because of his habit of breaking down in laughter at his own jokes. He was popular with one particular set at Gordonstoun, however. Girls had recently been admitted to the school and they all fell over themselves to get close to the young prince. Andrew had a revolving door of young girlfriends and acolytes, who came to be known as Andy's Harem. Amidst this romantic pell-mell, Andrew had a couple of relationships that were long-lasting or serious enough to bring the girl back to Buckingham Palace during the holidays. One was Kirsty Richmond, an 18-year-old student at the school, and another was an American girl, named Sue Garnard. Back in London, he was also dating regularly and attending nightclubs such as Tramp which, in the future, he would become infamously connected with.

Although Andrew developed a reputation as being polite and charming around women, the same couldn't be said for his treatment of subordinates. In my book *Who Killed Epstein?* Andrew's royal protection officer, Paul Page, described the prince shouting and swearing at other members of the team and treating them like personal servants. This is confirmed by other accounts, such as royal bodyguard, Ken Wharfe, who said Andrew's manners were "just awful." Another aide told of how he would throw things on the ground and demand they "fucking pick them up." This lack of diplomacy extended to public life, as well. On a visit to Lockerbie, following the bombing of Pan Am flight 103, which crashed into the Scottish town, killing 11 people on the ground and all 259 passengers and crew aboard the plane, Andrew told grieving locals that the disaster had been "much worse" for the Americans.

Meanwhile, Andrew's education continued apace. He scraped three A-levels at Gordonstoun and sought admission to Cambridge University, where Charles had studied. However, he was unceremoniously turned down as not having the required grades. Instead, he decided to pursue his brother's chosen career directly, by applying to the Royal Naval College in Dartmouth. Andrew already had a pilot's licence and was brave and physically active but, again, he failed to make a particularly good impression with his peers who, according to Cawthorne, thought he was "arrogant" and "played the big 'I am the prince' routine." The wife of one of the instructors compared him unfavourably to Charles, who had studied there before, saying, "Andrew isn't popular with the staff or cadets… He never lets you forget who he is." Another senior officer described him as a "mummy's boy."

During Andrew's flight training to become a naval helicopter pilot, his fellow trainees resented his airs and graces, with one of them complaining that they had to "bow and scrape" and even salute the prince's car when he was driving around the base. Andrew finally passed out as a sub-lieutenant and was awarded best pilot. However, his classroom performance had been less spectacular and, according to Cawthorne, he was known as "Golden Eagle" amongst his classmates, because of the number of clangers he dropped when questioned by teachers. This perhaps summed Andrew's character up neatly – a doer more than a thinker, to put it diplomatically.

Andrew's first tour of duty brought more unfavourable comparisons to his older brother when he served on HMS Hermes, the same aircraft carrier Charles had served on previously. He was again noted for being overly conscious of his own royalty, and he made a bad first impression on Hermes' captain when he introduced himself by saying, "Hi, I'm Prince Andrew, but you can call me Andrew." To which the captain replied, "And you can call me Sir."

On his first shore leave in Florida, the prince earned his nickname "Randy Andy." He was photographed at a strip club, ogling topless dancers. The dancers all commented to the press about how much Andrew had enjoyed the show, and one even re-named her act the "Randy Andy Eye Popper." It makes one think of the later, less light-hearted testimony of 'Tiffany Doe,' a stripper hired for Epstein's private parties, who commented on how Andrew couldn't take his eyes – or other parts of his anatomy – off her breasts, even putting his head between them and "motorboating."

Despite his less-than-gentlemanly antics, Andrew's reputation was about to reach its apogee. On 2 April 1982, Argentina invaded the Falkland Islands: British-held overseas territories in the South Atlantic. UK prime minister, Margret Thatcher, declared war and a naval task force was immediately dispatched to the south Atlantic, including two aircraft carriers, one of which, the HMS Invincible, carried the 22-year-old Prince Andrew on board.

During the conflict, the young prince saw active duty and performed well. One of his roles as a Sea King helicopter pilot was to protect the Invincible from Argentine Exocet missiles, which involved using his helicopter as a decoy to draw the missiles away from the carrier. Andrew described to the press how the Sea King would hover behind the vessel, presenting a large radar target then, when the Exocet had diverted its course towards the helicopter, he would rise quickly to a height which was beyond the missile's operational capacity, allowing it to fly harmlessly underneath. It was certainly a dicey activity and Andrew was engaged in just such a role on 25 May, when the Argentines launched an Exocet against the Invincible. The hovering Sea Kings managed to divert the missile but it struck a nearby supply ship, the Atlantic Conveyor, instead.

Andrew was involved in the rescue mission, flying his helicopter over the stricken ship and saving eight members of the crew, while Argentine shells dropped all around. He also came under danger from his own side on three separate occasions when British Sea Wolf defence missiles locked onto his aircraft as a potential target. The terrible south Atlantic weather was as much a risk as the enemy and one of Andrew's first missions was to rescue the single surviving crew member of a Sea King that had ditched into the sea during a storm; it was one of 20 helicopters that would be lost in similar circumstances over the course of the 10-week war.

Rightly, Andrew was hailed by the press as a Falklands hero. But apart from all the patriotic furore, some more astute journalists noticed that Andrew had grown as a person through his experiences. John Witherow in *The Times* noted that, "It almost seemed as if a different character had emerged. He was more articulate and less self-conscious than before." Andrew's newfound popularity wasn't fully to sink in until he returned home later in the year. In November, he was due to switch on the Regent Street Christmas lights. The crowd was packed with women screaming, "We want Andy!" Police struggled to restrain the pushing crowd and some women actually fainted and had to be lifted over the barriers. Andrew had hit pop-star levels of adulation, and the store manager of the shop from which the lights were switched on compared it to Beatlemania. Hard as it is to imagine now, Andrew's popularity surmounted even Princess Diana's, who had switched on the lights the year before.

To go with the pop-star image, Andrew added the pop-star love life. He dated Miss UK and a string of other models and curvaceous pin up-types, including cover girl Kim Deas and topless model Joanne Latham. The string of beauties culminated with Koo Stark, the beautiful star of several Hollywood erotic films, such as *Emily, Cruel Passions* and *The Blue Film*. Stark was thought to be Andrew's first experience of real love and the two had a relatively long, serious and, for the most part, secret relationship, until the paparazzi caught up with them on a holiday in Antigua. From then on, the relationship went downhill and ended in 1983.

In the meantime, Charles had married Diana – Andrew was the best man and, in typical fashion, attached a 'just married' sign written in lipstick on the back of the couple's car – and Charles' first son, Prince William, had been born. Amidst all the popularity, this was a major turning point in Andrew's life and career as a royal. He was now no longer second in line to the throne and thus no longer quite as special as he had been before. He had gone from a possible future king to just another royal hanger-on.

Andrew was great friends with Diana – according to Cawthorne, he told his naval friends in the Falklands that there were only four women in his life; his mother, grandmother, sister and Diana. They had known each other before Diana became romantically involved with Charles, and it was through Diana that Andrew met Sarah Ferguson, or Fergie, as she was more commonly known. Diana, who had written to Andrew throughout the Falklands conflict, keeping him up to date with the family gossip, understood the perils of the endless tide of women throwing themselves at England's most eligible bachelor and engineered a match with her childhood friend, Sarah, the daughter of King Charles' polo manager, Major Ron Ferguson. Andrew met Fergie in 1985, at a party in Windsor Castle during Royal Ascot week. Within a week, they were dating and, by February 1986, Andrew had proposed.

The young couple were married by the Archbishop of Canterbury at Westminster Abbey on 23 July 1986. The televised event drew huge crowds and, as a national spectacle, almost rivalled Charles and Diana's own wedding. Fergie was a real character – bubbly, loyal and fun. She and Diana had tried to crash Andrew's stag party by dressing up as policewomen. At the wedding after-party, she encouraged everyone to jump in Windsor Castle's swimming pool and, according to Cawthorne, persuaded Diana to do the Can-Can. However, she was famously bad with money and always seemed to be looking for ways to make up for her over-spending, which was unbecoming for a royal, such as demanding money for interviews and asking designers for free clothes. She was also lax with her royal duties and engagements which, combined with her spendthrift ways, earned her the nickname "Freeloading Fergie." By 2010 alone, the duchess was reported to have gotten herself into £5 million worth of debt. One cartoon, shown to John Sweeney by royal biographer, Andrew Morton, summed up the Duchess of York's clueless behaviour with money. The cartoon, according to Sweeney, shows Fergie holding up a five-pound note saying, "But I'm sure I left with 50,000 this morning."

But there was a less humorous side to Ferguson's profligate ways. It was her mounting debts that would later tie her to Epstein who, it was reported, lent her $15,000, which she accepted, even after his initial Florida conviction. Sweeney even believes Ferguson's debts might have tied Andrew into his disastrous trip to visit Epstein in Manhattan in 2010. Sweeney speculated in our interview that the photograph of Epstein and Andrew strolling in Central Park during that visit might have been a carefully set up PR stunt to launder the paedophile's reputation, in return for bailing Fergie out of her financial difficulties.

In fairness to Fergie, much of her over-spending was probably to compensate for her husband's long and frequent periods of absence. Andrew still had a burgeoning naval career and was overseas more often than at home. In fact, after four years of marriage, the duchess complained that they had only spent forty-two nights a year together during the whole time. Even worse, when Andrew was at home, he spent most of his time playing golf. The births of their daughters, Beatrice in 1998 and Eugenie in 1990, didn't save the floundering marriage. In the early 90s, Fergie began hitting the town and was soon photographed sunning herself on holiday with Texan oil tycoon, Steve Wyatt. When the pictures were published, Andrew asked for a divorce and the couple publicly separated on 19 March 1992.

Andrew's public reputation began to decline after his split from Fergie. Again, the revolving door of glamourous girlfriends re-opened, as did the nicknames Randy Andy and Handy Andy, the latter due to his propensity for wandering hands around beautiful women. One party-goer told *The Times* about Andrew's behaviour, "He is a boobs-and-bum man. There is nothing sophisticated about it. One minute you're having your bum pinched, and the next he is reminding you he is Your Royal Highness." In my interview with John Sweeney, he confirmed from personal experience, how Andrew's behaviour around women could be uncomfortable to the point of embarrassment. Sweeney's ex-wife was a mature student at the London School of Economics when Andrew paid an official visit. Sweeney's ex, Tomiko, was asked to be one of several top-performing students to meet the prince. However, being a beautiful young woman with blonde hair, Tomiko found that the prince was fixating on her in a way that she found so uncomfortable, she eventually invented an excuse and left the meeting. As well as confirming his reputation as somewhat of a lech, Sweeney's ex also described the prince as "entitled and dim," thus corroborating other suspicions about his character.

Andrew also confirmed his reputation for enjoying strippers by touring strip-bars in a red-light district on the Thai island of Phuket. With his police bodyguard in tow, Andrew danced with topless young women, many of whom were probably prostitutes. It was all the worse as the prince was on a trade mission for the UK government.

It is hard to comprehend the British government's decision in 2001 to make Andrew the UK's Special Representative for Trade and Investment – a role that involved promoting UK exports and businesses around the world – given his well-known predilection for gaffes, blunders and his general lack of diplomacy. He had already proved his incapacity in a diplomatic role on a 1984 trip to the US. His behaviour on the visit was so bad, the British press nicknamed him "the Duke of Yob" and their American counterparts commented that it was "the most unpleasant royal visit since they burned the White House in 1812". Part of the problem was his habit of playing practical jokes, which were unstatesmanlike, to say the least. On one occasion, during a tour of a poor housing project in the Watts district of Los Angeles, the prince was handed a paint sprayer, which he laughingly turned on a group of reporters. The jape went so badly wrong that Buckingham Palace had to pay $1,200 for damages to one journalist's camera. This particular stunt led to Philip and Elizabeth finally "reading him the riot act" according to *Vanity Fair* journalist, Sue Arnold, but the PR damage had already been done.

Now, in 2001, this man would become the face of British trade and investment overseas. The results were swift and predictable and, within months, complaints were stacking up at the Foreign Office. Diplomats reported that Andrew never stuck to agreed itineraries and "left a trail of glass in his wake." His behaviour was "rude" and he lashed out at people to "lay down the law." He refused to fly commercially and was ferried around the globe by private jets at taxpayers' expense, to destinations that often appeared to have little to do with his trade missions, such as golf tournaments, football matches and the pads of his various girlfriends. This gave birth to a new unflattering sobriquet to add to his collection – "Airmiles Andy." Rather than a public servant, Andrew seemed to regard himself as some kind of travelling superstar, along with his personal entourage of six staff, including a valet to look after his wardrobe and appearance. He even went as far as assuming, like a rock or film star, he could demand his own personal rider, one time, according to Cawthorne, phoning ahead to demand that the water be served at room temperature. No wonder his personal taxpayer-paid expense account was £620,000 in one year alone.

Fellow envoys described him as "boorish" and "rude." And his nickname amongst the British diplomats in the Arabian Gulf was "HBH" – "His Buffoon Highness" – because he always did the opposite of whatever was agreed at the pre-visit meetings. At a party in Italy, he dismissed a famous fashion designer with the phrase, "Never heard of you." And in Australia, he refused routine security screening at the airport, leading one of the airport staff to comment, "What a pompous prick."

It was around the same time he was representing the UK so badly that Andrew fell into the company that would ultimately seal the last nail in his reputation's coffin. In 2000, Andrew was photographed with another middle-aged man on a yacht in Thailand, with several topless women. The other man was billionaire financier, Jeffrey Epstein, not particularly famous at that time, but well known in the New York social circle as a financial whizz, who only did business with the most exclusive – and richest – clients. The same year, Andrew was seen on at least five occasions with Epstein and their mutual friend, Ghislaine Maxwell. One of these occasions was a combined royal birthday party held at Windsor Castle, called the 'Dance of the Decades.' The party celebrated Prince Andrew's 40th birthday, his sister Anne's 50th, Princess Margaret's 70th and the Queen Mother's 100th and was attended by the queen and 600 other select guests. Epstein and Maxwell went on a shooting weekend at Sandringham just before Christmas the same year, and Andrew had also hosted Epstein at Balmoral the year before, as well as flying on the Lolita Express to Epstein's island, Little St James.

It seems the men had been introduced by Ghislaine Maxwell, who had once been Epstein's girlfriend but was now managing his affairs and acting as his madam, helping to recruit up to five underage girls a day for sexual massages. Andrew had been friends with Maxwell since the early 80s, when she was a student at Baliol College, Cambridge, studying modern languages. There were rumours about a romantic involvement at the time but, if it did happen, it was probably just a brief fling. Maxwell was more interested in dating rich tycoons and Andrew preferred buxom blondes or red-heads. But the two became close friends and the duo became a trio in the late 90s, when Maxwell introduced Epstein to the prince.

Epstein wasn't the only dodgy contact Andrew made as his jet-setting lifestyle hit new heights. In the same summer of 2000, he took Fergie and his two daughters to visit fashion tycoon Peter Nygård, on his estate in the Bahamas. Nygård, it has now been revealed, was a serial sexual abuser of underage girls, on a scale rivalling even Epstein. Another of Andrew's new acquaintances was Saif al-Islam, son of Libyan dictator, Colonel Gaddafi, a man later to be charged with crimes against humanity for inciting violence and murdering protestors. There was also Sakher el-Materi, son-in-law of the deposed Tunisian leader, Zine al-Abidine ben Ali, who was sentenced to 16 years in prison for corruption. Trips to see despotic rulers like the presidents of Azerbaijan and Kazakhstan and holidays with gun smugglers like Libyan gun runner, Tarek Kaituni, followed.

It was the Kazakh president's son-in-law, Timur Kulibayev, who bought Andrew and Fergie's dilapidated former estate, Sunninghill Park, in 2011, for £15 million – £3 million over the asking price. The deal seemed highly suspicious. The Berkshire property, built by the Yorks in the 80s, was given to Andrew and Fergie as a wedding present by the queen. It was something of an architectural monstrosity, compared by some to a Tesco supermarket. The Yorks had moved out by 2014, transferring to the Queen Mother's old Royal Lodge in Windsor. By 2011, when Kulibayev bought the property, it had been on the market for five years and was almost derelict, which makes the extremely steep price he paid for it somewhat fishy. Kulibayev did nothing at all with the property for eight years, before having it demolished. He then kept the site empty for another three years before rebuilding. It soon came to light that Andrew had been acting as a fixer for Kulibayev, introducing him to clients, as well as attempting to arrange for Coutts, the queen's bank, to take him on as a client. Clearly, the sale of Sunninghill was a way of taking payment from the dictator's son-in-law, for services rendered.

But it was Andrew's association with Epstein that would land him in the hottest water. In 2010, the infamous photos were published of Andrew's visit to Epstein's house in New York, to celebrate the paedophile's release from prison. Over the next year, the prince's relationship with Epstein produced a steady stream of criticism in the press, which only intensified when it came out that he had arranged for Epstein to pay off $15,000-worth of his ex-wife's debts. Friends had tried to warn him off Epstein but, according to one friend, quoted in a 2011 *Vanity Fair* article, during an argument over the phone, Andrew told her that being loyal to friends was a "virtue" and that he would remain loyal to Epstein. However, the damage to his reputation was too much and, in 2011, he was forced to step down from his role as UK trade ambassador. He also, reputedly, cut all ties with Epstein.

But the controversy didn't stop there. Soon, the picture of Andrew emerged with his arm around Virginia Roberts, Epstein's personal masseuse and sex slave. The story that accompanied the picture wasn't long to follow. Virginia's story emerged in the press and subsequently in court. She had been recruited for Epstein by Ghislaine Maxwell, as a 16-year-old working as an attendant at Donald Trump's famous Mar-a-Lago resort in Palm Beach, Florida. According to Virginia, Maxwell lured her with promises of training to become a professional massage therapist. However, her job 'interview' at Epstein's Palm Beach home quickly turned from a simple massage into sexual intercourse. Virginia had been a runaway from home since the age of 13 and had been sex-trafficked before, so she was extremely vulnerable. She quickly fell into Epstein's orbit and went from regular sexual massages at his El Brillo Way mansion in Palm Beach to jetting around the world with him as his personal 'masseuse.'

It was on one of these trips in March 2011 that she first met Prince Andrew. Virginia, Epstein and Maxwell had flown into London and were staying at Maxwell's townhouse in Belgravia, when Maxwell informed Virginia that, later that day, she would meet a prince. Maxwell took her shopping for new clothes and, in the evening, Andrew arrived. The old friends talked for a while, according to Virginia, mostly slagging off Andrew's ex, Fergie. At one point in the conversation, Andrew was invited to guess Virginia's age and he guessed correctly that she was 17. Maxwell then joked that she would soon be getting too old for Epstein. The group then headed out to a restaurant. It was in the taxi that Maxwell told Virginia she was expected to supply the same services to Andrew that she did for Epstein. Virginia was shocked that a royal would engage in such nefarious activities and felt anxious about making the prince happy.

After dinner, they went to Andrew's old haunt, Tramp nightclub in Mayfair, the same place where he had met his ex, Koo Stark. Virginia recounted that she danced with the prince, who was a terrible dancer and sweated all over her. They then returned to Maxwell's house, where Virginia asked Epstein to take a photo of her with the prince. The now-infamous picture was taken by Epstein using Virginia's camera and showed the prince with his arm around the 17-year-old's waist on the landing of Maxwell's house, with Maxwell herself floating in the background. After the photo, Virginia and Andrew retired to the bathroom to take a bath, where Virginia alleged that Andrew kissed and licked her toes and the arches of her feet, followed by going to the bedroom, where they had sex. Virginia described it as the longest ten minutes of her life.

The next day, Virginia was told that she had done well and had made the prince happy. Epstein paid her $10,000 for the encounter, more than she had ever received for such services. Unfortunately, she spent most of the money on partying and drugs, to mask the increasing pain her lifestyle was causing.

Virginia next met the prince in the following spring of 2002. She was lying in her room at Epstein's Manhattan mansion, when she received a call to come down to Epstein's study. She was surprised to see Andrew grinning at her from the couch. Virginia alleged that Maxwell took her by the hand and led her over to sit on the prince's lap. Andrew had a Spitting Image puppet of himself, which Maxwell had given him as a present. He allegedly used the puppet to grope Virginia's breasts and did the same to Johanna Sjoberg, another Epstein sex slave, who was also present. Virginia took Andrew to what she called "the dungeon," Epstein's massage area. There, she proceeded about her normal massage routine, starting with the feet and massaging up the legs. The prince flipped over before she had even made it to his calves and the massage allegedly turned into oral sex.

The third time Virginia allegedly had sex with Andrew was, she testified, on Epstein's island, Little St James. This was an alleged orgy, in which eight other girls took part, all of whom looked underage and were from eastern Europe or Russia, speaking little or no English. Virginia recounted how Epstein joked with Andrew about the girls' lack of English, saying they were the easiest kind of girls to get on with.

Virginia eventually escaped the clutches of Epstein, after he sent her to Thailand for a six-month massage therapy course. The predator had earlier told Virginia that he wanted her to have his baby. The shocked 18-year-old prevaricated, saying she wanted to get the massage qualifications he had promised her first, before committing to the pregnancy. While in Thailand, she met Robert Giuffre, an Australian backpacker, and the two quickly fell in love. Virginia returned to Australia with Robert after a shotgun marriage in Thailand and went on to have a family of three children. She wanted to forget Epstein forever but, with his first Florida conviction and subsequent private lawsuits, she found herself dragged back into the case, and began sharing her story with the press and US courts.

With Virginia's allegations, Andrew's reputation was at an all-time low. Yet still, the storm might have blown over, if it hadn't been for Epstein's arrest in July 2019 and subsequent charges of trafficking minors for sex. All the stories about Andrew and Virginia resurfaced in the press, along with fresh allegations. Documents appeared, showing that Johanna Sjoberg had also accused Andrew of sexually assaulting her in New York with the Spitting Image puppet, thus corroborating Virginia's story. As we have seen, the mounting pressure led to Andrew's fateful and disastrous decision to appear on the BBC Newsnight interview. Following the car-crash interview, organisations associated with the prince began pulling their backing, including KPMG, Aon,

Standard Chartered, Adweek, AstraZeneca, Barclays, the Royal Philharmonic, the National Ballet and Yorkshire Air Ambulance. As Andrew increasingly became a pariah, the inevitable happened. Within four days of the interview, he stepped down from all royal duties, saying, "The circumstances relating to my former association with Jeffrey Epstein have become a major disruption to my family's work and the valuable work going on in the many organisations and charities that I am proud to support."

But worse was to come. New allegations began to surface about Andrew's sexual predilections and his ties to Epstein. One former friend of Maxwell told the *Daily Beast* that she had been invited by Ghislaine to a party at Andrew's private apartments in Buckingham Palace. Once there, it became clear to the woman that she was present as a "sex object," with Andrew fawning all over her. She also claimed that Ghislaine acted for Andrew in a similar way as she did for Epstein, procuring women for the prince, although there was no allegation that any of these women were underage. It was alleged that Maxwell also arranged massages for Andrew, as she did for Epstein. That Andrew allegedly expected at least some of these massages to be sexual was illustrated by the story of one professional masseuse. Monique Giannelloni, recommended to Andrew by Maxwell, told of how she arrived at the palace ready to massage the prince, but was surprised when he disappeared into the bathroom and allegedly reappeared naked.

The fallout from the interview and the subsequent revelations meant Andrew was now radioactive. His removal from royal duties also meant a loss of income. He was stripped of the £249,000 a year he received from the Sovereign Grant to perform royal duties. Perhaps feeling the pinch, Andrew and Fergie failed to pay an £8 million bill on their jointly-owned £23 million ski chalet in Verbier, Switzerland. The unpaid debt forced the couple to put the property up for sale for £18.6 million. However, other aspects of the prince's lifestyle belied his ostensible poverty. He could still be seen playing golf and relaxing at the most exclusive resorts around the world and he still drove a £170,000 Bentley with the personal number plate DOY.

It seems likely that Andrew had built up a sizeable nest egg from corrupt deals with some of the dodgy acquaintances he made during his stint as trade ambassador. Leaked emails surfaced of a deal brokered by Andrew for Greek and Swiss firms to bid for infrastructure contracts in Kazakhstan. The prince was due to earn a 1% commission, or £3.83 million, on the agreement. Add to this the dodgy sale of Sunninghill Park to Kazakh oligarch, Timur Kulibayev, and it seems extremely unlikely that such deals were one-offs for the prince during his time as trade ambassador. The press had voiced surprise as to how Andrew had afforded the £13 million purchase of his luxury ski chalet in Verbier in 2014. Well here, it appears, was the answer – by allegedly using his privileged position as UK trade ambassador to make money from crooked side deals with corrupt regimes.

One of the many dubious claims Andrew made in the Newsnight interview was that he was willing to co-operate with US law enforcement investigations into Epstein. Shortly after Epstein's arrest in 2019, Gloria Allred, the lawyer of one of Epstein's anonymous victims, Jane Doe 15, wrote to Andrew, asking him to provide sworn testimony in her client's case. She was ignored. Lisa Bloom, the attorney for another five Epstein victims, also made a public appeal for Andrew to voluntarily come to the US to answer questions. She too was ignored. Then, in June 2020, news reports emerged that Geoffrey Berman, US state attorney for the southern district of New York and the man in charge of the Epstein investigation, had officially requested the UK government for Prince Andrew's testimony in the case. Again, ignored. Incredibly, Berman himself held a press conference, in which he stated, "Contrary to Prince Andrew's very public offer to co-operate with our investigation into Epstein's co-conspirators, an offer that was conveyed through press release, Prince Andrew has now completely shut the door on voluntary co-operation." Although Berman's boss, United States Attorney General William Barr, made it clear that extraditing Andrew was not on the table, several hints and whispers from the US have made it clear that this might yet be a possibility. It would certainly be foolish of Andrew to visit the States, as it seems likely he would be subpoenaed for questioning.

In the meantime, Andrew has made some attempts to put the Epstein affair behind him and launder his reputation, and he has been aided in some ways by the media spotlight transferring to Harry and Meghan. After months of hiding from the press, Andrew and Fergie made a tentative appearance packing care parcels for the NHS in April 2020, to help with the coronavirus pandemic. However, Andrew's image was obviously still considered too toxic for him to be aired at Princess Beatrice's wedding, later that year. Although Andrew walked his daughter down the aisle at the ceremony on 17 July 2020 at Windsor Castle, both Andrew and Fergie were conspicuously absent from all the official wedding photographs.

In September 2022, Prince Andrew joined the funeral procession taking the Queen's coffin to Westminster Abbey. "Andrew, you're a sick old man," yelled a heckler, who was extracted from the crowd and detained by the police. The royal biographer, Tina Brown, said on breakfast TV: "That's it for Andrew. You saw how bereft he looked because his one protector has gone… Andrew is done. That was the last time, I think, that you are going to see him in public life."

It remains to be seen whether Prince Andrew will manage to stay out of the news in future or whether he will be sucked back into the Epstein and Virginia Giuffre cases. Ghislaine Maxwell's court proceedings were a key event where all ears were pinned back for any mention of the prince or other powerful associates of Epstein. However, Maxwell protected her co-conspirators in what many believe was a quid pro quo for soft prison time and an early release on appeal.

Another possibility is the release or leak of video or photographic evidence of Andrew having sex with Virginia Giuffre or some other Epstein survivor. Virginia herself made it quite clear that she believes there was video footage of her and the prince, captured at Epstein's New York mansion. Considering the reports from Virginia herself and other witnesses about the extensive CCTV system in operation at the East 71st Street property, it seems likely that this footage is still around, possibly in the hands of the FBI, who removed several boxes of evidence from the house on the day of Epstein's arrest.

Whether Andrew will ever have to officially answer allegations against him or not, one thing seems clear – his reputation will forever be tarnished, and rightly so. However, Epstein victims – some of whom consider themselves Prince Andrew victims too – will hope that the entitled prince will one day stand trial in a more official setting than the court of public opinion.

CHAPTER 3

LORD MOUNTBATTEN'S LUST FOR BOYS

If the general public were shocked and surprised by Prince Andrew's alleged sexual predilections, or the bad company he kept, perhaps they shouldn't have been. His family had history.

From King Charles' friendship with Britain's most notorious paedophile, Jimmy Savile, to his close relationship with the paedophile bishop, Peter Ball, the royals seemed to have a habit of befriending the wrong kind of people. But perhaps the most insidious of all was the case of Charles and Andrew's great-uncle: Lord Louis Mountbatten.

Mountbatten's full title – Admiral of the Fleet Louis Francis Albert Victor Nicholas Mountbatten, 1st Earl Mountbatten of Burma, KG GCB OM GCSI GCIE GCVO DSO ADC PC FRS, sums up perfectly the man's long record of achievements. Apart from being a war leader, a major political player on the world stage and a friend to people like Gandhi, Mountbatten also served as a close mentor and advisor to both his nephew, Prince Philip, and Philip's son, Charles, with Charles in particular seeing him as the grandfather he never had. Like Prince Andrew, Mountbatten served in the navy. Like Andrew he was seen as a war hero and a focus of national pride. But, like Andrew, his past – and his reputation – are beginning to be radically reconsidered.

Mountbatten was born with the (comparatively) humble title Prince Louis of Battenberg on 25 June 1900, in Frogmore House, Windsor. His parents were descended from German nobility, Prince Louis of Battenberg and his wife Princess Victoria of

Hesse and by Rhine. His maternal grandparents were even more distinguished – Queen Victoria and her consort, Prince Albert of Saxe-Coburg and Gotha. The godparents at his christening gave some indication of the world young Louis was born into – Queen Victoria, the Empress of India, and Alexander II, the last Tsar of Russia.

From an early age, the prince was nicknamed 'Dickie,' a moniker that would last his whole life. He was educated at home until the age of ten, before being sent to Lockers Park School in Hertfordshire. At the age of 13, he entered the Royal Naval College, Osborne, on the Isle of Wight, before finishing his naval education at Dartmouth, just as Charles and Andrew would do years later. The First World War erupted while he was still undergoing military training but he graduated in 1916, in time to see some action. His name also changed to Mountbatten during the war, as the German family name of Battenburg sounded unpatriotic, given the nature of the enemy.

Mountbatten's first naval role was as a junior midshipman on the battlecruiser, HMS Lion. He was stationed on the fore bridge, which was an excellent place to watch the captain and other commanding officers, as well as any action going on at sea. In August that year, he did see his first action. Lion was ordered to defend the port city of Sunderland from a German naval bombardment. The destroyer narrowly escaped being hit by a mine and a torpedo during the engagement. In 1917, Mountbatten transferred to HMS Queen Elizabeth and, for the last months of the war, he was promoted to sub-lieutenant, second in command of 50 officers and men aboard the small escort and anti-submarine vessel, P31.

After the war, Dickie was sent to Christ's College, Cambridge, for two terms as part of a scheme to improve the education of 400 young officers whose training had been interrupted by the war. It was here that Dickie made the first of his royal contacts and, as in the rest of his life, made the most of them for his own advancement. Two of the king's sons, Bertie (the future king) and Henry, were also studying at Cambridge at the time Mountbatten befriended them. Hearing their brother and heir to the throne, David (officially known as Edward), was setting off on a world tour the following year, Mountbatten requested that Bertie ask the Prince of Wales if he could join him. The heir to the throne agreed and Dickie was ready for his next adventure.

The tour to Australia, New Zealand, the Pacific and the West Indies was a way of formally thanking Britain's overseas territories for their help in the war. Mountbatten was officially posted to the ship, HMS Renown, as flag-lieutenant but his real role was to be a kind of minder and companion to the future king, who was deeply in love with his mistress, Freda Dudley Ward, and was desperately unhappy to be leaving her for such a long time. On the trip, the two became close friends and, according to Dickie, shared things with each other that neither of them had said to anyone before, especially about affairs of the heart. Although he attracted the jealousy of other officers aboard the ship, Mountbatten made such a good impression on the Prince of Wales that he was invited to accompany him on another tour, this time of India and Japan, in 1921, where the friends' relationship deepened even further.

In the meantime, Dickie had fallen in love with Edwina Ashley, the granddaughter of the Earl of Shaftesbury on one side and Sir Ernest Cassel, a merchant banker and one of the richest men of his day, on the other. The two had met several times across various social functions and each had been fascinated by the other, but it was on a cruise along the coasts of Belgium and France that the two fell in love, sitting up late at night on deck holding hands and visiting the local nightclubs at each stop on the tour. Thrown together in grief by two sudden deaths in their families – Mountbatten's father, Prince Louis, and Edwina's grandfather, Sir Cassel, both of whom died of heart attacks within ten days of each other – the young couple spent several days together, during which Dickie declared his love.

Edwina travelled out to meet Mountbatten in Bombay during his tour with the Prince of Wales. They spent three days together in February and, on Valentine's Day, Dickie proposed. They were married in St Margaret's church next to Westminster Abbey on 18 July 1922. Most of the royal family were in attendance and the Prince of Wales was the best man.

The following year, Mountbatten's naval career was almost cut short by severe post-war defence cuts, which meant 350 lieutenants would have to be retired, mostly those, like Mountbatten, who had their own private income. Dickie's influential connections saved him, however, with the future king himself putting in a word for his friend. Mountbatten was subsequently posted to the battleship HMS Revenge in the Mediterranean Fleet.

Saved from the axe, Mountbatten put all his energy into succeeding in his naval career, and during the interwar years, he enjoyed a meteoric rise through the ranks, so that by 1934, he had been given his first ship, HMS Daring, to command. In 1936, he was made a personal aide de camp to his old friend David, who had now become King Edward VIII. However, the new king's reign didn't last long and, in May the following year, Mountbatten attended the coronation of his other royal friend, Bertie, as King George VI, following Edward's abdication. By the time the Second World War broke out, Mountbatten was a full captain and in command of the destroyer HMS Kelly.

At the outbreak of war, Mountbatten took charge of the 5th Destroyer Flotilla. Close scrapes appeared to follow him wherever he went. In May 1940, Kelly was hit by a German torpedo off the Dutch coast. Mountbatten was unharmed but the ship was seriously damaged, so he switched his command of the flotilla to HMS Javelin. Later the same year, Javelin was hit by two torpedoes in a fight with three German destroyers off the coast of Cornwall. Mountbatten returned to Kelly, which had since been repaired, only to have it sunk by German dive bombers in 1941, during the battle of Crete. Mountbatten was subsequently given command of the aircraft carrier HMS Illustrious, which was docked in Norfolk, Virginia, for repairs.

Perhaps due to his bad luck or lack of judgement, his days of commanding vessels didn't last long. In October 1941, he was promoted to Chief of Combined Operations, a staff role that would look for opportunities to mount amphibious assaults on Hitler's Fortress Europe, with an eye to an eventual full-scale invasion. How did a captain who had two vessels torpedoed and one sunk under him, in two cases at least due to questionable decisions, achieve such an important role so quickly? For one, he was a favourite of Churchill, who saw his buccaneering spirit as an antidote to the staid, cautious decision-makers, who were failing to prosecute any kind of war on Germany. Secondly, he had a genius for PR and self-promotion that meant he could turn disasters into personal triumphs.

Losing his first ship, HMS Kelly, should have earned Mountbatten a court martial – he had signalled needlessly using a bright Aldis light, thus giving his position away. Mountbatten, however, became a public hero for bringing the stricken ship back to dock in the Tyne. He used the ensuing press attention to lobby for a Distinguished Service Order, which was subsequently awarded, despite the fact it was his own carelessness that had led to the disaster.

When Kelly capsized off Crete after being hit by dive bombers, Mountbatten's friend, the film-maker Noel Coward, decided to make a film about it. The propaganda piece, In Which We Serve, was a great hit and the commander of the movie's stricken vessel, played by Coward himself, was such a thinly disguised portrait of Mountbatten that everyone knew who it really was. Mountbatten played a large part in the making of the film, providing script advice and even 200 wounded sailors to act as extras. Not surprisingly, he enjoyed the film immensely and watched it three times.

However, failure was to follow Mountbatten in his staff role as well. After two successful commando raids – Bruneval, which captured important intelligence information, and St Nazaire, which destroyed the German's largest Atlantic dry dock, Mountbatten was promoted to acting Vice Admiral. He and his staff planned the disastrous Dieppe raid in August 1942, which would see over

6,000 Canadian troops frontally assault the well-defended port city of Dieppe, without adequate air or naval cover. The operation was ill-prepared and conceived, mostly as an exercise in showing the beleaguered Russian allies that the western powers were doing something positive to attack the Nazis in Europe. Of the 6,086 men who landed, 3,623 were killed, wounded or taken prisoner, and the landing forces were obliged to withdraw after ten hours, having achieved almost none of their objectives.

Mountbatten insisted the lessons learned for a future D-Day landing were worth the casualties and Churchill, still a fan, supported him. However, Mountbatten's shortcomings as a strategist meant he would not get the job many thought Churchill was grooming him for, as overall commander for D-Day preparations. Instead, he was transferred again, this time as Supreme Allied Commander of South East Asia Command (SEAC), and promoted to acting Admiral. In South East Asia, Mountbatten did manage to turn around the Allies' perilous situation. With several innovations, he dramatically reduced the number of casualties from malaria, improved troop morale and enabled them to fight through the monsoon season, thus surprising the Japanese. Consequently, the Japanese advance in Burma was halted and British troops began to advance, eventually retaking the country in May 1945. Following the surrender of the Japanese on 15 August, Mountbatten led Allied forces back into Singapore, which had been humiliatingly captured by the Japanese in 1942. With British troops back in the city, Mountbatten personally oversaw the formal surrender of Japanese forces in the South East Asia region on 12 September, recording in his diary that it was "the greatest day of my life."

SEAC was disbanded in May 1946 and Mountbatten returned to England as a rear admiral. Later that year, he was made a viscount, with a seat in the House of Lords. But greater honours and responsibilities – perhaps overwhelmingly great – were about to be bestowed. In 1946, he was offered the position of Viceroy of India with a mandate to transfer power back to the Indians, by no later than June 1948 and with the minimum of turmoil and bloodshed. Mountbatten reluctantly agreed with several conditions, including that his ambitions for furthering his naval career would not be hampered by the position. In February 1947, he was appointed Viceroy of India and took up his post in Delhi in March.

The political situation in India was extremely unstable, with constant violence against the British ruling regime, as well as inter-faith clashes between Hindus and Muslims. Muslim League leader, Muhammad Ali Jinnah, was demanding a separate homeland for India's roughly 94 million Muslim inhabitants. Mountbatten privately voiced concerns that he and his wife Edwina would end up with bullets in their backs and his reluctance was justified.

The Mountbattens' arrival in Delhi led to huge riots. Mountbatten was well-known for his diplomatic abilities and he required all of these to get all the conflicting factions pulling in something like a similar direction. He was already friendly with Jawaharlal Nehru, the independence activist, after Nehru had visited Singapore in 1946. Mountbatten had recognised that Nehru might become the first prime minister of an independent India and had stayed up long into the night chatting with him. Mountbatten took the time to get to know the other key political players, such as popular Muslim leaders Muhammad Ali Jinnah and Liaqat Ali Khan, and Congress Party leader, Sardar Patel, inviting each of them to the massive 377-room, 175-acre Viceroy House for private conversations.

Gandhi was one of the visitors and, like Nehru, he established an instant rapport with the Mountbattens. However, the Muslim leader, Jinnah, was a different case, coming across as fanatical and with a persecution complex that made him intransigent in his demands for five independent Muslim provinces. Indeed, sectarian strife was becoming so bad that Mountbatten quickly came to the conclusion that there would soon be civil war. He decided that the deadline of June 1948 was, in fact, too far away and that acceptance of partition and a prompt announcement of a quicker date for independence were essential, to avoid outright armed conflict.

It wasn't difficult to convince the differing parties of the necessity for partition. Mountbatten's main challenge was to find a plan that everyone would agree on. After an initial scheme to allow all 17 provinces to choose their own destiny was rejected, Mountbatten and his aides came up with Plan Partition, which would allow for two central governments, both to be included within the Commonwealth and both with their own assemblies. Nehru, who had been critical of the first plan, agreed and, crucially, so did Jinnah. The date for partition was set for 15 August, just 72 days from the official announcement. Some thought the haste of the plan showed decisiveness and a clear intent to hand over power, others that it was reckless and the product of over-eagerness on the part of Mountbatten to wash his hands of the problem and get out of India, regardless of the deaths and turmoil it would cause.

Nevertheless, partition went ahead and, at midnight on 15 August 1947, India and Pakistan gained their independence, with three north-western provinces, Baluchistan, North-West Frontier and Sindh, joining Pakistan and three other provinces, Punjab, Bengal and Assam, being partitioned between Pakistan and India. Mountbatten became the first Governor-General of India, in order to ease the transition of power, and was also promoted from a viscount to Earl Mountbatten of Burma. He stayed on as Governor-General of India for 10 months until June 1948, a period which saw terrible massacres committed by Indians, Muslims and Sikhs, particularly in the border territories. Many of these deaths were blamed on Mountbatten for keeping the decision on the geographical placement of borders a secret until partition.

When his time as Governor-General was over, the Mountbattens left India and returned briefly to Britain before moving back to Malta, where Mountbatten was made commander of the First Cruiser Squadron of the Mediterranean Fleet. He had been offered jobs as Governor of Malta, Governor General of Canada and ambassador to both Moscow and Washington, but he was more interested in his naval career, even though it meant he was now further down the chain of command. As before, however, Mountbatten rose through the ranks quickly, becoming Fourth Sea Lord, then Commander-in-Chief of the Mediterranean Fleet and NATO Commander Allied Forces Mediterranean. It wasn't long before he reached the top, becoming First Sea Lord, Chief of the Naval Staff, in 1955, the same position his father had held.

Meanwhile, Mountbatten's power and influence had extended in other directions. In 1952, following the death of her father, King George VI, Elizabeth was crowned queen. In 1947, she had married Prince Philip of Greece and Denmark. Philip was the son of Prince Andrew of Greece, brother of King Constantine I of Greece. After the disaster of the Greco-Turkish war, Constantine was forced to abdicate and Andrew and all his family were banished from Greece for life in 1922. Philip's childhood was itinerant and unstable. His father disappeared to Monte Carlo to live with his mistress and exercise his habit for gambling. His mother was diagnosed with schizophrenia and placed in an asylum. Philip, essentially an orphan, pinballed around Europe, living with various relatives and receiving education in schools in France, Germany and finally Britain. In Britain, Mountbatten's older brother, George, acted as Philip's guardian while Philip was educated at Gordonstoun, the same Scottish Highlands school which Charles and Andrew would later attend. When George died of bone marrow cancer, Philip, then 16, was placed in the care of Mountbatten.

Mountbatten had a close relationship with his charge, and the Earl, who had two daughters of his own, thought of Philip as the son he never had. It was Mountbatten who first arranged for Philip and Elizabeth to meet. In 1939, when 13-year-old Elizabeth was aboard the Royal Yacht cruising along the south coast, Mountbatten arranged for 18-year-old Philip, then a cadet at the Royal Naval College in Dartmouth, to escort the ship and have tea with the royal party. Philip and Elizabeth were seen to get along particularly well and Philip's was the last boat in the flotilla to turn away as they escorted the yacht on its departure.

Mountbatten was crucial in securing Philip's British nationality and getting him to sign a revocation to the throne of Greece, as well as Philip adopting the name Mountbatten from his mother's side of the family. All this was done with one eye on a possible marriage to Elizabeth and, no doubt, the raising of the Mountbatten name to the throne of England. His scheming was successful and, in 1947, Philip and Elizabeth were married in Westminster Abbey. However, his plan to have the Mountbattens become the ruling family of England was scuppered when the King insisted that Philip and Elizabeth's children would bear the name of Windsor, after their mother's family.

With Elizabeth's accession in 1952, Philip became consort and Mountbatten's influence over the crown was extended. There were worries and rumours at the time about Mountbatten's influence over Philip, especially focussing on his supposedly left-wing views, with some even branding him a communist sympathiser and others saying he was plotting to make Philip King Consort. The communist rumours even led to an MI5 investigation. Mountbatten himself wrote to his wife to tell her of rumours that he would be posted abroad to remove his influence over the young ruler and her husband. Interestingly, almost immediately after the coronation in spring of 1952, Mountbatten's post as Fourth Sea Lord, in which he had served just a year and a half, was terminated and he was sent to the Mediterranean to become commander-in-chief of the fleet.

But Mountbatten's influence wasn't to be negated so easily. He was still Philip's guardian and mentor and played the same role to Philip's eldest son, heir to the throne, Charles. Charles referred to his great-uncle as 'Honorary Grandfather' and followed in many of Mountbatten's footsteps, including a career in the navy and a lifelong love of polo. He also took Mountbatten's advice on affairs of the heart which, perhaps not surprisingly, included a potential marriage with Mountbatten's granddaughter, Amanda Knatchbull. Dutifully, Charles did court the young woman and proposed in 1979, but Knatchbull rejected his offer.

Worries about Mountbatten's influence may have been well-founded, given his role in the late 60s in an alleged plot to overthrow Harold Wilson's Labour government. Mountbatten had already long retired – his military career saw him serve as First Sea Lord until 1959 when he was appointed Chief of Defence Staff, a role he worked in for six years and during which he combined the three military branches into a single Ministry of Defence. By 1967, he was two years retired and 67 years old, but seemingly still active enough to take part in a scheme against the nation's government. Wilson's Labour government was beset by economic problems, overspending and union unrest. To add to this, there was widespread belief amongst the intelligence community that the Labour Party had been significantly infiltrated by the Soviets. There was even a claim by the head of the CIA's Counterintelligence Division, Jim Angleton, that Wilson himself was a Soviet agent.

According to initial accounts, the press baron, Cecil King, invited Mountbatten and his friend, the government's Chief Scientific Advisor, Solly Zuckerman, to a private meeting, in which King brought up the subject of deposing Wilson and setting up an emergency government with Mountbatten at its head. Zuckerman supposedly walked out, saying he wanted nothing to do with it and that Dickie shouldn't, either. Mountbatten supposedly agreed with his friend and the matter was ended. But subsequent sources, including MI5, alleged that Mountbatten had been far more interested in the potential coup than the original story let on. Harold Wilson's secretary, Marcia Williams, later told the press that Mountbatten was "a prime mover in the plan" and that he "had a map on the wall of his office showing how it could be done." Mountbatten's level of involvement in the conspiracy to overthrow the government might never be known, but it would certainly have appealed to his ambition and vanity. Friends and aides told of how he often talked about how he would have made a great politician and done a better job as prime minister than several of the incumbents.

Whatever the truth, the coup came to nothing and Mountbatten's political ambitions went back into retirement. Edwina had died in 1960 of artery coronary thrombosis during a visit to Burma and Dickie, now living alone, enjoyed a string of younger mistresses. As his retirement proceeded, he spent more time at the family home he had inherited from Edwina, Classiebawn Castle in County Sligo on the west coast of Ireland. Mountbatten would holiday there every August with his children and grandchildren throughout the 70s. The house was just 12 miles from the Northern Ireland border and near an area used as a cross-border refuge by the IRA. As early as 1960, threats were received on Mountbatten's life and, in 1971, he had a protection team of 12 policemen. In 1974, a police raid on an IRA safehouse in Southampton revealed that Mountbatten was one of 50 IRA targets, leading to a protection team of 28 in August that year. In 1978, an attempt to shoot Mountbatten aboard his fishing boat, Shadow V, was aborted at the last minute because the seas were too choppy for the sniper to get an accurate shot. Despite this and a spate of high-profile IRA killings that year, Mountbatten and the family still travelled to Classiebawn in August 1979.

The Mountbattens had a team of 28 protection officers that year. Yet strangely, Shadow V, identified as the biggest security risk by an army security officer, was not guarded during the day and had not been checked before Mountbatten took it out on Monday 27 August. On the morning of the 27th, Mountbatten and his family took Shadow V out to lift the lobster pots they had set the day before. With him were his elder daughter, Patricia, her husband, John, their twin sons, Nicholas and Timmy, Patricia's mother-in-law, Doreen, and Paul Maxwell, a boy who was holidaying in the village and helped with the boat. Mountbatten, standing at the wheel, took the boat out of the harbour and into the bay. At 11:45am, just as the boat reached the lobster pots, an

IRA detonation team, standing on a clifftop overlooking the bay, pressed a button that ignited the 50 pounds of gelignite they had stowed in the boat the night before.

There was a deafening explosion, followed by an equally deafening silence. Mountbatten was killed instantly, his legs blown off and his naked torso left floating face down in the sea. Along with him, 14-year-old Nicholas and 15-year-old Paul were killed. The others suffered serious injuries and Patricia's mother-in-law died the following day.

On 5 September, Mountbatten's funeral was held at Westminster Abbey. Attended by the Queen and the rest of the royal family, the ceremony, televised in over 20 countries, had been planned by Mountbatten himself, whose powers of self-promotion continued to serve him, even after death. His casket was carried to the abbey on a gun carriage drawn by 130 sailors and his body, like the corpse of some ancient pharaoh, was embalmed before being buried in Romsey Abbey near his home, Broadlands.

But behind the gaudy façade of pomp and circumstance, which marked the whole of Mountbatten's career and most of his life, there were secrets – dark sexual secrets that he seems to have succeeded, for the most part, in covering up. It had been known for a long time, almost since the beginning, that his marriage to Edwina was a sham. It took less than three years before Edwina had her first known affair with former army officer, Hugh Molyneux. After a ten-month relationship, she then started seeing a rich heir and polo player called Stephen Sandford. In 1926, her new lover was ex-cavalry officer, Mike Wardell. There followed an almost unbroken line of lovers throughout the rest of her life, including Hollywood star, Larry Gray, and possibly even Douglas Fairbanks Jr.

In 1931, things came to a head and Mountbatten threatened to leave, but Edwina persuaded him not to and they came to an agreement – Edwina could continue to have her lovers, as long as she was more discreet. The marriage became a one-sided open relationship. It became two-sided in 1932 when Dickie met Yola

Letellier, the third wife of Henri Letellier, a French newspaper magnate. She was young and beautiful and supposedly the inspiration for Colette's novella, Gigi. Yola became Mountbatten's main 'other woman' for the rest of his life but he had many other lovers besides.

Despite his many faults, Mountbatten seemed impervious to jealousy and many of his and Edwina's lovers became friends of the family, visiting openly and accompanying them on holidays. Still, Edwina's actions caused controversy, especially when she was found to be having affairs with black actor, Paul Robeson, and black jazz singer, Leslie 'Hutch' Hutchinson – quite a scandal by the racist mores of the time. Edwina was attracted to people of colour and, during and after Mountbatten's term as Viceroy of India, she had a long-term affair with India's first prime minister, Jawaharlal Nehru, who may well have been the love of her life. When Edwina was found dead in her hotel room in Burma, she was surrounded by Nehru's letters.

While an open marriage was a lot more shocking in Mountbatten's time than it is today, it seems there were other secrets and more sinister sides to Mountbatten's sexuality, which remained hidden, sides that might explain Edwina's early infidelities and the lack of sexual relationship between the two.

I interviewed Mountbatten biographer, Andrew Lownie, for my True Crime podcast. As Lownie told me, rumours about Mountbatten's bisexuality had followed him throughout his life. Mountbatten's close friend, the gay playwright and film maker, Noel Coward, said it was "beyond doubt" that Mountbatten had male as well as female lovers. Mountbatten's tiny mews house in Kinnerton Street in Belgravia was, according to one source that Lownie quotes, "Awash with young, good-looking Naval ratings bustling about the place to no apparent purpose." And a woman who worked in a clothes shop opposite the Kinnerton Street property told Lownie there was a constant procession of handsome young men visiting the flat. It seemed that Mountbatten used his position within the navy to obtain sexual favours from young serviceman, in return for career boosts. Nicholas Davies, who we have met before as Robert Maxwell's foreign editor at *The Mirror*, stated in his book, Queen Elizabeth II, which Lownie quotes, that he headed a *Mirror* investigation into a homosexual sex ring centred on the Life Guards barracks in London, in which a number of young guardsmen told him Mountbatten was involved.

Several men claim to have been Mountbatten's lover or to have seen him with male lovers. The murderer and conman, Roy Fontaine, claimed to be Mountbatten's partner during the war. He even claimed, according to Lownie, that Mountbatten's gay friends all knew him as 'Mountbottom,' while Fontaine himself called him 'The Queen.' And Lownie recounts another story from the actor, John Gielgud, who told how Mountbatten was caught in flagrante by his butler after he had invited a young man to strip and beat him. The man went about his business with so much enthusiasm, according to Gielgud, that Mountbatten's cries of pain attracted the butler who said, on finding his master in such a compromising position, "I thought you rang, sir."

Nothing is wrong with being a homosexual, obviously, but during most of Mountbatten's life, it was a criminal offence punishable by imprisonment, which explains and justifies his secrecy (nothing, of course, justifies the coercing of young men into sexual activities in return for career progression).

However, the secrecy may have concealed something disturbing. Mountbatten's driver from 1942-43, Norman Nield, alleged that he was paid extra to keep silent about Mountbatten's assignations with young boys, who ranged from eight to 12 years old, using brandy and lemonade to help seduce the boys. Nield also alleged that Mountbatten sometimes dressed the young boys up in baby girl outfits before having sex with them. Another source, Anthony Daly, who wrote a memoir about being a high-class rent boy in the 70s, told of how he'd heard that Mountbatten had allegedly had sex with a young Burmese boy in the back of a Dakota cargo plane in Ceylon (now Sri Lanka). According to Daly, he was told that Mountbatten had an alleged sexual preference for "well-bred and well-educated young men of good standing... ... from good families; or public school boys."

In 1980, stories surfaced in the press that made even darker claims. Writing for *Now Magazine*, Northern Irish writer, Robin Bryans, alleged that Mountbatten was part of a homosexual and paedophile vice ring, operating over both sides of the Irish border in the 70s. Bryans alleged that Mountbatten, along with other top establishment figures, took boys from the Kincora Boys' Home in Belfast and Portora Royal School in Enniskillen and abused them in homosexual orgies held in various stately homes across Ireland, including Mountbatten's own, Classiebawn. According to the article, Mountbatten's alleged preference was for public school boys around the age of 13 or 14.

Lownie managed to track down two of the survivors of Kincora, who both remembered assignations with Mountbatten. The first, calling himself 'Sean,' was 16 when he remembers being driven from Kincora to Classiebawn in 1977. There, he remembers being led to a darkened room where an older man gave him oral sex. In an interview with Lownie, Sean said: "He was one of those men who wanted attention, wanted you to chase him... I think he felt some shame. He said very sadly, 'I hate these feelings.' He seemed a sad and lonely person. I think the darkened room was all about denial." Sean only recognised the man from the alleged encounter as Mountbatten when he saw a picture of him on the news, following his assassination.

Another Kincora survivor, known as 'Amal,' told Lownie that he allegedly met Mountbatten four times in the summer of 1977 when he was 16. On each occasion, Amal allegedly met the sea lord in a hotel room in Mullaghmore, the town near Classiebawn. Amal told Lownie that on one occasion, "I remember he admired my smooth skin. We gave each other oral sex in the 69 position. He was very tender and I felt comfortable about it. It seemed very natural. I know that several other boys from Kincora were brought to him on other occasions."

Lownie also found official confirmation of Mountbatten's dark predilections. An FBI file from 1944, containing an interview with an intimate of the royal family, stated that, "Lord Louis Mountbatten was known to be a homosexual with a perversion for young boys." Although some of Mountbatten's FBI file was released following freedom of information requests, most of it is still secret. The same is true of British government files on Kincora which, although due for release in 2018, were extended for a further period. The official secrecy around Mountbatten's private life and the Kincora paedophile ring seems to indicate information that the authorities would rather not become common knowledge. According to Lownie, there is little doubt that what we currently know about Mountbatten's private life is just the tip of the iceberg.

Lownie has been leading the fight to gain public access to Mountbatten's diaries, which might contain more clues or evidence. The University of Southampton purchased the entire collection of Lord and Lady Mountbatten's diaries from 1918 to 1979 for almost £4.5 million in 2011, with the stipulation that the material would be "available to all". However, in researching his book on Mountbatten, Lownie discovered this wasn't the case. When he requested access to the archive in 2017, the university refused. Lownie complained to the Information Commissioner's Office (ICO), which ordered the university to release the files. Southampton University ignored the ICO's request for over a year, until the office took the unprecedented step in December 2019 of bringing contempt of court proceedings at the High Court to force the university to respond. The university, with the support of the Cabinet Office, which had vetoed the original release of the archive, appealed the decision and has repeatedly refused to publish files that they had previously promised would be open to the public, as well as delaying the date of the tribunal. Lownie has found himself struggling to take on the full legal might of the Cabinet Office and has been forced to launch crowdfunding campaigns to raise the £100,000 to fight the final case against a well-funded team of government lawyers. As Lownie states on his crowdfunding request, the stalling tactics of Southampton University and the Cabinet Office raise some important questions about the contents of the letters and diaries, as well as the motives behind the secrecy.

"Specifically:

(i) What is the genesis of the Ministerial Direction which "closed" the diaries and letters shrouded in secrecy? Despite four years of probing, neither the Cabinet Office nor the University has disclosed even the name of the person who signed it;

(ii) Why are Government and University spending large sums of money (with two QCs) on a legal case to prevent access to private diaries and letters bought with public monies and where the fundraising emphasised that the archive would open to all?"

As for Mountbatten, his life appears, under the microscope of the new revelations, to have been an almost schizophrenic split between the outward pomp and high achievement of his public career and the dark secrecy of his inner life. In his book, Lownie speculates about one potential cause – that Mountbatten may have himself been abused as a boy. When he was 13, the young Dickie spent several weeks in Bridport in Dorset, recuperating from whooping cough and bronchitis. During his stay, he was taught by a private tutor called Frederick Lawrence Long, who had left the Royal Navy to train as a church minister and was doing some private tutoring along the way. Lownie quotes some of Long's letters to Mountbatten, which appear to reveal a relationship that was oddly intense at the least:

"Dear Kid, I have one special pupil now – Prince John de Mahe. He is about your age & a decent enough kid but you need not be jealous as you know there is only one Dick in the world for me & there never will be anyone before or anywhere near him in my affections."

In a reply to a letter from Mountbatten congratulating him on his forthcoming ordination as a priest, Long wrote:

"You won't find that ordination makes me any the less yours

or you any the less mine: although I think I understand just what you felt. However many things there may be to do & think about there will always be time to think about you – and in the way that will be of most use. The use of those envelopes is a sound idea – very as I always have an idea you wish to say more, in some ways, than you cared to do… you are constantly in my thoughts. Best of love, your devoted, Lawrence."

As Lownie points out, as well as the extremely familiar tone of the letters, why did they need to be sent in double envelopes? For the answers to this and other pressing questions about Mountbatten's private life and the various skeletons in his closet, we must hope that the full tribunal for Lownie's case against the University of Southampton is successful. But maybe it is advisable not to get too excited. The government appears committed to censoring the private diaries and correspondence of Lord Louis Mountbatten and no doubt has further dirty tricks up its sleeve, in order to do so.

CHAPTER 4

GLOBAL HUMAN TRAFFICKING

'Sarah' met her new boyfriend when she was working at a fast-food job. Although 'Paul' didn't seem to have a job of his own, he did have lots of money and treated her better than anyone had before. She quickly fell for him and left her job.

Little did Sarah know that Paul worked for a human trafficker, spotting girls who could be manipulated easily and selling them on. When Paul took her to meet his 'friend,' Sarah entered a life of slavery. She was repeatedly raped and beaten and force-fed large doses of drugs to get her addicted quickly. Within days of leaving her job, she was sleeping in a dog crate, only being brought out to have sex with clients she was sold to over the internet.

Fortunately, Sarah managed to escape and the trafficker was brought to justice, but her case is far from unique. Millions of other victims of human trafficking around the world live lives of similar degradation and despair.

In the US, Sarah's hellish predicament is becomingly increasingly common. In the States, a child is taken by human traffickers every two and a half hours, contributing to a $975 million a year industry. Half of all human trafficking victims are children and 95% of them are female, with an average age of 12-14 on entry into the human trafficking system. Once taken, they have an average remaining lifespan of seven years.

Young vulnerable girls are targeted by traffickers or middlemen like Paul, who know the best places to entrap their victims. It could be grooming them by starting up relationships online or it could be looking for runaways or girls recently released from the foster-care system. Ex-CIA agent and human trafficker hunter, Nic McKinley, whom I interviewed for my True Crime podcast, told me, "These human traffickers, this is their business and they are good at it because they've got a lot of reps at it, and they were trained and mentored by people who were good at it because they had a lot of reps at it. So they know to go hang out at bus stops in the United States and look for what appears to be runaways, they know to hang outside of community colleges and fast-food restaurants, and they know how to target the types of people that they are looking for."

Once traffickers have victims in their clutches, they repeatedly beat and rape them – a process they call 'seasoning' – in order to break their spirit and acclimatise them to having sex with strangers. They then quickly get them hooked on opiates, usually heroin, to make them completely dependent on their traffickers. According to McKinley, "Traffickers get them hooked on increasingly high levels of, usually, heroin. And then, if they get out of line, then what they'll do is, they'll just withhold the heroin. And the trafficking victims we've talked to, addicted to these high levels of heroin, many of them don't even know how to shoot themselves up. They are completely reliant on the trafficker."

Once the girls are no longer of use to the traffickers, there are usually only three ways out, according to McKinley. One is death, often at the hands of the traffickers themselves if the girls get too out of line. This is where the heroin addiction comes in handy again because, according to McKinley, traffickers can simply give the victim a 'hot shot' of heroin and, when police find the body, they think it's just another overdose victim. The other routes out are being dumped – literally on the side of the road – or by becoming sex traffickers themselves, often starting out as their own trafficker's 'bottom girl' – essentially a business manager – before beginning to accrue their own 'stable' of victims.

Mckinley's own story is worthy of a Hollywood film in itself, which is perhaps why he was contacted by Amazon when it was set to launch its new Jack Ryan series, as a real-life example of the fictional CIA special agent. McKinley's talents manifested early when, at high school in 90s Montana, he hacked into the school attendance system to show a full year's attendance when in fact he had been skipping class to go skiing. After school, he joined the air force and became a para rescue man, a special forces operative who parachutes into crash or combat situations to rescue downed or injured personnel. After 10 years in the service, he went to work for Wall Street, doing private personnel recovery work. In his own words, that meant, "Some very wealthy investment banker went overseas, did something stupid, usually involving alcohol and women, and then I was the guy who had to go and get them out of that situation before the financial analysts found out and their stock price went down." With the US fighting in Iraq and Afghanistan, McKinley was soon poached by the CIA to become a special agent in the field, where he served in some of the most hostile environments on the planet, working with other field agents and special forces operatives.

It was while doing this that McKinley first became aware of the human trafficking problem, an awareness that culminated in Helmand province in Afghanistan. While working for the US Joint Special Operations Command, McKinley received intelligence about a bomb maker, who was using child slaves to test his bombs. "We found the human trafficker who was actually selling children to bomb builders, and the bomb builder was using the children to test their bombs because they wanted to make sure the bombs wouldn't go off if a child stepped on them. It wasn't because they cared about the child but because they were trying to kill US and British soldiers." The bomb maker was burying pressure plates for anti-personnel mines in a field and had young boys walking around the field to test that the plates would not be set off by the weight of children or animals.

McKinley was shocked, but even more surprised that there was no agency, unit or office to report this intelligence to. "So think about that – we are two of the most powerful countries and empires the world has ever seen militarily, from an intelligence capacity, from a law-enforcement capacity, from a technology capacity, from an economic capacity, by any way you measure it. I'm talking about the western world is more powerful now than it's ever been in any point in history, and yet we can kill people with flying robots from 6,000 miles away, but we don't have anybody who's solely focused on the human trafficking problem."

McKinley began asking his friends in US and UK special forces whether they had ever been involved in missions to take out human traffickers. "All I know from my life… … I know the best of the military operators from both sides of the pond, and when I start asking all my friends, have you ever done a human trafficking mission? I couldn't find a single one who said yes." McKinley was so profoundly shocked by the lack of interest in tackling the human trafficking problem, he decided to do something about it himself. In 2015, McKinley set up DeliverFund, a private agency, applying his and his colleagues' counter-terrorism expertise to fight human trafficking by supplying law enforcement with the necessary intelligence to arrest the perpetrators.

What McKinley discovered was that the lack of will to fight human trafficking ran right through the system from top to bottom. There hadn't even been a unified piece of legislation tackling human trafficking in the US until 2000. The US government had no agency or department to fight human trafficking and spent only around $22 million a year on the problem, as compared to over $50 billion annually on the war on drugs. Even worse, he discovered that police forces had no funding to fight human trafficking and, in many cases, didn't even have a dedicated unit to work on trafficking crimes. Individual officers and detectives were so poorly trained in fighting human trafficking that often, when they found victims, they would arrest them on prostitution charges, not even realising that these were victims of human trafficking operations. Then there were the sentences – human trafficking carries a minimum mandatory sentence of 15 years at the federal level in the US, with parole being granted sometimes after just five years. Compare this with a possible 30-year term for money laundering and you have a legal system which appears to have its priorities wrong.

With DeliverFund, McKinley used intelligence-based counter-terrorism strategies to go after the human traffickers themselves, of which he estimates there are between 25,000 and 50,000 in the US alone. These prey on an estimated 100,000 new children a year entering the cycle, who contribute to what McKinley estimates could be as many as 1.4 million victims of human trafficking in the US alone. Trying to tackle the problem from the victim's side is almost impossible to keep up with so, as a sheer numbers game, McKinley found that going after the traffickers themselves made much more sense.

With McKinley at the helm, DeliverFund has had some remarkable success stories. Most notably, its take down of the classified advertising website, Backpage.com, which was being used by traffickers to advertise and sell sex trafficking victims. Backpage was a classified advertising platform much like Craigslist. Like Craigslist, it had a number of categories, such as 'personals,' 'automotive,' 'rentals' and 'jobs,' as well as an 'adult' section where sex workers could offer their services. As is probably now clear, many of these were not independent sex workers but victims of sex traffickers who were taking the majority of their profits, and some were children.

In 2018, Backpage.com was seized by the Department of Justice and the company's executives were all arrested on 93 indictments around prostitution, sex trafficking and money laundering. DeliverFund had been part of the operation, providing important intelligence that helped secure the arrest and provide evidence for the prosecution. Backpage's executives deny any knowledge of sex trafficking on their site but McKinley says evidence shows they were openly talking about it between themselves. He also claims there is evidence they knew about underage victims advertised on their site. He gives one example of a human trafficker who advertised a 12-year-old girl with a picture and her actual age.

According to McKinley, Backpage simply changed the girl's age to 18 and let the ad go through. Seven of Backpage's executive staff were arrested and are awaiting trial. Of course, Backpage was not the only website facilitating sex trafficking and child prostitution and DeliverFund are currently gathering intelligence on 32 other platforms with similar 'adult services' advertising.

Part of DeliverFund's strategy is to gather intelligence on human traffickers via their social media posts, which are shockingly open about what they are doing, giving an illustration of just how prevalent a part of culture sex trafficking has become in the US. These posts on sites like Facebook and Instagram are full of pictures of the money and 'bling' the traffickers have made from selling their victims. In one series of posts, shared by DeliverFund on its YouTube channel, a pimp shows the takings from each of his victim's 'dates' with a 'John.' The posts cover a 24-hour period and include $810 in takings. This amounts to $295,000 a year from just one victim. When one considers that many traffickers have a 'stable' of three or more girls, it's easy to see how their Instagram posts are full of 100-dollar bills, diamond jewellery and gleaming sports cars. What is more worrying is the explicit promotion of the trafficker lifestyle that goes with these posts, including advice on how to treat victims. Social media trafficking memes, shared by DeliverFund, include messages such as, "If the bitch don't fall asleep in the car as soon as u lift her she wasn't down long enough." Or "It's not how many hoes you breakin,' but how many dollars you makin'". Pictures that go along with these messages show traffickers or their victims with hands, sometimes tables, sometimes beds, filled with dollar bills, showing off new jewellery, or posing in and around top-range cars. Others show off their victims' bodies, sometimes capturing their branding marks – tattoos such as a crown, which identify the victim as owned by a specific trafficker. The human trafficking lifestyle is so heavily pushed online that those interested in subscribing to the lifestyle can literally buy manuals on how to become a successful pimp or human trafficker.

One of the most successful manuals is called the '48 Laws of Pimping'. The 48 Laws begins with the rather philosophical line, "There are only two categories of people: pimps and hoes." Some of the 48 laws include: "Don't chase 'em, replace 'em"; "keep a ho in arrears"; "prey on the weak"; "when pimpin' begins, friendship ends"; "ain't no love in this shit"; "keep hoes on their toes"; "play one ho against the next"; and "turn a tramp into a champ". The 48 Laws manual shares a concerning trend with the social media posts – they both paint the lifestyle of human trafficking as an aspirational career choice for born entrepreneurs, which benefits the sex workers as much as the pimps. One example of the nefarious 'inspirational' promotion of the lifestyle can be seen in this social media post by a pimp, shared by DeliverFund:

"I left her with 120, 48 hours later I get back to $1880 and she said it was kinda slow. I told her to take off she said she wanted me to come back to something. Things like this make me go to the mall and surprise her with a new purse or something."

The reality behind this seemingly mutually beneficial, even affectionate, relationship, is that the victim would have had to have sex with around 9 or 10 clients in a 48-hour period to earn this money, all of which would have been handed to her pimp and a miniscule percentage, if any, returned to her own pocket.

This blatant use of social media reflects the move of sex trafficking from the street to the internet. According to the Human Trafficking Institute, in 2019, 83.7% of solicitations for sex in criminal sex trafficking cases occurred online. Prostitution and sex trafficking does still occur on the street or 'track' as it's known; however, on the street, the lives of independent sex workers are made even more fraught by sex traffickers who harass, threaten and sometimes even attack workers who don't have pimps. Often, independent sex workers will be surrounded by traffickers, who will force them to choose one and then pay a 'choosing fee' to the trafficker. And it shouldn't be assumed that this is merely an issue of men degrading women. According to the International Organization for Migration, 42% of traffickers are women. Neither is it just strangers who treat victims this way. According to the same source, in 46% of trafficking cases, the trafficker is known to the victim. Indeed, a large proportion of sex trafficking occurs within the family unit. This is particularly prevalent with child sex trafficking, where the trafficking victim leads an ostensibly normal family life but in reality is being regularly sold for sex by their own family members.

Such was the case of Melanie Cholish, who shared her story on Upworthy after seeing an advertisement about child sex trafficking that showed a child tied up in a basement. Concerned that this was giving the wrong image of what child sex trafficking really looks like, Melanie told her story of being sex trafficked by her own father from the age of five. Melanie told of how she would be dropped off by her father in the dressing room of an amusement park. Another man would then come in looking like he was searching for his daughter and would leave holding hands with Melanie, who would be given a 'treat' such as an ice cream cone for being sexually abused by the stranger. Melanie described how many victims, such as her, are not tied up, beaten or treated as slaves but praised, told they are 'special' and that what they are doing is 'good' – mixed messages that become particularly hard to process as the child grows up.

This is the secret side of sex trafficking. The other aspect, which sees victims paraded on the street and online as commodities, is the more brazenly public-facing side. Here, victims are not only branded with their traffickers' tattoos but are actually traded like cattle in 'conventions,' often held in strip clubs where they are traded between pimps and taken to different parts of the US to ply their trade. Ideas and terms like branding, stables and cattle markets aren't just tasteless and uncaring linguistic conventions, however; they mark a worrying trend towards the treatment of sex trafficking victims less as humans and more like commodities, from which the maximum value is to be extracted.

On my podcast, I interviewed Andrew Wallis, the CEO of Unseen UK, a charity fighting modern slavery. Wallis told me this trend of commoditisation of victims is especially prevalent in the UK. According to Wallis, "You can exploit someone during the day, say, in forced labour situations and then, at night, you can exploit them with sexual exploitation... ...and at the end of the process, you might as well exploit them for organ trafficking."

Wallis explained that organ trafficking often centres around the trade in kidneys. These kidneys often come from the black market, where they are extracted from victims of human trafficking who have outlived their value as a sexual or labour commodity. Otherwise, victims might be people from impoverished backgrounds in poor countries in Africa and Asia, who are targeted and offered money to give up their kidneys for transplant. However, as Wallis detailed, the transaction often doesn't turn out the way the victims expect. He gave the following example:

"The trafficker will go to, say, a remote village and some will give you $5,000 for a kidney, even one kidney. They will arrange it, arrange everything – the hospital and everything else. You think about it, you've got to get them to a hospital and the sterile environment it's got to be done in... They will take them to the hospital, they'll often fly them to a country where the hospital and everything will appear legit in that whole process, and it is because they are selling the kidney to the trade. They have the operation, they come round and they are then told, 'I'm sorry, the cost for flying you there and looking after you and the hospitalisation was $5,000. So 5,000 minus 5,000 is zero. Hey, we don't owe you anything.' And you haven't got a kidney. And then they are sent back home. And remember, they're in a remote place. They won't have access to the medicines that they need to live successfully with just one kidney."

According to Wallis, this isn't uncommon; in fact, much of the kidney transplant trade is supplied by such practices. With kidney transplant waiting list times of two-to-three years in the UK, many patients opt to fly abroad where they can pay to have a kidney transplant done privately. In that situation, as Wallis says, "Maybe you don't ask, where did that kidney come from, what was the situation in which that donor gave that kidney in the whole process? Now, I'm not saying in every incident, it has come from that, but there is a likelihood that there is a victim at the end of that trade."

Wallis's journey, like McKinley's, involved several close encounters with human trafficking that brought the issue close to home. He first came across the human trafficking problem 14 years ago, when a colleague who had been visiting Ukraine ended up paying off a trafficker to prevent someone being sold into slavery. The problem was highlighted again when another friend came back from a summer in Ukraine, working with young people in orphanages. The friend told Wallis that orphans were being picked up by traffickers the exact day they left the orphanages at age 16. The traffickers literally knew the days the children turned 16 and were ready and waiting to sell them into slavery.

Wallis was shocked but still thought of it as a distant problem. That was until he read an article about how human trafficking victims were smuggled from eastern Europe to the US, using the UK as a staging post. The article listed the regional airports smugglers used to avoid major hubs like Heathrow. Wallis was shocked to find that Bristol airport, near where he lived, was one of those being used. Appalled to find the problem in his own back yard, Wallis went about writing to all the MPs in the Bristol area, as well as all the members of the city council and the chief constable, asking what they knew about the issue and what he could do to help. Wallis's tenacity gained him a behind-closed-doors meeting with a senior police officer, in which he discovered that the problem was much bigger than he had ever imagined. Like McKinley in the US, Wallis was stunned by how little was being done or could be done by law enforcement to tackle the issue. The meeting ended with the police officer asking Wallis what he could do to help. It turned out that a major problem in Bristol was a lack of safe houses. Similarly to the situation in the US, because of the lack of targeted legislation against human trafficking or slavery, in order to rescue sex trafficking victims, the police would have to arrest the victims, in order to remove them from the situation. But due to the lack of safe houses, they would have to put the victims up in B&Bs or hotels overnight before they could interview them. During this time, the victims would almost invariably return to their traffickers, denying the authorities the chance to question them and find out the identities of their traffickers.

Wallis set up Unseen UK and established the first safe house in the south west for victims of human trafficking in 2011. In 2013, Unseen created an ongoing resettlement service for the victims. Through Wallis's new police connections, he began working with the Home Office and the UK's Human Trafficking Centre and he chaired a report by the Centre for Social Justice into modern slavery. Just six months after the report was published in 2013, the Home Secretary said, based on the report, that the government was going to build targeted legislation to combat human trafficking. The Modern Slavery Act was established in 2015 and, like the Trafficking Victims Protection Act of 2000 in the US, was the first single piece of legislation to consolidate various slavery, trafficking and exploitation crimes under one set of laws. Wallis was involved in the process of draughting the new legislation, which propelled Unseen on to greater things. As he said, "I lost two years of my life in Westminster on the Modern Slavery Act, and through that we've grown the charity and we now run the UK's modern slavery helpline. We work with businesses, policing, the general public and governments around the world, so it's been a bit of a whirlwind."

But as Wallis himself admits, the fight against human trafficking has barely even started. The human trafficking industry is estimated to be worth $150 billion dollars a year, which is more than the combined profits of Apple, Google, Microsoft and Starbucks. In 2016, there were an estimated 40.3 million people held in modern slavery, of which a large proportion were children – 1.2 million are estimated to be trafficked a year. This means that, despite the so-called 'abolition' of slavery in the 17th century, there are currently more slaves on the planet than at any other point in history. Human trafficking is the fastest growing international crime in the world and the second largest behind the arms trade, having recently overtaken the drugs trade in size. The reason? It is easier and pays better. There is less risk in smuggling a person across a border than a quantity of narcotics, and you can only sell the narcotics once, while you can sell the person again and again. This means, according to McKinley, that for sex traffickers, the profit margins are 80%-90% or even more.

Of all the countries in the world, India ranks highest in the 2014 Global Slavery Index for human trafficking, with 14 million victims. China comes second with 3.2 million victims and Pakistan third with 2.1 million victims. Asia accounts for two thirds of all human trafficking around the world. One of the prevalent forms of human trafficking in Asia is forced marriage, where a woman or an underage girl is forced into marriage without her consent and forced to have sex and/or treated as a domestic servant. The UN estimates that 39,000 girls under the age of 18 are forced into early marriages every day. Another disturbing form of human trafficking is so-called birth trafficking, where women living in impoverished circumstances are lured away from their homes with promises of lucrative work, only to be forced to bear children for their traffickers. Such is the case in Myanmar, where it accounts for 20% of the trafficking of women. These women are lured to what they think are factory jobs in China, where they are forcefully injected with sperm and compelled to bear children for Chinese men. In Africa, the process is even more brutal. Young women are lured with similar promises to camps in Nigeria where they are repeatedly raped before and throughout pregnancy until they give birth to a child, which is promptly taken from them and sold into a life of misery of its own. These babies might be sold illegally to adoptive parents, forced into child labour, trafficked into prostitution or even ritually killed.

Such crimes can feel like they happen in another world but the effects of human trafficking are far closer to home than anyone might expect. Labour trafficking accounts for 32% of all human trafficking cases, making it a close second behind sex trafficking (43%) as the most common form of human trafficking. Labour trafficking has a huge influence on the industries that impact on our everyday life, such as food and beverage, hospitality, technology and clothing. Consider the chocolate in your cupboard. More than two million children work in the cocoa industry in Ivory Coast and Ghana. Many of these are children of farmers but others are sold as bonded workers – slaves essentially – from neighbouring Mali and Burkina Faso. These children work long hours in dangerous environments, exposed to agro-chemicals and using sharp tools. An in-depth study by French Professor, John Dumay, showed that big companies like Nestle, Cadbury and Mars, who source their cocoa from the Ivory Coast, are contributing to this human-trafficking-driven industry. This means if you have chocolate snacks produced by any of these companies lying on your shelf, you are likely to have contributed unwittingly to the modern slave industry.

Then there are smartphones. The batteries that power our phones rely on cobalt, a rare metal which is found mostly in the Democratic Republic of Congo in Africa. More than half the world's cobalt comes from mines in DRC, one fifth of which, according to Amnesty International, are mined by 'artisanal,' ie non-professional miners. There are 40,000 child miners working in DRC, some as young as seven, many of whom work in cobalt mines. Child miners who spoke to Amnesty International told the charity they worked up to 12 hours a day, hauling 20-40kg of cobalt a day for $1-2 per day. Exposure to cobalt can cause dermatitis and inhaling cobalt dust can cause hard metal lung disease – a potentially fatal condition, yet children have no gloves or masks to protect them. One 14-year-old boy, who started mining when he was 12, told Amnesty that he often spent 24 hours down the mines, arriving in the morning and leaving the following morning.

What about the clothes we wear? Fashion is the second largest industry in the world that contains slavery in its supply lines. In India alone, it is estimated that over 200,000 girls have been trafficked to work in clothing production. China, Pakistan, Bangladesh, and Uzbekistan are other countries where trafficking victims contribute massively to clothing manufacture. Workers are exposed to toxic chemicals, hot irons and other dangerous conditions and are locked inside workplaces, where they are overworked and might be tortured, beaten and abused. One of the prime causes of slavery within the clothing industry is the West's demand for 'fast fashion' – low-quality cheap clothes that can be replaced regularly at low cost. We have all probably bought a garment like this during our lives, if not regularly, so it is important to understand the contribution such clothing items are making to global human trafficking.

The fact that many of the world's largest and most essential industries rely on human trafficking means that, just by living our normal everyday lives, we come into contact with 40-60 victims of modern slavery every day, according to Wallis. And if you think you never come into contact with the victims themselves, think again. What about the Indian or Chinese takeaway you enjoyed the other evening? How about that hand carwash down the road, where all the workers are eastern European? The chances are that some of the workers behind these products and services are victims of human trafficking.

One sector badly compromised by human trafficking is the modelling industry. Modelling is the front that Epstein used for his own nefarious ends, at first often by pretending that he was a modelling scout for Victoria's Secret, who could get aspiring models a foot in the door, and later on a much more industrial scale with MC2, the modelling agency which he ran with fellow child trafficker and paedophile, Jean-Luc Brunel. With bases in New York and Miami, MC2 trafficked thousands of girls from eastern Europe, Russia and South America to the United States, many of them smuggled in on tourist visas and many of them underage. The girls were housed in Epstein's brother, Mark Epstein's apartment block, where up to four girls had to share a single room. Brunel charged the girls $1,000 a month rent and Brunel and Epstein took thirty percent of their earnings. If these earnings didn't come from traditional modelling, the girls would be used to make pornography or were farmed out to rich clients as escorts. By far their most 'prolific' client was Epstein himself, who boasted of sleeping with more than a thousand of Brunel's girls. Judging by Epstein's tastes, we can surmise that the great majority, if not all, of these thousand-plus girls were underage. One of Brunel's underage trafficking victims even became one of Epstein's many 'personal assistants' / sex slaves. This was Nadia Marcinkova, who took over the role from Virginia Roberts. Marcinkova was 14 years old when Brunel brought her into the States.

Similar operations to Epstein's and Brunel's are, sadly, common in the modelling world. According to DeliverFund, thousands of "lower-level Epsteins" – that is, sex traffickers and pimps – are running fake modelling agencies online to lure in unwitting girls. DeliverFund has found lots of examples of women being advertised as models on websites and platforms like Instagram and, on other sites, the same women being trafficked as prostitutes.

One recently exposed wannabe-Epstein is Colombian model, Liliana del Carmen Campos Puello. The Instagram star was arrested in 2018 for recruiting underage girls for a sex-trafficking ring based in Cartagena, on Colombia's Caribbean coast. Campos Puello lured more than 250 minors to Cartagena in just one year on the promise of modelling careers. On arrival, the young girls from poor backgrounds were stripped of their belongings and documents and forced to work as prostitutes in Cartagena's thriving sex-tourism industry.

Ukraine is a major supplier of women and underage girls for sex trafficking and, in 2007, the Ukrainian police uncovered one sex-trafficking operation under the guise of a modelling agency. Over 100 Ukrainian and Russian girls between the ages of 15 and 23 were lured to the UAE on the pretence of modelling at a two-week fashion show, with payment of $500. On arrival in the

UAE, the girls' passports were taken away and they were sent for medical examinations, after which they were forced to serve as prostitutes for the two weeks of their stay, before being sent back to the Ukraine.

One aspiring model who fell afoul of a model agency front was Airica Kraehmer. Kraehmer was 20 years old when she moved from Tennessee to New York to work for what she thought was a legitimate modelling agency. The agency housed her in an apartment with only two bedrooms and 21-30 other aspiring models. It also told her that, unlike normal modelling agencies, it wouldn't find her work, she had to do that herself. The girls were also closely monitored. They had to report everywhere they went and weren't allowed to see any friends outside the agency. When modelling work started to dry up, the agency required Kraehmer to work in nightclubs, where she was supposed to just stand around "looking pretty." It was at one of these clubs that she was drugged and raped by one of the managers at the agency. Afterwards, she tried to escape but was followed and caught. She was drugged again and woke up tied to a bed. She had been sold to sex traffickers. Kraehmer was repeatedly beaten and raped on the bed for three days, before the traffickers moved her to a different location. On the journey, she managed to escape by causing a commotion in the back of the car, then fleeing when one of the traffickers opened the door. Kraehmer now runs an organisation that helps survivors of sex trafficking and has written two books about her ordeal. It goes without saying that not every victim of sex trafficking is fortunate enough to escape, as she did.

According to Anti-Trafficking International (ATI), the modelling industry is so ripe for the kind of abuse that Kraehmer experienced because it has no unions or policies and nothing more than a recommended age limit. Although agencies represent models, the women are considered independent contractors, not employees. This means that models have no guaranteed salary, no health insurance and no minimum wage. By bypassing regulations and union oversight, modelling agencies in America can take as much as 50% or 60% commission from their models. This compares to 10% for actors, where commission rates are limited by union rules, alongside other rights such as mandatory breaks, scheduled payments and overtime wages, all of which are absent from the modelling industry. Because of the lack of regulation around age limits for models, 54.7% of models begin working between the ages of 13-16 years old, according to Model Alliance. And more than half of these child models say their parents rarely or never accompany them to castings. Because of the control agencies have over their models, particularly foreign ones, many of them are basically debt slaves from the moment their contracts are signed. Ashley Mears, a sociologist who went undercover as a model, wrote in her book, Pricing Beauty, "20 percent of the models on the agency's books were in debt to the agency. Foreign models, in particular, seem to exist in a kind of indentured servitude, often owing as much as $10,000 to their agencies for visas, flights, and test shoots, all before they even go on their first casting call."

These factors, combined with a low average income of less than $20,000 a year, creates "a haven for predators", according to ATI. Many models are asked to perform sexual acts during photoshoots, according to the organisation, and are reported to their agencies, or not paid, if they fail to comply. One model who tried reporting an abusive photographer to her agency was told, "That's just Terry." Another model said about sex with photographers or casting agents, "Sometimes it's alluded to during the arrangement; sometimes it's agreed to beforehand. But in most cases, sex is just expected. Comply, or you don't get a plane ticket home…" And sex trafficking of models for money appears to happen throughout the industry, even at the highest levels. London-based model, Jazz Egger, told *The Daily Mail* that big agencies and established models are paid up to $2 million dollars to spend the night with male clients.

And lest we make the mistake of thinking that Epstein and Brunel are the only big names who have used modelling as a cover for sex-trafficking, let's not forget fashion tycoon, Peter Nygård, whose massive sex-trafficking operation (which rivalled even Epstein's own) we will discuss in the next chapter.

CHAPTER 5

BILLIONAIRE PREDATOR PETER NYGÅRD

LEGAL DISCLAIMER: At the time of publication of this book, Nygård is incarcerated for charges of sex trafficking and rape, but is unsentenced, which carries a presumption of innocence. Therefore, all of the accusations in this chapter must be classified as allegations.

Jane Doe 1 was a naïve 14-year-old girl, out shopping with her sister and cousin in a local mall when her innocence was taken away.

As they walked past a new clothes shop that was opening, two models standing outside the shop beckoned the girl inside. They asked if she would like to try on a pair of pants and she followed them inside. When she got to the changing rooms, Jane Doe 1 found that they had no curtains or doors and, when she asked the women if there was somewhere else to change, they said no. They then began taking pictures of her. At that moment, an older man walked in and began taking her measurements. As he did so, he began rubbing her inner thighs and buttocks. He asked her what grade she was in at school and she replied Grade 9. The older man then asked her if she had considered a career in modelling, as she had the body for it. She said yes, she had always dreamed of being a model. Seeming pleased, the man told her to give her phone number to one of his assistants to arrange something.

Just a few days later, she received a call asking her to be ready in a dress, heels and makeup, to be picked up at 6pm. At the appointed time, a white SUV arrived outside her house and drove her to a gated mansion with acres of palm trees and its own white sand beach. She waited inside a dining area with two other young girls, while the older man from the clothes shop played poker. Eventually, he pulled her aside and asked her if she was ready to "discuss business." He led her upstairs, but instead of taking her to an office as she had expected, she found herself in a bedroom. The girl became nervous. The older man turned on a television which, was showing porn of a man rubbing faeces over a woman's body. The man then opened a closet and produced a dildo and some K-Y Jelly. He instructed the girl to apply the jelly to the dildo and insert it into his anus. The girl tried to protest that she was only there to discuss modelling, but the man became more forceful until, afraid, the girl complied.

The older man masturbated while the girl inserted the dildo, then he told her it was her turn to have some fun. The girl asked him to stop, but the older man unzipped her dress, kissed her and opened her legs. Ignoring her protests, he forced himself inside her and proceeded to rape her. When it was done, he handed her an envelope of cash and told her to leave. Her makeup smudged with tears, the 14-year-old girl stumbled downstairs, where an employee drove her home to start the process of dealing with life-long trauma.

This story could be any one of hundreds of Epstein encounters. Except it isn't. The perpetrator was another wealthy and influential impresario, who used his connections to run a human sex-trafficking ring of almost unbelievable scale, solely for the purpose of satisfying his own perverted needs. The man is Peter Nygård, a fashion tycoon with an international clothing empire. As we shall see, his story and his methods are strikingly similar to Epstein's, not least the scale of his sex-trafficking operation.

Arrested in 2020, 80-year-old Nygård faces over 115 allegations of sexual abuse or rape, spanning six countries and 50 years. Like Epstein, he operated a pyramid-scheme of sexual exploitation, where abused women and girls would recruit more victims to satisfy their master's endless sexual appetite. Like Epstein,

Nygård liked them the "younger the better" and, like Epstein, he used a gated Caribbean island property and a private Boeing 727 jet to facilitate his crimes. Like Epstein, he paid the girls off after sex and, like Epstein's partner Jean-Luc Brunel, if the girls said no, Nygård would drug them and rape them anyway. As we shall see, some investigators think the scale of Nygård's operation out-shadowed even Epstein's, making him what one investigator called "the most prolific sexual offender that our world has seen to date."

How did the world find a rival to Epstein's international industry of sex abuse so soon and why are the two cases so similar? We need to begin with Nygård's background, to see what produced such a comparable giant of evil.

Nygård's life began in the frozen tundra of northern Finland. He was born to Hilkka and Eeli Nygård on July 24, 1941. His parents were farmers, who eked out a life in an area so snowbound that Nygård later claimed he could ski before he walked. His sister, Pirjo-Liisa Nygård, was just a year younger than him and they were to remain lifelong companions. One of her earliest memories was of shearing sheep at the farm, when Nygård cut all her hair off as a prank. When Nygård was just three, the remote area of his birth suddenly became a ferocious battleground of the Second World War as the Nazis – formerly allied to the Finns to repel the Soviet invaders – now turned on them, in an attempt to gain control of their nickel mines. The war devastated the region so, soon after the war ended, the Nygårds moved to seek better fortune in Finland's capital city, Helsinki. They opened a bakery but, as the post-war Soviet shadow began to loom over Finland, they soon decided to flee their homeland and seek asylum in Canada.

They chose the small town of Deloraine in the province of Manitoba. According to Nygård's later claim, his father chose this location because it was just a centimetre away on the map from where his brother lived in Hibbing, Minnesota, not realising that this was on the other side of the United States border. If the

Nygårds had expected an easier life in Canada, they were wrong. Later, Nygård would describe his first house in Canada as a converted coal bin. It was around eight feet square inside and had no running water or heat, except for an ancient stove in the centre of the room. Nygård described the entire family sleeping in a single bed where they all sagged into the middle, and a laundry-strewn kitchen table made of bottles they had collected. The only toilet was 200 yards away and would have to be braved in temperatures of -40 degrees centigrade during the winter months.

But the Nygårds were upwardly mobile – a trait that Peter would share with his parents. They soon moved out of Deloraine and its coal bin to Winnipeg, Manitoba's capital. There, Peter's father got a job in a bank. Winnipeg was where Nygård did most of his growing up. According to investigative journalist, Melissa Cronin's book on Nygård, *Predator King*, his earliest entrepreneurial endeavours were collecting discarded bottles, which he could sell for two cents apiece. Later, he graduated to the more civilised activity of a paper round, which he used to fund the purchase of his own bike. Later, while in high school, Nygård worked as a lifeguard, saving enough money to buy his first car, which he later sold to help his parents open a bakery. After high school, Nygård attended the University of North Dakota, just across the border in the US. There, he focussed less on the sporting activities that had preoccupied him in high school and more on business studies. He studied hard, living what he later claimed was an almost monastic existence, in order to absorb as much as he could from his lectures and his activities as the president of the university's business fraternity. By his last year, he claimed, he was almost a straight A-student.

He graduated with a business degree in 1964 and quickly found employment in Eaton's, Canada's largest chain of department stores. He started off with the lowly tasks of stacking shelves, sweeping floors and carrying bags of manure, but within three years, he had risen to an executive position, overseeing more than $250 million in sales. But he gave up this position of power to risk everything on an up-and-coming clothing company called Tan Jay. Nygård put all his savings plus a loan of $8,000 into purchasing 20% of the business from owner, Nathan Jacob. It was a real risk as the clothing line was not profitable yet. However, within three years, he owned the company and had renamed it Nygård.

The key component to Nygård's success was his targeted business model. Starting business during the post-war baby boom, when everyone was targeting younger customers, Nygård spotted a niche by doing the opposite. He later said, "Everyone was telling me that half the population is under the age of 25 and, you know, I sort of cleverly figured out, if half is under 25 the other half must be over 25, you know, and if everybody's going after this then maybe I should go over the 25." Nygård's garments targeted an average age of 40, with a style aimed to flatter middle-aged body shapes. It worked. His company grew quickly and became the first North American clothing line to expand into Asia. Nygård developed a distribution system that was the fastest the world had ever seen. He became one of the pioneers of what today is called 'fast fashion' and reaped the rewards. His net worth had reached nearly $900 million by 2010, when Forbes crowned him the 'Polyester Phenom'. He had more than 170 dedicated stores across North America and employed more than 15,000 staff. His distribution network shipped 20 million clothing items a year, for total revenues of more than $1 billion.

But behind the scenes of this outward success, another Nygård had been evolving, a sexual predator and paedophile, who would build a secret sex-trafficking empire to rival his own business one.

Perhaps the first sign that Nygård wasn't as wholesome a character as he liked to portray occurred in the mid-70s. According to Cronin, he had gone into partnership with a talented fashion designer called Nancy Ebker. Ebker was the president of Susan Thomas Sportwear Division, a conglomerate of several clothing lines. However, when the parent company, Genesco, announced they were pulling out of the clothing market, Ebker was left stranded, needing $1 million of her own money to continue the lines herself. Just as she was getting desperate, Nygård stepped in and offered a great deal, whereby Ebker would get to continue two of the lines herself and Nygård would be strictly hands-off in terms of how the business was run. But at the last minute, in a move that is reminiscent of Robert Maxwell's shady business practices, Nygård refused to sign the written contract, instead demanding an informal verbal agreement. Trustingly, Ebker accepted and went to work. It was a decision she would regret for the rest of her life.

Nygård soon started micro-managing Ebker and her staff, taking over decision-making, slashing salaries, even removing the office water cooler, and moving Ebker's personal office into a tiny storage room. It soon became clear that Nygård was taking de facto control over the whole business but, when Ebker complained, he reminded her that she had nothing in writing and would need to pay him $1 million to buy back control. If she didn't, he said he would ruin her reputation in the industry. She sued and, although the judge found Nygård's actions to be "unseemly," he didn't order Nygård to pay any compensation, concluding, bizarrely, that Ebker had brought nothing to the partnership in terms of assets and so had nothing to lose. Ebker was ordered to pay her own court fees. She later claimed that Nygård had ruined her life.

Despite the bullying and misogynistic business tactics, there was as yet no indication of the sexual deviance for which Nygård would later be exposed. In fact, Nygård was outwardly gushing about his love and respect for women, often talking publicly about how he thought they were equal to men in every way. His personal life, however, was littered with broken marriages and relationships. His first marriage to Winnipeg model, Carolyn Knight, ended after two years, in 1970. He then married flight attendant, Patricia Bickle, with whom he had three children, while having another child in 1974 with model, Helen Jaworski. This was probably seen as relatively normal for a high-flying 70s playboy like Nygård (he went on to have 10 children with eight different women). The first sign of something untoward didn't come until 1980, when an 18-year-old girl from Winnipeg accused him of rape. Nygård was arrested and forced to pay $7,500 bail, but the court case never got off the ground. The woman refused to testify in court and the case was stayed.

Although the 1980 case was the first public accusation of sexual misconduct to surface, it has now become clear that, behind the scenes, Nygård had already embarked on his career of sexual abuse and rape in earnest.

Casey Allen was a 17-year-old recent high school graduate, who enjoyed dancing at the local Winnipeg night clubs with her friends in 1979. Allen said in a Canadian Broadcasting Corporation (CBC) documentary about Nygård that she always saw him in her favourite nightclub, Bogarts, on the prowl for women. "He was circling," she told the CBC. "He was sort of a shark buying drinks, checking everybody out and being very unsubtle about it." Allen said everyone knew who he was and that most girls knew to stay away from him because he was "pushy." However, one night at Bogarts, when Allen wanted to go home but her friend wanted to stay, Nygård overheard their conversation and offered to give Allen a lift home. Allen agreed but, instead of home, Allen soon found herself being taken to Nygård's warehouse, with him saying he had to pop into his office to get something. Allen followed Nygård up some stairs and found herself in Nygård's office-cum-bedroom with a couch that transformed into a large circular bed, adorned with a tasteless animal skin rug. Allen said that Nygård threw her onto the bed, ripped her knickers off and began to violently rape her. Although five-foot-eleven, Allen struggled with all her strength, but said Nygård was "strong and he was practiced at it. It was clear to me that this was not his first time." She added, "He was accomplished. He was good at being a rapist."

Afterwards, Nygård drove her home to her parents' house. Allen said she didn't tell her parents what had happened, for fear that her dad might do something "really drastic" and she didn't want to cause trouble. Although Allen never accused Nygård publicly, she was thrilled when the 1980 rape case was announced and hoped to testify herself. She then received a call from Nygård in the run-up to the case, in which he offered to pay her off for not testifying. Allen refused and took the opportunity to tell Nygård exactly what she thought about him. "The joy and the beauty of that moment for me was he couldn't hang up on me," Allen told the CBC, "and I yelled at him for so long I lost my voice. I called him every expletive I know alphabetically. And so I had my day in court or, at least, an hour in court with that man."

But it wasn't just the nightclubs of Winnipeg where Nygård did his stalking. It has since become apparent that Nygård's offices and warehouse nurtured a culture where sexually inappropriate conduct was normalised. Women had to put up with crass sexual humour and comments and inappropriate touching as part of the normal workday environment. One employee, for whom things went even further, was seamstress Jonna Laursen. She had emigrated from Denmark to Canada in the early 70s when she was in her 20s. She was headhunted by Nygård and went to work for him in 1980. Laursen told the CBC that she'd heard about the rape case and asked several questions but was told that it was just a woman trying to take advantage of Nygård for his money. She said she was made to feel comfortable at Tan Jay but that Nygård himself gave her the creeps. The first indication of something seriously wrong was when she was asked to go on stage to model her own latest clothing line. Nygård jumped onto the stage and touched her breast, saying she had to lift it because her breast was too low. Laursen was shocked, not just by the inappropriate act but by the lack of reaction from the 10 men in the room, who acted as if this was perfectly normal behaviour.

Despite her shock, Laursen felt she had to continue at Tan Jay, as her career was progressing swiftly and she was trying to build a new life in Canada. Soon, she was accompanying Nygård on international business trips. On one trip to the Far East, Laursen was given a luxury penthouse suite that even had chocolates and stationery with her name on it. However, she was concerned that the room was connected to an adjoining room by a door. She asked a hotel employee to lock it and was relieved when he did. She had jet lag and fell quickly to sleep but she was woken at 1:30 in the morning, to find somebody else was in bed with her. Nygård covered her mouth, telling her not to worry, then raped her. Afterwards, he warned her not to go to the police, then left.

Laursen tried to put the event behind her and get on with her work while avoiding Nygård as much as possible, but he soon started following her home. Laursen made it plain that she wanted no more of Nygård's advances and that she was repulsed by him. This led, she claims, to Nygård firing her in 1981. When she was told the news, Laursen exploded and told the executive who had fired her that she was going to the police about the rape. Soon afterward, two Nygård employees turned up on her doorstep, offering her $8,000 to remain silent. Laursen didn't feel she had any other option but to take the money while she looked for a new job. However, she soon found that all doors to the Canadian fashion industry had been closed to her. Nygård, it seemed, had used his influence to make Laursen untouchable, much in the same way that Jean-Luc Brunel would persecute models who refused his advances. Laursen struggled on as best she could but eventually had to give up and return to Denmark, her Canadian dream ruined by her former boss, the man who had raped her.

Several sources have made it clear that there were always rumours of nefarious goings-on at Nygård's offices in Winnipeg but that somehow – apart from the 1980 case – nothing made it into the courts or the press. One investigation by local newspaper, the Winnipeg Free Press, came close in the 90s, when reporter Catherine Mitchell began investigating Nygård. Mitchell said she'd heard rumours about Nygård's predatory behaviour since she started at the paper in the mid-80s. But it wasn't until a decade later that Mitchell was able to get her first story about Nygård's behaviour, when a trio of women employees came forward to talk about his sexual misconduct in the workplace. One of the women, Judy Shier, told how often, when she entered Nygård's office, she would find him masturbating. She said he often made lewd comments about her breasts and, on one occasion, sent her to fetch something from the closet in his office / bedroom. When she opened the cupboard, she found a box full of pornographic pictures of Nygård with other women.

For Allison Adams, the abuse began on her first day, when her new boss patted her bottom while commenting on how beautiful she was. He followed her to a bar one evening after work and fondled her bottom again, suggesting Adams follow him to a corner to "neck" in private. Adams got away by introducing Nygård to her friends but the sexual harassment continued at work. Once Nygård got the message that Adams wasn't interested, the verbal abuse began and, just like Laursen, she was soon fired. The third woman, Mary Ann, also testified to walking into Nygård's office to find him masturbating. According to her report, she turned her back on him in disgust, hoping this would give him a chance to stop what he was doing, but when she turned around again, he had actually pulled his pants down further and was openly masturbating while ogling her.

Mitchell's story was a front-page splash and, as soon as it hit the press, the paper's phones were inundated with calls from similar Nygård victims. It was then that Mitchell came across Joanna Laursen's rape story. Mitchell was working on a series of stories, including Laursen's, when the newspaper's publisher inexplicably shut down the investigation and all other stories about Nygård's sexual exploits.

The Free Press's journalists were so shocked at the decision that they organised a petition and handed it, in person, to the publisher, Rudy Redekop. The journalists were shocked to see Redekop take the petition and, without even looking at it, throw it in the bin. Perhaps sensing he had gone too far, from the shocked looks on the journalists' faces, Redekop removed the petition from the bin and said he'd look at it later. Later, word came back from Redekop that he didn't want to be "the first publisher of the Free Press that sends hundreds of Nygård jobs out of the city," according to Mitchell. Mitchell says it was the first and only time she could remember a story being pulled by the publisher in this way.

Other stories about workplace abuse are numerous and similar in content. Debra McDonald, an employee who joined the company in 1978, told the New York Times in 2020 of Nygård repeatedly trying to grab her breasts. She finally left, after being called into a meeting to find her boss watching pornography. A colleague of Laursen, Dale Dreff, told Toronto Life that Nygård had called her into his office and spoken to her while sitting on the toilet with his pants down – an act of disrespect that is strikingly similar to how Robert Maxwell treated his staff. Another woman, Deborah Wagner, was tasked with organising Nygård's evening activities at his California offices. She spoke about how he had five different bedrooms in his office suite, each of which had locks on both sides. On one occasion, she recalled several girls being locked inside separate bedrooms so they couldn't stumble into one another.

If the abuse was bad at the Winnipeg and California offices, it was nothing compared to the industrial scale it would achieve at Nygård Cay, Nygård's gated residence in the Bahamas, not far from its capital, Nassau. Like Epstein, Nygård would become more practised in his recruitment of women and more insatiable in his desires, until he had built up a massive pyramid scheme-style operation, which centred around so-called 'pamper parties,' thrown at the 150,000-square-foot beachfront estate. Bought by Nygård in the late 80s, the property, at the north-western tip of the Bahamas main island, New Providencia, was based around a Mayan theme, designed by Nygård himself. According to Cronin, it featured a 50-foot replica of a Mayan pyramid from Guatemala, and an 80-foot-high manmade mountain, based on the Matterhorn. Around the mountain were scattered twenty open-plan cabanas, more than three hundred palm trees and dozens of Mayan-based rock sculptures that acted as braziers during the evening. Elsewhere, fake volcanoes spurted out dry ice and statues of nude women – modelled on Nygård's exes – dotted the grounds. To add to the tasteless nouveau-riche vibe, the property sported a helipad, a 1,176-square-foot beachfront gym, an underground kitchen catering for up to 800 guests, a disco hut with underfloor cameras, a shark pool, a dolphin pool, an underground cave housing 30 cars, a 3,000-CD audio system, a colony of peacocks and a chunk of the Berlin Wall.

This was the mind-and-eye-boggling backdrop to Nygård's pamper parties, wild music and alcohol-driven events held every Sunday, where 150 to 200 women, mostly local Bahamians, would visit Nygård Cay to be treated to the high-life. Or that was the pitch. Starting at 3pm, the parties offered food and drink, volleyball on Nygård's Olympic-quality beach volleyball courts, swimming in the luxury pool, as well as massages, manicures and pedicures, and that was just during the daytime. At night, the party really got going, with the disco often continuing until 6am on Monday morning. The guestlist was almost exclusively female and mostly those who fitted Nygård's ideal of beauty – slim but with a large bottom. Guests were expected to wear bikinis and, according to one Nygård employee, Natasha Codner, Nygård had a selection of Brazilian-cut bikinis to hand out to those who hadn't brought the appropriate swimwear. As the alcohol flowed, the parties would get wilder, with girls taking their tops off and dancing naked. Ex Nygård employee and masseuse, Richette Ross, told the CBC how, at one vampire-themed pamper party, she had witnessed women in the jacuzzi performing oral sex on each other, right next to the bar.

The main point of the parties, however, was not for the women to enjoy themselves, but for Nygård to prey on the pick of the bunch. Supposedly, it was a chance for Nygård's favourites to get a chance to become models but, in reality, being selected by Nygård meant one thing – sex with the fashion mogul, either consensually or otherwise. Nygård or one of his staff would approach girls he had picked and ask them to accompany him to a private room, ostensibly to talk about modelling. But when there, they would be expected to have sex with Nygård. If the women refused to accompany him, they would be drugged and led away from the party. Nygård's masseuse, Ross, recalled a number of occasions where she saw bartenders drop pills into girls' drinks. She told CBC, "When I was coming up to the bar, I saw the bartender drop a pill while he was handing the female her drink. It was in the middle of his finger and when he handed her the drink, he dropped it in. And I said, 'What did you just put in that girl's drink?' And he told me, 'That's the party pill.'"

There would usually be a guard outside Nygård's bedroom to stop the girls escaping but if, somehow they did manage to flee the room, there was no escape from the Cay. On one occasion, Ross saw a girl who had tried to flee from Nygård's bedroom. "She was naked," Ross told the CBC, "and she ran straight to the gate and she tried to climb it. And his bodyguard came and he dragged her down the fence and he carried her back." Afterwards, the girls were paid off with envelopes of cash and left to try and get on with their lives, all promises of potential modelling careers conveniently forgotten. Worse, if Nygård suspected they might tell anyone, they were threatened with retribution, including murder. Other girls were paired off with the few male guests who might be present – often high-ranking Bahamian police or government officials – to supply them with sexual favours.

Although it was more common for Nygård to invite younger girls to private events, there were still many underage girls at the pamper parties. Ross described seeing girls at the parties whose breasts "weren't even developed."

The organisation and recruiting of girls for the pamper parties was a small business operation in itself, according to Cronin, staffed by an entire department of Nygård's company – the Corporate Communications Coordinators (ComCor). ComCor staff would lure victims to the parties from the streets, at shopping malls or via social media. Nygård himself would often promote the events on his own channels, advertising them as a way of saying thank you to his female customers. Nygård stores were used as a particular hunting ground and high school girls were even targeted via Facebook messaging. Nightclubs were another fertile hunting ground and, on the rare occasion when male guests were invited, it would be on the condition that they brought five beautiful female friends. At one point, the operation was so co-ordinated and slick that a shuttle bus brought guests to and from Nygård Cay.

Once on site, the girls were subjected to a screening process where they submitted their personal information, including phone numbers and email addresses, and had head and full-body snapshots taken. These were emailed directly to Nygård, sitting upstairs in his bedroom, who scanned them and used them to identify his handpicked victims for the evening ahead, rating them from A to D in beauty, based on his tastes. His selection criteria? According to a 2020 class-action lawsuit by 10 Nygård victims, it was "an eight in the face and a nice toilet". Toilet was Nygård's term for bottom, the disgusting reason for which will soon become apparent.

One of the victims of Nygård's pamper parties was 'Jane Doe 5' from the 2020 lawsuit. As a 16-year-old Bahamian girl, she was thrilled to be invited to one of the famous events by her teen friend, who told her she would receive free massages and manicures. At the party, the two friends explored the grounds and drank lots of alcoholic drinks. While they were on the beach, Nygård appeared and gestured for Jane Doe 5's friend to follow him. The friend motioned for Jane Doe 5 to come along because she didn't want to go alone, so the two friends accompanied Nygård to his bedroom, where he gave them more drinks. The girls started to feel drunk and Nygård told them to start touching each other sexually. They complied, according to the lawsuit, and Nygård himself soon joined in. However, Nygård went much further. According to the lawsuit, he "sodomized Jane Doe 5 against her will". The 16-year-old was thrown $200 and left bleeding from her anus.

Like Epstein, Nygård had many famous visitors to his Caribbean retreat. They included, according to Cronin, Jessica

Alba, George H W Bush, Barbara Bush, Sean Connery, Robert De Niro, Lee Iacocca, Michael Jackson, Lenny Kravitz, Sylvester Stallone and members of the Kennedy family. It's unclear how much of what was going on was apparent to these guests but, certainly, Jessica Alba was disturbed enough by what she saw to want to leave as quickly as possible. According to a Finnish newspaper, Alba spoke on a press tour about a party she witnessed at Nygård Cay while shooting the film 'Into the Blue.' Alba described it as "gross," saying, "These girls are like 14 years old in the jacuzzi, taking off their clothes."

Like Epstein, one of Nygård's most high-profile visitors was Prince Andrew. He visited Nygård Cay in 2000 with ex-wife Fergie and their two daughters, Beatrice and Eugenie. One photo from the visit, obtained by Cronin, shows Nygård smiling with his hands on the shoulders of the two princesses, aged 12 and 10 at the time. It is unclear how much Andrew or Fergie knew or saw regarding Nygård's nefarious activities but, with what we know about Nygård now, the photo has a spine-tingling creepiness to it.

Irrespective of what his celebrity guests did or didn't know, the big question remains, how did Nygård get away with such public displays of his crimes for so long? Like Epstein, was there a reason that he chose a Caribbean island to be the main location for his pyramid scheme of sex trafficking, and the Bahamas in particular? The answer, it turns out, is yes. The Bahamas has a dubious culture of sexual violence towards women, which makes it a perfect location to get away with the kinds of crime Nygård was perpetrating. In 2007, the Caribbean nation had the highest number of rapes in the world and, until today, it has a US travel advisory warning that "sexual assault is common". In Bahamian culture, rape and sexual violence towards women is considered a private affair that is dealt with amongst families, to the extent that the term for rape in the Bahamas is 'hush.' Until 2007, rape within marriage wasn't a crime under Bahamian law.

Add to that the level of corruption in the Bahamas and you have a perfect recipe for committing sex crimes on Nygård's scale and getting away with it. Nygård's former masseuse, Richette Ross, when asked by the CBC why she hadn't reported Nygård's crimes sooner, said her reports would have fallen "on their face" adding, "Just like many others long before me put in their reports and put in their complaints. It had to be help from outside of the country to come in to rectify the situation." Ross described the Bahamas as "the devil's backyard" in terms of corruption and said, "This country has been bought and at the price of many young girls, many women." She described how many of Nygård's victims had relocated away from Nassau because they were so scared of the repercussions once the stories started coming out. She even recalled a time when she had heard Nygård speaking on the phone to a wealthy American. He was telling his friend that he should set up shop in the Bahamas because of the corruption and the ease with which to find young kids if you wanted to do "a certain dance."

Nygård was right about the corruption. It began in the Bahamas in the 1960s when Castro's takeover of Cuba forced crime syndicate boss, Meyer Lansky, to move his operation off the island. Lansky chose the Bahamas as his new base. Casinos were quickly legalised on the islands. International banks followed and the Bahamas soon became an offshore tax haven, where illicit money could be made to disappear. With the sudden boom in criminal activity and the huge influx of illicit cash, political corruption became endemic and has continued to this day. According to a 2016 survey by Transparency International, corruption "is rooted in the fabric of Bahamian society", with one in ten Bahamian citizens having been forced to pay a bribe to obtain public services, within just one year of the survey. However, only 6% of residents had reported corruption and a grand total of zero had had anything done about it. When asked why they never reported such crimes, 44% of respondents said they were "too afraid of the consequences".

That Nygård was up to his neck in the corruption seems indisputable. Former Nygård employee, Natasha Codner, told

CBC that police officers would come to Nygård Cay every day to collect envelopes filled with cash but particularly on Mondays because that was "pay-out day." And Ross confirms that pay-outs were handed to politicians, as well as police. She recalled an occasion when Nygård instructed her and two "notorious gangsters" to stuff some fish with around $150,000 in cash, then freeze them overnight before delivering them to the house of a prominent Bahamian member of parliament.

In one investigation, detailed by a New York Times article in 2020, a Times report into Nygård's sexual abuse of two Bahamian sisters – including the anal rape of one at the age of 10 – was stymied when the sisters suddenly changed their story and said they had been lying the whole time. Subsequent investigations by the Times uncovered that Nygård had used a corrupt police insider, Camalo McCoy, to bribe the sisters to change their story and to claim that former Nygård masseuse, Richette Ross, had paid them to invent the allegations.

In fact, Nygård's influence went to the top. Like Epstein, Nygård used his wealth to fund politicians and parties that he hoped would best represent his interests. Nygård's choice was the Progressive Liberal Party or PLP. So strong was his financial influence over the party that, when they returned to power in 2012, Nygård posted a video titled 'Nygård takes Bahamas back', in which he celebrated the victory as if it were his own. There were also clips of Nygård celebrating with prominent PLP members at Nygård Cay, including the deputy prime minister, the minister of health, and the minister of education. The message that the new government was in his pocket couldn't have been clearer.

Indeed they were. Since their fall from power in 2007 – thanks mainly to a scandal that included one prominent politician being bribed to allow Nygård's former girlfriend and glamour model, Anna Nicole Smith, to settle in the Bahamas – Nygård had paid hundreds of thousands of dollars illicitly to PLP politicians. One of these payments was the fish delivery that Ross spoke about. Ross also talked about seeing stacks of $10,000 bills bagged up ready for delivery. One of the recipients was former Minister of Immigration and Labour (and Anna Nicole Smith's corrupt friend) Shane 'Shameless' Gibson. According to the Bahamas Tribune, Gibson received over $94,000 from Nygård companies in 2012 and 2013 alone. All in all, the Bahamas Tribune estimated that Nygård donated around $5 million to the PLP party in the run up to the election, as well as claiming he rolled up £100 and $300 notes in PLP T-shirts while handing them out to onlookers at PLP rallies.

Nygård was, of course, rewarded for his 'loyalty' to the party. Not long after the election win, he was granted the extension to Nygård Cay that he required, in order to build a stem cell research facility, of which more later.

Caribbean island homes and underage girls weren't the only tastes that Nygård and Epstein shared. They also had the same eye for a good private jet. Both owned reconfigured Boeing 727s, decommissioned passenger jets that could carry over a hundred passengers, with a range of over 2,500 miles. And both men opted for similar furnishings, which hinted at the dark goings-on that took place inside. While Epstein's Lolita Express had its own private bedroom and en suite, Nygård's own 'N-Force' jet was, according to pictures obtained by Cronin, scattered with beds and banquettes, situated beneath mirrored ceilings. A chrome stripper pole was the centrepiece of another room.

Flight manifests, obtained by Cronin, give an indication of some of the women or girls who were sharing N-Force flights with Nygård. Their nationalities included American, Canadian, Bahamian, Brazilian, Czech, Belgian, Estonian, Dominican, Ethiopian, Lebanese, Ukrainian, and Yemeni.

Interestingly, the Boeing 727 design features a rear door with retractable staircase, which makes for easier embarkation and disembarkation in smaller out-of-the-way airfields and runways and which could even be opened in-flight. Charlie Robinson speculated in one of our interviews that this design feature may have been one of the reasons why Epstein chose that particular aeroplane, as it facilitated the dropping off of sensitive packages, such as drugs or armaments. Robinson speculated that it could even be used to dispatch victims who had perhaps proved overly troublesome while on board. Might Nygård have chosen the 727 for similar reasons? It is another mystery to which we might never know the answer.

Another similarity the two men shared was their 'philanthropic' spending, especially when it came to funding science, and fringe science in particular. Nygård's foremost interest was stem cell research. Like Epstein, Nygård was a health fanatic and supremely vain about his physical appearance, so the aging Nygård was naturally drawn to stem cell technology for its promise of reversing the aging process. Nygård wanted to open his own stem cell research facility and scoured the world in the 2000s for the best place to host it. In the end, he settled on the Bahamas but he was faced with a problem – the islands didn't have the necessary legislation in place to begin stem cell research. Coincidentally enough, when the PLP returned to power in 2012 with Nygård's help, one of the first items on their agenda was the pushing through of the Stem Cell Therapy and Research Bill in 2013. As we have seen, they also granted Nygård permission to extend his property to house a stem cell research facility at Nygård Cay.

However, to Nygård's fury, the Bahamian government didn't quite uphold its end of the bargain. It appointed an independent regulatory ethics committee that would decide who could and couldn't open stem cell facilities in the Bahamas, meaning that Nygård's influence over the procedure had effectively disappeared. Frustrated and privately complaining that his $5 million in bribes had been wasted, Nygård took his project to nearby St Kitts, just a short hop away from Epstein's own island, Little St James. More coincidences followed. In 2013, the PLP party was founded in St Kitts and Nevis by a politician called Timothy Harris. Despite his party winning only one seat at the 2015 election, and amidst rumours of shady campaign donations, Harris was elected prime minister of the country. In 2016, Harris's government gave Nygård permission to open a stem cell research and treatment centre at St Kitts's Joseph N France General Hospital.

Unfortunately for Nygård, however, the government's chief medical officer, Dr Patrick Martin, inspected Nygård's private wards in the hospital one day and found that the doctors were not licenced to practise in St Kitts and that they were not keeping medical records for their patients. Martin quickly closed down the operation and was just as quickly relieved of his post by the St Kitts government. In subsequent press investigations, one local news source claimed that Nygård had been taking stem cells from the placentas of mothers who had given birth in the hospital, without their knowledge. Former Nygård employee, Richette Ross, confirmed Nygård's interest in placentas for his stem cell research, saying he had told her that he forced women he had gotten pregnant to have abortions, then used their placentas to treat his own aging process. Nygård claimed that because his own DNA was in the placentas, they were an even better match than usual, when treating himself. This was confirmed independently by Nygård's 'girlfriend' Suelyn Medeiros, who told the story in her memoir of how Nygård had once propositioned her to get pregnant by him, then abort the foetus, in order to provide "a life's supply" of stem cells.

Medeiros was Nygård's girlfriend in the same way that Ghislaine Maxwell was Epstein's. And this was another similarity between the two perverts – they both kept an inner core of girlfriends / personal assistants / recruiters, who formed the top level of their sex trafficking pyramid scheme.

As with Epstein, the victims that Nygård found most attractive and pliable were kept on in permanent roles, in what he called his 'harem.' They accompanied him on his business trips around the planet and were always seen with the most impeccable hair and makeup and the most fashionable designer dresses. But life was far less glamorous beneath the surface glitz. As the 2020 lawsuit detailed, the average day in the life of one of these girlfriends went something like this:

"They must awake every day at 5:30am to prepare his breakfast and ensure that it is ready for him to eat the moment he awakens. They are also required to, among other things, give him his medications on schedule, prepare his clothes, bathe him, clip his toenails and prepare all of his meals… to prepare his bags with marketing and public relations materials for his business meetings relating to Nygård Companies, attend his business meetings, otherwise act as his personal servants, and to model company clothing for company executives."

And that was just the day job. Behind the scenes were the sexual services. Two former 'girlfriends,' who spoke to the CBC about life with Nygård, talked of how he would require sex or sexual acts at least once a day. Some of these sexual acts were "inhumane" and "sadistic," according to one of the women, Celebrity Harvey. What were these inhumane sexual acts? Well, the clue comes in Nygård's term for a woman's behind – 'toilet.' It turns out that Nygård had a thing about faeces. He liked women to defecate on him and, according to Harvey, even to eat their faeces. Harvey claims that, as a 'girlfriend,' she even had to maintain a strict diet to ensure that her faeces was of the right quality for Nygård's needs. She told the CBC, "He wanted me to have a clean bowel movement. I was able to give that to him, where a lot of girls they were on cocaine which is a laxative, so they couldn't defecate properly."

According to the 2020 lawsuit, Nygård's faeces fixation was a common theme amongst the complaints of sexual assault. In the indictment, 14-year-old Jane Doe 1 reported how, after Nygård lured her to his bedroom, he turned on a porn film showing a man rubbing faeces onto a woman's body. Fourteen-year-old Jane Doe 2, who became a regular at pamper parties, testified that on one occasion in 2017, "Nygård insisted that she defecate and / or urinate in his mouth." She refused and Nygård offered to give her drugs to help, but she continued to refuse and never went back to Nygård Cay again. Fifteen-year-old Jane Doe 6 also alleged that, when lured to an upstairs jacuzzi with Nygård, he asked her to defecate onto his face. She refused and Nygård attempted unsuccessfully to rape her anally before raping her vaginally. And 15-year-old Jane Doe 10 told how Nygård had offered her "$10,000 to defecate into his mouth". Jane Doe 10 also refused and was anally raped by Nygård.

According to the 2020 indictment, girlfriends were required to sleep with other men, friends of Nygård, just as Epstein's 'personal assistants' and 'masseuses' were. The other, unnamed, girlfriend who spoke to the CBC confirmed this, saying that she and three other women were asked on one occasion to go up to one of the top bedrooms in the Nygård Cay complex and perform sexual services for a guest, who was a TV star. She also described parties at Nygård Cay that took place on Saturdays. Unlike the 'pamper parties' on Sundays, these parties had a lot more men in attendance. The former Nygård 'girlfriend' described these as "a kind of auction" where Nygård's women were paired up with the various men to have sex or perform sexual acts, in order to keep the recipients in Nygård's pocket.

Indeed, this was how the woman first met Nygård, according to her interview with the CBC. As a young Canadian model travelling to the Bahamas to meet Nygård with her manager, she was shocked to find her boss in a grotto, taking part in a "full-blown orgy." When she later confronted her manager about what he had been doing, her boss told her that he had "traded her" with Nygård for the three women he'd been having sex with.

Like Epstein's 'assistants,' Nygård's 'girlfriends' would be expected to recruit what he called "fresh meat" or "sacrifices." According to the 2020 lawsuit, they would be expected to use drink and drugs to get their victims loose and were told by Nygård to target girls, telling them "the younger the better". As with Epstein, they would be paid more for acting as recruiters but it seems that many of the 'harem' did it more as a way of getting out of having to have sex with Nygård themselves.

But the recruiters weren't the only enablers for Nygård's sex trafficking operation. Investigations are beginning to show that staff throughout his business empire were actively participating, complicit, or at least aware of, what was going on. Pamela Erickson worked as a director of marketing in Nygård's LA office. She told the CBC that she had personally witnessed company money used to make allegations against Nygård go away, and that she was personally involved in cover-up attempts in the 2000s, when she was asked to sign false affidavits saying she had never been aware of anything untoward within the company.

Erickson told the CBC that the whole company was aware that, if you tried to say anything publicly about Nygård, you would face the full financial might of the company in court, and this was done with the full knowledge and backing of the executives. One of these top-tier enablers appears to be long-term senior executive, Greg Fenske, who, after Nygård's arrest in 2020, deleted more than a thousand company documents that had been requested by subpoena. Another is Tina Tulikorpi, a Toronto-based executive and friend of the Nygård family, who was instrumental in covering up abuse and putting pressure on victims to stay quiet, according to the CBC. Another is Nygård's employee and niece, Angela Dyborn. Dyborn was in charge of communications and personally responsible for checking in guests at the pamper parties and uploading their photos and information to Nygård's database. According to victims' lawyer, Lisa Haba, Dyborn was not only aware of the rapes happening at the pamper parties but was instrumental in the "clean up" side of the operation – making sure that girls were aware that, if they spoke about what had happened, things wouldn't go well for them. And Greg Gutzler, another lawyer for the victims, said that the number of enablers within Nygård's companies would have had to be "in the hundreds."

One distinct dissimilarity between Nygård and Epstein was that Nygård had children – 10 of them in total. Were they aware of what their father was up to? And what was it like to be in the immediate family of such a monster? Kai Zen Bickle, son of Peter Nygård and his former wife, Patricia Bickle, was probably as close to Nygård as any of his children. Kai, whom I interviewed on my Attwood Unleashed show, worked for the Nygård empire and was seen at one point as Nygård's natural heir. Now he speaks out against his father's crimes and is a leading advocate for Nygård survivors.

Kai's earliest memories of Nygård are not good. He was the youngest of three children born to Nygård and his mother, Patricia, during a tempestuous 14-year relationship. Kai was just three when his parents split and he remembers constant fights and Nygård leaving. His mother had to take Nygård to court to fight for child support. Kai said his first seven years after leaving Nygård were in therapy and that the whole family was in therapy after the trauma of the split. He said his mother hinted that there were terrible secrets about Nygård but that she wouldn't tell him the details until he was older. Growing up, Kai only saw Nygård on occasional trips at holiday seasons. In his teens, Kai started to spend more time with his father in the Bahamas and the warehouse in Winnipeg. It wasn't until he was 15 that he suddenly found out he had a half-brother, when the younger boy came to visit Nygård Cay. After that, Kai began to realise that he had more and more step-siblings and that the family of three children was actually 10. Still, he tried to stay neutral and not judge his father.

Kai developed a desire to work in his father's company and, when he was 21, he moved to Los Angeles to undergo a personal apprenticeship with his dad in running the company. "I lasted about three years before I totally burnt out," Kai he said in an interview with the CBC. "By the time I was 24, I was a shell of myself. I walked into that situation confident, happy and vibrant and three years later I look at pictures of myself and I look like I'm dying. I've lost weight. I'm not taking care of myself. I look depressed, I am depressed. My self-esteem is shot and I really had ended up with a quarter-life crisis."

Kai said he attended a lot of dinner parties that Nygård threw in LA. There were always women and it always looked like his dad was going to get with one or another of them, but he never suspected there was anything nefarious involved. In fact, he remembers Nygård speaking respectfully about women. It wasn't until 2019 that Kai finally realised what a monster his father was, and the revelation couldn't have been more shocking. It was at one of the LA dinner parties and Kai noticed with a sense of unease that Nygård had an eight-year-old girl sitting in the chair on his righthand side. Kai thought of as this seat as the 'girlfriend chair' because it was the place where Nygård always sat the woman he wanted to sleep with that night.

As the dinner wore on, Kai watched with increasing discomfort as Nygård would lean over and whisper in the girl's ear. Kai continued to keep his eye on the situation and, when the party transitioned to a game of poker and everyone stood up, Kai noticed Nygård's hand behind the girl's back, resting on what appeared to be her bottom or upper thighs. "I see his elbows start gyrating back and forth," Kai told the CBC, "like he's moving his hand and immediately I got these terrible like butterflies and anxiety, and I said to the mother, 'He's feeling up your daughter. Get him away from her right now.'"

After the girl's mother dragged her away, Kai remembers being filled with adrenaline as he stared into his father's eyes. "I was thinking to myself, who is this guy? Did I just see what I really thought I saw? And that means that so many other things that I could have maybe suspected, maybe they were real rumours from the past, like all of this information was hitting me like an avalanche." Kai left the party with his brother, still trying to process what he had just witnessed. Outside, he told his brother, "I think our dad is really, really sick. I think he just felt up this kid." After that, Kai said, "I went home and I curled up into a little ball and I was just in the foetal position."

Kai said he confronted his father about the incident sometime later on the phone but that Nygård turned the tables on him, telling him that he must be sick and twisted to think he had seen something like that, and that he had been "brain damaged" by his mother. Unsure of what to think, Kai began looking into his father's past. What came up was story after story of rape and abuse. When Kai questioned Nygård about his findings, his dad told him nobody had ever got any dirt on him and never would because he was like "a choirboy" and had no skeletons in his closet. But it was too little too late to convince his son. Kai is now one of the leading advocates and campaigners for Nygård survivors.

And Kai is not the only son who has turned against Nygård. The growing ranks of the civil lawsuit against Nygård now include John Doe 1 and John Doe 2, both of whom are his sons. The two men claim that Nygård paid a sex worker to rape them when they were 14 and 15 years old respectively. Both children said that Nygård flew them to the Bahamas with the plan of having the same sex worker – one of Nygård's long-term 'girlfriends' –have sex with them on separate occasions. According to the lawsuit, the girlfriend, who is unnamed, would have been "punished, including loss of pay and benefits, had she not followed Nygård's instructions to rape his sons."

The turning of Nygård's sons was one of many body blows the serial predator has received in the last two years, but the writing may have been on the wall since 2013, when his hold over the Bahamian authorities first appeared to desert him. Nygård had been in a long-running feud with his neighbour, international hedge fund manager, Louis Bacon. Much of the argument surrounded the use of a shared drive between the two properties and the overbearing noise of Nygård's pamper parties, which disturbed the peace of the reclusive Bacon. However, Bacon was also a staunch environmental campaigner, who had spent much of his own money to preserve local wildlife habitats in the Bahamas. Bacon soon discovered that Nygård had been illegally dredging the sea floor around his estate to enlarge his section of the coast to more than double its original size.

Bacon immediately threw his financial backing behind a local environmental group called 'Save the Bays,' which was seeking to halt the millionaire's illegal activities in court. With Bacon on board, Nygård was, for once, not able to resort to his tried and trusted tactic of outspending his rivals in prolonged court battles. The persistence of Smith and Bacon paid off and, in 2013, a Bahamian supreme court judge ordered Nygård to stop the illegal dredging. Predictably, Nygård did no such thing and his repeated attempts to dredge the coastline outside his property led to three contempt of court convictions and a fine for breaching the ban. Nygård was to pay Save the Bays $3 million in legal fees. When payment didn't materialise in 2018, the judge ordered the court to seize Nygård Cay from the Bahamas' most flamboyant resident. In a later breach in 2019, the same judge ordered Nygård to be placed in jail for 14 days but the Finnish millionaire was elsewhere and hasn't returned to the Bahamas since.

With Nygård's presence no longer so keenly felt on the island, the tyrant's reign of terror began to fade and, feeling safer, survivors of his sexual abuse began to come forward. One of the first to turn was his former masseuse, Richette Ross. Ross had previously felt close to Nygård. He had never tried to sexually assault her and she had often listened to him share some of his most private thoughts during massages. However, in 2014, Ross's feelings towards her boss changed irrevocably. Nygård had set up a camp for teenagers at the Cay, where over a hundred children at a time would be invited to various charitable events. Ross's younger 14-year-old sister was at one of these camps when, during a lunch break, she realised she hadn't seen the younger girl for some time.

Ross searched the compound and eventually found her sister following Nygård up to his room in her swimsuit. Ross asked what she was doing and her sister replied that Nygård wanted her to model something for him. Shocked, Ross ordered her sister to leave and stared at her boss in disbelief. In response, Nygård merely smirked. "When he did that, everything in me just left," Ross told the CBC, "because you didn't just cross a line, you just blatantly disrespect everything in me, you broke everything."

With six dependants, Ross couldn't afford to leave Nygård's

employ but, from that day on, her demeanour changed markedly from one of friendship to strictly business. However, her ordeal wasn't over. One day, just before a massage, one of Nygård's 'girlfriends' offered Ross a glass of wine. At first, she declined but the woman became oddly insistent. Thinking nothing of it, Ross downed the glass and hurried upstairs for her massage appointment with Nygård. Nygård was on a call and, while she waited, Ross noticed that the feeling in one of her arms had gone dead. Ross turned to tell Nygård she was feeling ill and that was the last thing she remembers. Ross regained consciousness briefly to find Nygård giving her oral sex before blacking out, then coming to again to find Nygård raping her.

When she fully regained consciousness, day had turned to night. Ross threw on her clothes and hurried out but not before Nygård had pressed a wad of rolled-up dollars into her hand. Still, Ross was forced to return to work. But when Nygård told her she was required to perform regular sexual favours, she refused. She was taken off the roster and tried to find work elsewhere, but Nygård used his influence to stop her. She was eventually forced to beg for her job back, and when she returned, her duties had changed to less salubrious enterprises, such as delivering fish stuffed with money to corrupt local politicians.

Ross's nightmare continued until 2017, when the PLP lost the election, but she was also collecting a lot of damaging information about her boss. With Nygård's cronies out of power, Ross felt safer to act. She approached Fred Smith, a human rights lawyer, who had been helping Save the Bays in its legal fight against Nygård's dredging activities. Ross not only told Smith her own story but started rounding up other survivors who were willing to talk to the lawyer. Ross received financial help from Nygård's neighbour, Louis Bacon, to relocate to a new apartment. It was good that she did because, soon after, her old apartment was found riddled with bullet holes.

The number of Nygård accusers began to grow. Smith put the girls in touch with American lawyers, Lisa Haba and Greg

Gutzler, and in February 2020, a class action civil lawsuit was launched by 10 survivors, who all claimed to have been raped by Nygård.

Later in the same month, the New York Times ran a series of exposés on Nygård. The Times reporters had interviewed 270 people connected to Nygård and detailed the massive scale of his pyramid scheme of sexual abuse. Days later, FBI agents stormed his Times Square headquarters in New York and his Marina del Ray property, search warrants in hand. Soon after the raid, Dillard's, one of Nygård's biggest American distributors, announced that it would no longer supply his brand. And hours later, a spokesman announced that Nygård was stepping down immediately as president of Nygård International. Despite this, a judge said there was no evidence that Nygård had actually resigned and that he still owned 100 percent of the company's shares.

Soon after, another 36 women joined the civil lawsuit, bringing the total to 46. By July, the number had risen to 57. On December 15th, the inevitable happened – Nygård was arrested in Winnipeg, where he faced extradition to the US. In February 2021, he was denied bail. On 1st October, it was announced that Nygård had agreed to be extradited to the US, where he faced nine charges involving seven victims who said their livelihoods and movements depended on having sex with Nygård. On the same day, he was charged with six counts of sexual assault and three counts of forcible confinement by Toronto police. Nygård was flown to Toronto, where he has since been held. In February 2022, he was denied bail again and he currently awaits trial. In the meantime, Nygård International has been declared bankrupt and liquidated.

It remains to be seen how Nygård's legacy of sexual abuse will stack up alongside Epstein's. So far, more than 120 survivors have come forward with stories of sexual abuse involving the fashion tycoon. No doubt there are dozens, perhaps hundreds, more victims out there, who haven't spoken out yet or never will.

A more intriguing question is whether Nygård and Epstein

knew each other. The two billionaires' sex trafficking pyramid schemes were so similar, it is tempting to wonder if they shared notes. Nygård's masseuse, Richette Ross, recounted how she once heard him bragging on the phone to a friend about life in the Bahamas, saying how easy it was to get away with stuff down here, especially if you wanted to do a "certain dance" with young girls. It sounded like Nygård was trying to encourage the friend to purchase his own place in the Caribbean paradise. We will, of course, never know, but it is intriguing to speculate whether the person on the other end of the line was Jeffrey Epstein.

CHAPTER 6

GHISLAINE MAXWELL MEETS EPSTEIN

It is 7th November 1991, the Canary Islands. The world's press are huddled ashore next to the super-yacht, the Lady Ghislaine. They are waiting to hear the reaction of the Maxwell family to the death of one of the world's richest, brashest and most colourful tycoons.

It is Robert Maxwell's youngest child, Ghislaine, who steps forward to address the media. She reads a prepared statement, then answers questions from the press. She is just turning to leave when a reporter shouts, "How did your father die?"

Ghislaine turns back to the throng and says in a loud clear voice, "I think he was murdered."

This was not the official line. The autopsy concluded that death was caused by cardiovascular failure. Maxwell, it was thought, had suffered a heart attack and stumbled to the side of the boat to gasp for air. His great weight – 22 stone or 140kgs – would have been enough to send him crashing through the relatively flimsy metal cord and into the sea below.

Why, then, did Ghislaine think her father had been murdered? And who did she think had done it? Maxwell's business empire was in billions of dollars of debt. In increasingly desperate attempts to fend off his creditors, the tycoon had for years been illegally borrowing money from some of his companies to pay the debts of others. Things had gotten so bad that, according to the authors of the book, *Robert Maxwell, Israel's Superspy*, he had even been taking money from the various intelligence agencies he was working for, including Mossad and possibly also the Russians. Needless to say, spy agencies don't take well to agents stealing their money.

Others alleged the same thing. Former Israeli intelligence agents, Ari ben Menashe and Viktor Ostrovsky, both claimed that Maxwell had been assassinated by Mossad agents, who snuck up on the Lady Ghislaine in a high-powered speed boat, grappled their way on board and injected Maxwell with a lethal agent while he was taking one of his customary night-time pisses over the side of the boat.

I go into more detail about the alleged assassination of Maxwell in my book, *Who Killed Epstein?* For our purposes, it is enough to know that Ghislaine wasn't the only one who suspected foul play, and – tellingly – it was those in the know about Maxwell's intelligence connections who suspected it most. Did this mean, then, that Ghislaine was one of those in the know? Other evidence suggests she was, and perhaps intimately so.

Mirror reporter John Jackson had flown to the Canaries with the Maxwell family to cover the story. He said that, when he accompanied Ghislaine aboard her father's yacht after his death, she scurried about his private suite, pulling documents from drawers and cabinets, which she ordered the crew to shred immediately. Clearly, she had some knowledge of the more sensitive aspects of her father's dealings, and that they had to be destroyed. Perhaps Ghislaine was more immersed in the secretive spy world of her father than has previously been acknowledged. One writer and researcher goes even further, claiming that Ghislaine was Robert Maxwell's apprentice spy, groomed for over a decade in the dark arts for just such a moment, when she could take over the reins.

Kirby Sommers is the author of more than ten books on Epstein and Maxwell. I have interviewed her several times and her insights are always interesting and backed up by excellent research. Sommers herself has a story that is uncannily similar to Epstein survivor, Virginia Giuffre. Like Giuffre, she was the live-in sex slave of a rich businessman. In Sommers' case, the billionaire tycoon was the son of Israeli financier, Meshulam Riklis, a man who had extensive links with Robert Maxwell, Leslie Wexner and Jeffrey Epstein. Like Giuffre, Sommers managed to escape her life as a sex slave and is now a full-time writer, with over a dozen books to her name.

Sommers points to several factors, which illustrate that Maxwell was grooming Ghislaine to be his successor in the underworld of secret intelligence. Sommers points out that, in the early eighties, Maxwell replaced his wife, Betty, with daughter Ghislaine at the various functions he attended around the globe. "He also took her to the White House," Sommers told me. "He took her to the Kremlin. He took her to Israel. He took her on tonnes of trips, introducing her to everyone. Who introduces their daughter to the heads of countries and states?"

According to Sommers, these trips were all part of Ghislaine's training. She also points to the salary Maxwell was paying her. In 1991, when Maxwell died, Ghislaine was receiving £100,000 per year from his Mirror Group newspapers for doing essentially nothing, under the title 'fashion director'. As Sommers pointed out, Maxwell was notoriously tight with money and had once fired an employee for stealing fifty pence. That he would pay someone, even his own daughter, £100,000 to do nothing simply doesn't add up.

Then there was the Simon Wiesenthal memorial dinner. Wiesenthal was a holocaust survivor and renowned Nazi hunter. Robert Maxwell was a co-chair at the annual dinner held in his honour at the Simon Wiesenthal Center in Los Angeles. In 1991, Maxwell was unable to attend the dinner because he was in Russia meeting Russian president, Mikhail Gorbachev. Ghislaine was sent to attend the event in her father's place. She delivered a speech that went down well and, flushed with success, phoned her father in Moscow with a run-down of the evening. However, instead of the praise which she might have expected, Maxwell gave her a dressing down for her inadequate description of the event.

Ghislaine responded with a letter of apology which read:

"I am very sorry that my description of the dinner this morning was inadequate and made you angry. I should have expressed at the start of our conversation that I was merely presenting you with a preliminary report of the evening and that a full written report was to follow."

She followed the apology with a long description of every guest present at the event and a note that she would call him again to get his "precise instructions for the Kennedy wedding." On one level, this was typical Maxwell treatment of an employee. But on another level, it illustrates something deeper – why would Maxwell require such detailed information from the Wiesenthal dinner, and give such precise instructions for a wedding?

"It seemed to me that he was using her for her social skills," Sommers told me. "… So that he could get information from the people where he sent her to… She could wrap men around her finger and they enjoyed talking to her. And, as we know, men like to brag to a pretty woman. So I can well imagine that she got a lot of information from the men she met at this event."

If Maxwell was using Ghislaine to gather information on key players at these global events, it sheds a new light on her 1990 trip to New York. Ghislaine had been sent to the States to hand-deliver a sealed envelope containing nine forged share certificates, showing Maxwell's ownership of Berlitz, the international language school. Maxwell's lawyer in New York then re-registered the shares to a private company owned by the Maxwell family. After a stint shopping in Manhattan, Ghislaine returned to London the next day with another envelope, concealing part of the nearly $1 billion that Maxwell stole from the Berlitz shareholders. The story has always been told that Ghislaine was an unwitting mule, who had no idea what was inside the envelopes. But for someone who was so intimate with Maxwell's business affairs, could this really be the case? "Come on!" Sommers exclaimed in our interview. "She didn't know! Do you really think she didn't know?" she asked me. I thought then, and I think now, that it's highly unlikely.

Perhaps the most dramatic evidence of Ghislaine's secret spy side came from her own lips. Nigel Cawthorne's book, *Ghislaine Maxwell*, tells the story of a dinner at Ghislaine's house in London, where Prince Andrew was the guest of honour. Sikh billionaire, Vikram Chatwal, recounted Ghislaine telling the guests about a time in Colombia when she flew a Black Hawk helicopter over a supposed terrorist camp and fired a rocket, destroying a tank. Chatwal drooled, "After that, my perception of her completely changed. I said, 'You have to be the coolest person alive.'"

But, like her supposed ignorance of the Berlitz operation, this seems a tall story. Perhaps it was downright fabrication from someone who took after her father when it came to lying. After all, it was said about Robert Maxwell, according to journalist John Sweeney, that you could tell he was lying if his lips were moving. More likely, it was an overly-elaborate version of an event that actually happened. Ghislaine was a trained helicopter pilot. Perhaps she had been invited to test her skills on a training simulation exercise, while visiting a Colombian military base. Who knows? But the fact that she would tell the story at a dinner party fits into another researcher's interpretation of Ghislaine and Epstein as second-rate spies, who pretended they were something more. "Jeffrey has always had that kind of desire," Frederic Ponton told me in one of our many interviews, "that desire to be mysterious, to be a kind of James Bond and have access to so many things... And I think that Ghislaine Maxwell was somebody who was rubbing off that... implying that she was a lot more than she actually was."

However deep her involvement in intelligence work, it seems clear that, at some level, she was obtaining illicit information for her father. Whether that was for commercial purposes or for deeper, state-level espionage can't, at present, be established definitively, but is a matter we will return to later.

Part of Ghislaine's duties as Robert Maxwell's social and travel companion was to accompany him to New York in March 1991 for his triumphant takeover of the city's *Daily News* publication. Ghislaine stood beaming next to him as he held up traffic on

East 42nd Street and gave a speech about how his takeover was going to save the ailing but historic newspaper. Maxwell got a great reception in the Big Apple, where he was treated like a hero – one of the reasons, Sommers believes, why Ghislaine chose to move there after her father's death. However, an incident later the same day reveals another side to Maxwell that was different to the confident smiling face the public saw.

In her book, *Ghislaine Maxwell: an Unauthorized Biography*, Sommers recounts how, on entering the 36-storey art deco headquarters of the *Daily News*, Ghislaine noticed that Maxwell's new office was smaller than the newspaper's editor, Jim Hoge's room. Maxwell immediately determined to have this fixed. He took Hoge aside and asked him, "Would you mind if I stood here with the door open and shouted at you for a while?" Nonplussed, Hoge agreed and stood there silently as Maxwell went into a forty-second tirade, banging his fist on the desk and demanding that Hoge fix the office situation. When he was done, he whispered, "Thank you," and left the room. Hoge later discovered that the whole scene had been staged for Ghislaine, who was standing just outside the door.

Maxwell clearly had a complicated relationship with his daughter, on the one hand domineering and sometimes even abusive, on the other hand desperately seeking her respect and approval. In the latter case, it seemed he was successful. That Ghislaine loved and worshipped her father is evidenced by her reaction to his death. Various sources agreed that Ghislaine could not stop crying, and she barely managed to hold herself together for her address to the media. *Mirror* journalist John Jackson said Ghislaine was "shaking like a leaf" before the press event. Other witnesses said she was "catatonic" with grief.

There would be more grieving to come, with a full state funeral on the Mount of Olives in Jerusalem. Maxwell's burial was attended by Israel's president, Chaim Herzog, its prime minister, Yitzhak Shamir, and six former heads of Israeli intelligence. But despite the family's public show of grief, it was a different story on board the Maxwell private jet back to London. In his biography of Ghislaine, Nigel Cawthorne records how the pilot, Captain David Whiteman, said, "It was champagne, chocolates and laughter. No tears."

Perhaps the family thought, with their stingy father out of the way, that they would get more access to his money. If so, they were wrong. Maxwell's umbrella company, Maxwell Communication Corporation, was already creaking under an insupportable weight of debt. With Maxwell's death, it collapsed and was put into administration with $4.4 billion of debt. Worse was to come. It was soon discovered that Maxwell had been raiding the pension funds of his Mirror Group employees to fend off creditors. Kevin and Ian Maxwell, who had inherited the reins of MCC, were tried for fraud in 1995. Although the brothers were eventually acquitted, up to $1 billion of the Mirror Group pension funds remained missing, and thousands of loyal employees lost their pensions. Kevin Maxwell was declared bankrupt and Maxwell's wife, Betty, was forced to sell the family home, Headington Hill Hall, and all its contents, and move into a friend's apartment.

Amidst all this, Ghislaine was flitting back and forth between London and New York. With typical insensitivity to her father's pension-less employees, she flew on Concorde with tickets she had saved from when her father was still alive. While in London, though, she had the good sense to wear a blonde wig to conceal her identity. Like the rest of her family, it seems she was suffering from a lack of funds. She kept her mews house in London and was renting a one-bedroom apartment in Manhattan for just $500 a week. It's unclear whether this was from necessity or just appearances. Ponton thinks the latter. "They were watching her," he told me, "watching what she was doing, and she just literally did what any intelligent person would do – she kept a low profile and started to disseminate this myth that she was broke."

Whatever the state of her finances, acquaintances agreed that she was still reeling from the death of her father. One friend, who spoke to her at a house party in Manhattan, said she looked "shell-shocked" and was "vibrating with anger and bitterness." It wasn't just the loss of her dad that had hit Ghislaine hard. Before Maxwell's death, Ghislaine had broken up with her partner, Count Gianfranco Cicogna, heir to the Italian CIGA hotel empire. Observers agreed that Ghislaine was deeply in love with Cicogna and had hoped to marry him. Cicogna had the effortless style and grace of those born into money. He instructed Ghislaine on how to dress and the best places to get her hair cut. He also loved flying, which perhaps influenced Ghislaine to learn to fly herself. But there was a darker side to Cicogna's family history than the glitz and glamour of European royalty.

As Sommers relates in her book on Ghislaine, Cicogna's grandfather, Count Giuseppe Volpi di Misurata, was the Italian finance minister for Mussolini's fascist government. He was also a freemason and the last doge of Venice. In the early 1900s, he took over the CIGA hotel chain, including Venice's world-famous Hotel Excelsior. Cicogna's father, Guiseppe Asconia Cicogna Mozzoni, was a producer and screenwriter in the Italian movie industry. Guiseppe, known as Bino, owned a famous nightclub in Rome called Number One, which catered to the rich and famous, and served cocaine alongside its expensive cocktails. In 1971, the club was raided by police and Bino fled to Brazil to avoid arrest. Later that year, Bino was found dead with his head in the oven. His death was ruled as a suicide but many of his friends suspected murder.

Gianfranco was just ten years old when his father died and he inherited his title and empire. He was a financier and entrepreneur who imported fruit and vegetables to Europe from Africa and South America. Known as Italy's Rockefeller, he spoke five languages and loved flying – a passion that would ultimately lead to his death in 2012 at an air show in Africa, where his plane crashed into the ground in front of hundreds of shocked spectators. Cicogna and Ghislaine's relationship lasted from 1986 until 1990m when he left her for British TV presenter, Tania Bryer. Ghislaine was said to be devastated and, followed by the sudden death of her father the following year, it could explain her low ebb in New York.

Whatever the truth about her mental health and her wealth, one thing is clear about Ghislaine's early years in New York – neither stopped her partying. Aided by her connection to Prince Andrew, she was soon accepted into the highest echelons of New York's social scene, and was spotted at practically every go-to event. She was seen dating veteran Hollywood star, George Hamilton, and rubbing shoulders with the likes of the Trumps and the Kennedys. Observers saw her as part of a group of 'it girls,' whose prime objective was to find a rich husband. It was the Kennedy family in particular that Ghislaine had her sights set on. Apparently, her father had always wanted her to marry into the Kennedy clan and, as Sommers records in her Ghislaine biography, press reports circulated about Ghislaine having brief affairs with John F Kennedy Jr and Joe Kennedy Jr.

Robert Maxwell had a long connection with the Kennedy family and had sent Ghislaine to the wedding of Kerry Kennedy and Andrew Cuomo in 1990. This was the event Ghislaine had said she was awaiting her father's "detailed instructions" about. It seems that Robert Maxwell's interest in the Kennedys had more than just social motives behind it. The internal dealings of such an important political dynasty would have been interesting to the intelligence agencies of countries like Israel and the USSR. Not to mention the groom, former New York governor, Andrew Cuomo. As Sommers told me, "Andrew Cuomo's family for decades have had sinister connections to the mob. They have been denied, downplayed for a very long time but once again it circles back to some of the people connected to Epstein."

In 1991, Ghislaine attended the wedding of Mathew Maxwell Kennedy to Victoria Anne Strauss in Philadelphia. But despite the various Kennedy events she attended, she didn't find her rich man amongst the Kennedy clan. Instead, it was a relatively unknown financier by the name of Jeffrey Epstein who would become Ghislaine's knight in shining armour. At least, that's how it was supposed to go.

Ghislaine and Epstein are supposed to have met at a memorial dinner for Robert Maxwell in New York on November 24th, 1991. It is a story that has been disputed. Former Israeli spy, Ari Ben-Menashe told me in an interview that Epstein and Ghislaine had met and, indeed, started dating several years earlier. "There was a prior relationship," Ben-Menashe told me. "Actually, Daddy helped create that relationship. Epstein at the time was a young good-looking guy, Jewish boy from New York, and that was a good thing to have the daughter meet."

Ben-Menashe said he was working for Israeli intelligence at the time and had been tasked to deal with Robert Maxwell. He claimed to have met Epstein in Maxwell's London office as early as the early eighties and that Epstein could be found hanging out there all the time. If Ben-Menashe's account is true, it seems that Maxwell had a hand in encouraging the relationship between his daughter and Epstein. Does that mean he was eyeing the good-looking Jewish boy as the inheritor of his spying and money-laundering networks? It would certainly fit with what subsequently happened in New York.

However, Sommers finds Ben-Menashe's narrative fishy. The Ghislaine-Epstein affair doesn't tally with the Ghislaine-Cicogna relationship, which would have been running at the same time. Furthermore, she is suspicious about Ben-Menashe's motives. "I do not believe Ari Ben-Menashe," Sommers told me. "I think that he's a disinformation agent. I happen to know from insiders that he is put out there when they need someone to say something."

Sommers believes that Ghislaine and Epstein first met in different – but equally suspicious – circumstances. "I believe they met each other when Ghislaine Maxwell was on the yacht after her father died, going through the papers," she told me. "He had his number in all of the contact numbers and that is how I believe they met… I believe she got his phone number, she made a couple of phone calls, and that is how she met him."

Whatever the case, soon after the memorial dinner, Ghislaine and Epstein were seen out together, first at a restaurant opening, then regularly at social occasions. Friends said they were dating and even that Ghislaine was hoping he would propose. The same friends also noticed the similarities between Epstein and Robert Maxwell. If Ghislaine was looking for a replacement father figure to look after her, it seemed she had found him. This ties in with something Epstein survivor, Maria Farmer, claimed about the relationship. Farmer said Ghislaine had told her that Epstein had been asked to look after her, following her father's death. But why? And who had done the asking? Could it have been her intelligence handlers, the same people who had been dealing with Robert Maxwell? Ghislaine also told Farmer that the Rothschilds were the "great protectors" of her family, so perhaps her transfer to Epstein was something to do with them?

In any case, Ghislaine was soon running Epstein's social life, organising his calendar and accompanying him to social events. The line between girlfriend, friend and employee seemed to have blurred. Epstein himself claimed that Ghislaine was his "best friend" and organised much of his life for him. Although Ghislaine appeared dependent on Epstein, both emotionally and financially, this may have been strictly for appearances. Insiders claimed that Ghislaine was in charge of the purse strings, as well as the social calendar. In his biography of Ghislaine, Nigel Cawthorne quotes a New York acquaintance as saying, "I can't tell you how many times I said to Ghislaine, 'I hear Jeffrey's bought a house in Palm Beach.' She would say, 'Darling, that's my house.' I could never figure out why Ghislaine acted like a boss towards him."

The same friend alleged that Epstein was helping Ghislaine launder Robert Maxwell's money, probably including the missing *Mirror* pension funds. This would certainly account for Epstein's sudden explosion of wealth, enabling him to buy private airliners, real estate in some of the most expensive parts of the US and, eventually, his own private Caribbean island.

Another aspect of the relationship that appears to have started early was the alleged procuring of young girls. Maria Farmer first met Epstein and Ghislaine in New York in 1995, when she was studying at the New York Academy of Art. Farmer worked briefly as a receptionist at Epstein's new multi-million dollar townhouse – supposedly purchased from Lesley Wexner for just one dollar. Farmer reported seeing as many as five young-looking girls a day go up the stairs to the mansion. Supposedly, Epstein was interviewing them for modelling roles for Wexner's underwear company, Victoria's Secret. Farmer also remembers trips with Ghislaine in one of Epstein's chauffeur-driven cars, where the socialite would be on the hunt for 'nubiles' – young teenage girls whom she could introduce to Epstein. Farmer said of these trips:

"I began to see the dark side of Ghislaine when I worked at the mansion. She would come back from a shopping trip all giddy with happiness because she'd just shopped, and then a few hours later she would say, 'I'm going out to get the nubiles,' and her whole expression and manner would change to what I can only describe as evil. It was so sudden, it was like this Jekyll and Hyde thing."

Farmer claims Ghislaine insisted she worked for Wexner, not Epstein. Farmer and several other witnesses have said that Epstein's Manhattan town house was riddled with CCTV cameras, which could be viewed from a secret control room hidden behind a concealed door. This has led many to allege that Epstein and Maxwell were recruiting the girls for a sexual blackmail operation to entrap politically important figures, figures that would include the likes of Prince Andrew, Bill Clinton and Ehud Barak, no less. Whatever the case, it was clear the girls meant little to Ghislaine. A *Vanity Fair* article reported Ghislaine telling a friend, "They're nothing, these girls. They're trash."

While all this was going on, Ghislaine and Epstein were still the toast of New York, rubbing shoulders with the highest echelons of society, such as the Clintons, the Kennedys and the Trumps. Ghislaine is reported to have had dinner with Bill Clinton in LA in 2014, and she attended his daughter Chelsea's wedding in 2010. But the relationship may have gone much deeper. Maria Farmer alleges that Bill Clinton visited Epstein's

Manhattan townhouse several times in the mid-nineties when he was president. According to Farmer:

"He came to the house three times when I was there and each time everyone would have to clear out, except the chef, Andy, and the two maids. I was usually the last to leave and Ghislaine would be in a tizzy all day, sending people out to buy stuff and decorating the place with candles and ornaments. Ghislaine boasted about how much Bill Clinton loved her and she wanted the place to be as perfect as possible. No one will ever believe me about this, but I've seen the photos of him there and yes, as unbelievable as it sounds, the president of the US used to turn up at Jeffrey's house with no security detail, no announcements or anything – it was all very secretive."

Allegedly, Ghislaine and Clinton were having an affair, which shouldn't be that surprising, given their past sexual records. Ghislaine was well-known among her acquaintances for being highly sexed. Laura Goldman, a friend of Ghislaine's sister, Isabel, testified that Ghislaine had, "a superpower when it came to attracting men," and that, "all she ever talked about was sex, sex, sex." Ghislaine apparently liked to speak about oral sex techniques in casual conversation. She also enjoyed notching up big names on her bedpost. Virginia Giuffre alleged in her memoir that Ghislaine once returned from a party boasting that she had given George Clooney oral sex in the bathroom.

Ghislaine may also have been bisexual, which partially explains her involvement, alongside Epstein, in the alleged sexual abuse of many of his victims. Nigel Cawthorne's biography of Ghislaine includes a story from a young woman who met Ghislaine in London. According to the woman, Ghislaine persuaded her to drive her to a party, despite the fact that she couldn't drive. The woman said:

"I was so nervous but somehow she convinced me. It was a manual so, to help me as we set off, she put her hand on top of mine – but it stayed there the entire journey. If one was that way inclined, it could have been very erotic, a prelude to something."

Another friend alleged that Ghislaine told her she could get into anyone's pants and that girls were like "candy."

Ghislaine could also count royalty amongst her friends. She had apparently become pally with Prince Andrew during her time at Oxford University, but the relationship went into overdrive towards the end of the nineties, after she introduced Epstein to the prince. Andrew's name first appears in the Lolita Express flight records in February 1999, flying to the Virgin Islands. Over the period of a year, starting in February 2000, Ghislaine and Andrew were spotted together no less than eight times. The first was a holiday at Donald Trump's Mar-a-Lago club in Palm Beach, followed by a fashion show in New York. The next was a fundraising dinner for the London Symphony Orchestra in New York in March. The pair were spotted again in New York in April, followed by Andrew visiting Ghislaine in Florida in May. In June, Ghislaine and Epstein were invited by Andrew to attend his fortieth birthday party at Windsor Castle. In October, Andrew spent an evening partying with Ghislaine during an official trip to New York. And in December, Ghislaine and Epstein were back in the UK, this time staying at Sandringham Palace, where Andrew had organised a party for Ghislaine's thirty-ninth birthday. Finally, in January 2001, Ghislaine, Epstein and Andrew shared a beach holiday in Thailand, where the prince and the financier were photographed on a yacht, surrounded by topless women.

Ghislaine and Epstein were also friendly with Andrew's ex-wife, Sarah Ferguson. Epstein gave Fergie several cash loans to bail her out of her well-known financial problems. Ghislaine may even have had some form of relationship with Princess Diana, although it's unclear how close they were. Maria Farmer alleges that she heard Ghislaine laughing about how much she hated Diana, even on one occasion making her cry. Kirby Sommers says she has spotted Ghislaine and Epstein on footage of Princess Diana's funeral.

It was not long after Ghislaine, Epstein and Andrew started regularly hanging out that Virgnia Giuffre (then Roberts) first entered the scene. Giuffre became Epstein's personal masseuse and sex slave, whom he farmed out to various wealthy friends. Giuffre alleged to have been forced to have sex with Prince Andrew three times, once in Ghislaine's London townhouse, once in Epstein's Manhattan mansion, and a third time as part of an orgy with several underage Russian girls on Epstein's Island, Little St James. Giuffre has a photo of herself with the prince's arm around her waist and Ghislaine hovering in the background. With my cameraman filming, I knocked at the front door of Ghislaine's Kensington mews house and when the door opened, I saw the infamous white banister, confirming that the photo was taken on the landing, corroborating Giuffre's story. I go into more detail on Virginia Giuffre's story (and Maria Farmer's) in my first book on Epstein: *Who Killed Epstein?*

At around this time, Ghislaine moved into her own Manhattan mansion on East 65th Street, just around the corner from Epstein. The six-storey town house was bought for $4.495 million through a company registered to the same address as J. Epstein & Co. The purchase was overseen by Epstein's long-term lawyer, Darren Indyke. This is further evidence perhaps that Epstein was merely acting as the custodian of Ghislaine's own secret fortune, inherited from her father. The property was bought at $10 million under the market value, and the seller was someone with links to Epstein and Ghislaine – Lynn Forester de Rothschild. The bargain sale brings to mind what Maria Farmer claimed Ghislaine had said about the Rothschilds – that they were the "great protectors" of her family.

Ghislaine's new lavish lifestyle attracted criminals. In 2003, Ghislaine's butler and maid were arrested, after she had noticed several of her possessions had gone missing. Ghislaine surreptitiously entered the basement floor of her East 65th Street house, where the couple lived. She found $7,500 in cash plus assorted gifts from under her Christmas tree, alongside $10,000 worth of jewellery and clothes. The married couple were charged with possession of stolen property and grand larceny.

But police investigations were about to turn on Ghislaine herself. In 2005, Palm Beach police began investigating Epstein, after a woman reported that her 14-year-old daughter had been sexually abused by Epstein during a massage. Following the trail to another underage girl who had recruited the victim, police found that she had procured another six underage females for similar naked massages. The police began monitoring Epstein's El Brillo Way mansion in Palm Beach. Later the same year, they raided the house, finding numerous pictures of naked underage girls. However, many of Epstein's computers had been removed, leaving just the cables hanging. Someone on the inside had clearly tipped him off about the raid.

It soon became clear that Epstein was procuring underage girls, mostly from local high schools in deprived areas, in an industrial-scale sex trafficking scheme. Two to three girls a day would enter the El Brillo property to give Epstein massages. Some would be asked to strip while he masturbated, others would have to perform manual or oral sex, and others would be forced to have full sex with Epstein. For some reason, Ghislaine wasn't connected with the investigation at this time, despite her name being written on telephone notepads recording details of girls who were available for massages.

Epstein was arrested, but instead of numerous counts of the sexual abuse of minors, he was only charged with two counts of felony solicitation of prostitution, and procuring a person under the age of eighteen for prostitution. To add insult to injury, Epstein's schoolgirl victims had effectively been branded prostitutes. It turned out that a plea deal had been agreed behind the scenes. Epstein would plead guilty to the watered-down charges, in return for only serving thirteen months in prison and a further ten on probation, as well as registering on the sex offenders list. He would also be immune from any future prosecutions, along with four unnamed co-defendants. Incredibly, the plea deal was to be kept secret from the victims and their lawyers.

If the charges seemed lenient, Epstein's time behind bars

took the biscuit. He was given his own private wing of the Palm Beach county jail, where he was looked after by his own personal security guards, paid for out of his own pocket. After just three months, he was allowed out of his cell for up to sixteen hours a day, seven days a week, to work at a local office he had set up for the purpose. Here, he continued to receive visits from minors, while Palm Beach police officers waited discreetly outside.

While all this was going on, Ghislaine was continuing to party and socialise as usual, attending opening events, gala dinners and fundraising affairs, sometimes alongside Prince Andrew, even attending his daughter, Princess Beatrice's wedding in 2006.

Ghislaine's name wasn't connected with Epstein's crimes until 2009, when a federal lawsuit was brought against Epstein by a survivor, who would later be identified as Virginia Giuffre. Giuffre alleged that Ghislaine had procured her while she was working as an attendant at Donald Trump's nearby Mar-a-Lago club. Giuffre had told Ghislaine that she wanted to learn massage and Ghislaine had informed her of a wealthy gentleman who was looking for a traveling masseuse to accompany him around the world. Giuffre agreed to an 'interview' at Epstein's El Brillo Way mansion, which quickly escalated into full sex with Epstein, while Maxwell allegedly watched and gave instructions. I go into Giuffre's story in great detail in my first Epstein book. What is important for the present discussion is that Ghislaine's name had now been included in the allegations against Epstein for the first time. And, far from being a bit-part player, Giuffre alleged that Ghislaine was front and centre of Epstein's sex trafficking operation.

Over the next few years, Epstein would face more than a dozen similar lawsuits, paying out over $1 million to at least seven of the girls in out-of-court settlements. In 2010, Epstein completed his sentence and a release party was held in his honour at his Manhattan mansion. Allegedly, Prince Andrew was the guest of honour. On another trip to New York, Andrew was photographed walking in Central Park with Epstein. Another picture showed him waving goodbye to a young-looking girl from the door of Epstein's mansion. It was revealed that the prince had stayed at Epstein's house for three nights, while on an official visit to New York. The ensuing press furore effectively put an end to Andrew's relationship with Epstein.

Not long after the Andrew photos were published, Virginia Giuffre went public with her own story about allegedly having sex with Andrew, in an article in *The Daily Mail*. *The Daily Mail* also published the photograph of Giuffre and Andrew in Ghislaine's London townhouse.

Despite this negative press, Ghislaine continued to socialise at high-profile events, incredibly including a charity event in New York supporting STOP, an organisation campaigning against human trafficking. She was either completely oblivious to the nature of her crimes or had an extremely dark sense of humour.

Around this time, Ghislaine founded her own charity, TerraMar, which she set up in 2012, to create a "global ocean community" where people could become "citizens of the global commons". Donators to the charity could register for a digital passport for the sixty-four percent of the world's oceans that are free from national jurisdiction. She gave talks at the UN, the Council on Foreign Relations, the University of Texas, and a TED event about the project. Ghislaine was a trained diver and was even licensed to operate a certain type of diving vessel. Her passion for the oceans appears genuine, but it is interesting to note that someone so involved in international sex trafficking would be so committed to the conservation of the world's jurisdiction-free waters.

In the meantime, the Virginia Giuffre story had refused to go away. Allegations that Ghislaine was the mastermind behind Epstein's procuring operation were now in legal documents and in the press. Giuffre also claimed that Ghislaine participated in the sexual abuse of Epstein's underage victims and kept naked photos of minors participating in sex acts with Epstein. In 2015, Ghislaine decided to sue Giuffre for defamation. The scene was set for more secrets to emerge.

Perhaps in anticipation of the high costs of the court case, Ghislaine put her Manhattan mansion up for sale in 2015. It was sold in April 2016 for $15 million. But before Ghislaine could sue, Giuffre beat her to it, suing the Maxwell heiress for defamation, for accusing her of lying. In the lawsuit, Giuffre alleged that Ghislaine had "forceful" sex with underage girls almost daily. Giuffre also mentioned video evidence of her being sexually abused by several of Epstein's friends, which she said the FBI was holding. The case was about to go to court in May 2017, when Ghislaine decided to settle out of court. The court documents were sealed and the settlement details were kept secret.

Meanwhile, Epstein was defending himself in three more cases, settling all three for $5.5 million in October 2017. With their respective settlements concluded, Ghislaine and Epstein may have hoped the heat would dissipate, but the crusading journalism of the *Miami Herald* reporter, Julie K Brown, kept the story in the news. Brown's investigation found that Epstein's victims numbered at least eighty – as opposed to the thirty-six identified by federal prosecutors – and probably ran into the hundreds. The paper also filed a suit to unseal the court documents from the Guiffre-Maxwell case, but the motion was denied. *The Herald* appealed but, in the meantime, something happened that would ultimately seal the fates of Epstein and Ghislaine.

In 2015, court proceedings had commenced to find whether federal prosecutors had acted illegally by not notifying the victims of Epstein's 2007 sweetheart deal in Florida. In 2019, Florida federal judge, Kenneth Marra, ruled that this was indeed the case. With this, the dam broke and, in March 2019, the US Court of Appeals ruled that the Giuffre Vs Maxwell court documents could be unsealed. More importantly, the illegality of Epstein's non-prosecution deal paved the way for him to be prosecuted again. In July of that year, Epstein was arrested as his private jet touched down at Teterboro airport, New Jersey, just three days after the court had ruled that two thousand pages of previously sealed court documents could be revealed.

Epstein was found dead in his cell on the morning of 10th August. His death was ruled a suicide, despite a series of anomalies and 'coincidences' that all pointed to foul play. In *Who Killed Epstein?* I go into great detail about the reasons why I think Epstein was murdered and who the prime suspects are.

Epstein's death drove Ghislaine into hiding. Rumours were rife about where she was lying low, some saying the UK, others France, Israel or even Brazil. Later in August, a photograph appeared of her at an In-N-Out Burger restaurant in Los Angeles. The picture was soon debunked as a fake. The metadata on the photograph bore the name 'Meadowgate,' which was a company owned by Ghislaine's friend, lawyer Leah Saffian. The dog sitting at Ghislaine's feet was identified as Saffian's pet from her Instagram account. Ghislaine may have been thumbing her nose at her detractors, and her sense of humour, as ever, was darkly inappropriate. In the photograph, she is seen reading a non-fiction bestseller called *The Book of Honor: the Secret Lives and Deaths of CIA Operatives*. And behind her, there is a poster advertising an R-rated movie called Good Boys, which featured teenage sex. The advertisement had been photoshopped over the real poster, which was for a local hospital.

One rumour that persisted was that Ghislaine was hiding out with her boyfriend, Scott Borgerson, in the sleepy Massachusetts town, Manchester-by-the-Sea. Borgerson was a member of the Council of Foreign Relations and a tech entrepreneur, who founded CargoMetrics Technologies, a company that analysed global shipping data. Kirby Sommers believes Borgerson fit with the role of father-figure that seemed to attract Ghislaine. At six foot four and with black hair, he certainly matched the imposing physical presence of her father. He was also a millionaire playboy and allegedly could be "physically violent" and "extremely controlling," according to records from his divorce from former wife, Rebecca. The divorce records went on to claim that he had once threatened her, saying, "Don't make me beat you in front of the children." According to court documents, Borgerson allegedly beat his ex-wife in 2014 and was charged with assault. According to Sommers, Borgerson split up from his wife by sending her a video message of himself hugging and kissing Ghislaine. All of which definitely fits the sadistic and manipulative profile of Robert Maxwell, not to mention Ghislaine.

Like her father and Epstein before him, Borgerson looked after Ghislaine, helping hide her and aiding her in buying the house where she was ultimately found. The aptly named 'Tuckedaway' is a $1-million mansion in the small town of Bradford, New Hampshire. Described in a real estate listing as "an amazing retreat for the nature lover who also wants total privacy," the property was bought with cash in December 2019 by a man described as having a British accent. The buyers, apparently the man and his wife, said they didn't want their names on the paperwork, so the owners were recorded as Granite Realty LLC, a company created for the purpose. The real estate agent who made the sale later told the FBI that the couple both had British accents and called themselves Scott and Jen Marshall. The man said he was retired from the British military and was writing a book, and the woman said she was a journalist. The woman wanted to know about the flight patterns over the house, which the agent thought was "strange." It was only later, on seeing a photograph of her, that the real estate agent realised that 'Jen' was, in fact, Ghislaine. The identity of the man remains a mystery but it could well have been Borgerson putting on a British accent, or perhaps Kevin or Ian Maxwell.

Sommers believes that purchasing the mansion as a couple was all part of the ruse to keep Ghislaine hidden from the police. She told me, "The authorities were going to look for a single woman who looked like Ghislaine Maxwell. They were not going to be expecting a couple – because that's how they purchased the house, as a couple – and a couple who were married."

While secluded at Tuckedaway, Ghislaine had a team of security personnel with ex-British military backgrounds protecting the property. French activist Frederic Ponton finds the British nationality of the security guards suspicious and suspects there was more involved than mere protection. He told me, "When you hear about security which is Ghislaine Maxwell's, think more about what she knows about Andrew, how much she knows about Crown secrets, because these are Crown secrets at the end of the day… So she's got this British Crown intelligence apparatus watching over her every single move because of her knowledge of Prince Andrew and what he did and how this whole thing was organised, that's the only reason I can explain it."

Despite the security and the secrecy, the ruse didn't succeed for long. In the early hours of July 2nd, 2020, a convoy of fifteen FBI and local police vehicles roared up the dirt track through the woods that led to Tuckedaway. At the gates to the 156-acre estate, an FBI agent cut through the lock and twenty-six officers approached the house. Through the window, they saw Ghislaine wearing a T-shirt, reclining on the couch. She ignored their instructions to open the door, instead fleeing into another room, slamming the door behind her. The agents broke the front door down with a battering ram and found Ghislaine who, according to some accounts, was hiding beneath a bed.

Ghislaine was driven away to the Merrimack County Jail in the nearby town of Boscawen. Meanwhile, FBI agents searched the mansion. Amongst Ghislaine's possessions, they found a mobile phone wrapped in tinfoil – an apparently misguided attempt to maintain her secrecy. Amongst the other weird events of the arrest was the loss of Ghislaine's pet cat, which had scarpered into the woods in terror when the door was broken down. According to a *Daily Mail* article, federal agents spent four days looking for the cat before it was finally found, happy and in good health.

It would be tempting to quip that the authorities spent more time and resources hunting the cat than they did Ghislaine.

CHAPTER 7

MY TWO YEARS WITH EPSTEIN AND MAXWELL - JULIETTE BRYANT

Juliette Bryant watched the flashing lights of the forty-car police escort as they sped down the abandoned highway. She had to pinch herself to check she wasn't dreaming.

The 20-year-old budding model from Cape Town, South Africa, had never had more than a few rand to scrape together. Now she was part of an official cavalcade, following former US president Bill Clinton to one of his speeches.

"The whole highway was shut off," Bryant told me when I interviewed her in 2022. "I've never seen anything like it. There were police cars left, right and centre. It was just madness."

It was 2002 and Bryant had recently left her university in Cape Town to try modelling, in order to earn some money. She had grown up in Johannesburg until her parents had got divorced. Her mother had moved to Cape Town with the children and their life had been a continual struggle to make ends meet. Bryant had been approached by Elite modelling agency when she was fourteen but her mother had refused to allow her to become a model. Now, at age twenty, Bryant was trying hard to make it in the modelling world.

So she couldn't believe her luck when she was approached by a successful model, asking if she wanted to meet the "King of America," a man, she said, who could open the doors to Victoria's Secret, one of the most sought-after modelling jobs in the world.

Bryant, of course, jumped at the chance so the model took her to an upmarket restaurant called Beluga near the waterfront in Cape Town. There, she met Epstein for the first time. "He was sitting there with Bill Clinton and Kevin Spacey and Chris Tucker," Bryant told me. "They all stopped eating and stood up to meet us and I was like, 'Oh my God, this is amazing!' I was starstruck, to be honest." When it was Clinton's turn to be introduced, he took Bryant's hand and started speaking to someone else, allegedly without releasing his grip until it became uncomfortable. "He held onto my hand for almost a minute," she told me. "I was freaking out because I was just a young kid."

The next day, the professional model called to tell Bryant that Epstein had really liked her and wanted to see her modelling portfolio. She also invited Bryant to watch one of Clinton's speeches. Bryant said yes and that was how she found herself sitting in a police escort, rushing through Cape Town in a car behind Bill Clinton.

After the speech, Bryant was escorted back to the five-star luxury Cape Grace Hotel, where Epstein and the former president were staying. She grabbed her modelling portfolio and went inside. Bryant was first met by three women who said they were from Karin Models, the French modelling agency that Epstein's business partner, friend and fellow paedophile, Jean-Luc Brunel, had once headed. One of the women was Epstein's assistant, Sarah Kellen. During the casting session, Bryant says Clinton casually strolled through the room and said "hi" to the women. "It looked like they were sharing the presidential suite," Bryant said about Epstein and Clinton's sleeping arrangements at the Cape Grace hotel. The two men seemed "very close," she added. After looking at Bryant's modelling portfolio, the women ushered her though to another room, where Epstein was waiting.

Epstein looked at Bryant's modelling portfolio and told her she had the most stunning figure he had ever seen. He said he wanted to bring her to the US and set her up with Victoria's Secret. Bryant was blown away, not quite able to believe her luck. "It was like a dream," she told me. "All my dreams are coming true. Maybe I'll be able to go to New York and actually do really well and help my family."

The next day, Epstein and his entourage left. Almost immediately, Bryant started receiving calls from Epstein's assistant, Lesley Groff, who helped to arrange her US visa. It all happened fast. Within two weeks, Bryant arrived in New York, to find a driver waiting with her name on a board. "My mind was blown." Bryant told me. "I thought I was going to be a celebrity."

Little did she know, she had just taken the first step into a life of sexual slavery and abuse that would last two years.

Bryant was chauffeured to the infamous apartment block at 301 East 66th Manhattan, where hundreds, perhaps thousands, of Epstein victims would be held over the years. Owned by Jeffrey's brother, Mark Epstein, and bought from Victoria's Secret owner, Leslie Wexner, the apartment buildings would go on to house hundreds of young prospective models, shipped to New York from all over the world on the auspices of working for Epstein's partner, Jean-Luc Brunel, and his MC2 modelling agency. I go into great depth about the sex-trafficking front that was MC2 and the sordid goings-on at East 66th Steet in my first book on Epstein, *Who Killed Epstein? Prince Andrew or Bill Clinton*.

Bryant had hardly had time to drop her bags at the East 66th Street building before the phone in her room rang. It was Sarah Kellen, telling her to pack her bags for an immediate trip to the Caribbean. Bryant hadn't slept for twenty-four hours. Jet-lagged and starstruck by New York, she stumbled back down the stairs, where another car was waiting to take her to the airport.

It was when she stepped aboard Epstein's private plane that Bryant first realised something was seriously wrong. "Epstein was sitting there," Bryant told me, "and he patted the chair next to him for me to sit next to him. And as soon as the aeroplane took off, he started touching me. And I was so terrified, I immediately thought, he's going to kill me, I'm not going to see my family again."

Things would only get worse at their destination – Epstein's private Caribbean island, Little St James. On arrival, Bryant was shown to her private chalet next to the swimming pool but immediately she sensed that something was wrong. The property was covered with pictures of young naked women, including several naked pictures of Ghislaine Maxwell. In Bryant's bedroom, there was a disturbing picture of a walrus, seemingly about to rape a naked girl.

For the first day, Bryant felt lonely and trapped. Epstein's plane had landed on the neighbouring main island of Great St James and they had flown by helicopter to Epstein's island. She realised she was stuck on the island, with no way to escape. She had no phone and no way of contacting the outside world. Bryant says her name wasn't even on the flight records for that first trip to Little St James, which leads to the frightening possibility that anything could have happened to her on the island and no one would have known. When I asked her if she thought people were 'vanished' on Epstein's island, she answered, "I'm pretty sure."

Bryant found a disposable camera and spent the first day taking pictures of the island and the property, many of which she still has to this day. On the evening of the second day, she was invited to watch a movie with Epstein and another girl, Anna Hanks, who later went on to become Miss South Carolina. During the film, the other girl allegedly began to give Epstein oral sex, according to Bryant. "I was horrified," she told me. "… I just ran out of there crying because I was so freaked out. I just wanted to go home and I didn't know what to do."

Soon, it was Bryant's turn. She received a call to her chalet from Sarah Kellen, instructing her to visit Epstein in his room. Epstein's bedroom was pitch dark and ice cold, according to Bryant. She said she "checked out" of her body and let him do what he wanted. She tried to escape in her mind and pretend it wasn't happening. She also said that things happened with Epstein that terrified her so deeply she still can't talk about them. According to Bryant, Epstein "fed off the terror."

Bryant first met Ghislaine Maxwell on her third or fourth day on the island. "I was told that she was his girlfriend," Bryant told me. "So then I was even more confused because he was taking us to his bedroom. It just seemed so weird." Bryant never saw Epstein or Maxwell touch, hold hands, kiss or even hug and it soon became evident, she says, that the relationship was not romantic. Bryant described Ghislaine as "very scary" and said she tried to stay away from her as much as possible. Maxwell and Kellen were close, according to Bryant, and between them they ran the property and told the staff what to do. It would always be Maxwell or Kellen who ordered the girls to Epstein's room. Maxwell wasn't particularly interested in the girls, according to Bryant, and didn't have much to say to them, apart from hello and goodbye.

Someone else Bryant met on the island was another of Epstein's assistants, Andrea Mitrovich. According to Epstein researcher 'Agenthades,' Andrea Mitrovich was a former ballet dancer, who went on to work as a waste consultant for the Clinton Foundation, the Bill and Melinda Gates Foundation, and the World Bank. Bryant also met Epstein's house managers, the South African couple, Cathy and Miles Alexander. Bryant said the couple from her homeland occasionally gave her someone to talk to, but she noticed that the other staff were nervous around them. "I could see that all the staff were very scared of them," she told me. "They didn't really want to look them in the eye because they were very scary people. You didn't want to mess around with them, that was for sure."

Bryant said she saw other guests on the island, including a famous scientist. These guests didn't appear to be staying in any of the rooms that she knew of and she could never work out where they were actually sleeping. She says she now wonders if there was a secret underground area that she never had access to.

After five days on the island, Epstein and his whole entourage flew to his Palm Beach property. Bryant now began a two-year period in which she followed Epstein around as his live-in sex slave. She says she was raped as much as three times a day by

Epstein and that she saw at least sixty other girls come and go during this period. She describes the operation as a factory, a machine that Epstein was running. And allegedly Maxwell was the person operating it.

Her role sounds incredibly similar to that of Virginia Giuffre's and, according to Bryant, her stint with Epstein began just two weeks after Giuffre left. Indeed, Bryant remembers Epstein and Maxwell talking about a girl who they said was giving them trouble. But there was a crucial difference between Giuffre and Bryant – Bryant didn't receive any money for the sexual abuse and there was no longer any pretence about having an actual job, like a masseuse. Bryant says Epstein offered to pay her to stay with him but she always refused because she wanted to go home to her family. There was also the continual offer of recruitment money. "He said he'd give me $2,000 for any girl that I brought him – young girls and stuff – but I didn't do that. I used to just agree and then, when he asked me, I just didn't do it." On top of all this, not a single modelling contract materialised. It seems that Epstein and Maxwell had learned from their experience with Giuffre that, if anything, they should treat their live-in sex slaves more harshly. Bryant says she was too scared of Epstein to try to escape. "I was petrified of him," she told me, "totally petrified."

As part of her travels with Epstein, Bryant stayed at all his properties. The El Zorro ranch in New Mexico she described as "a very sinister place," adding that "weird things happened there that I still can't talk about." Bryant says she met several famous people at the ranch, including a famous Hollywood director. She also recounted a weird visit with Epstein to New Mexico governor Bill Richardson's mansion. Bryant was with another girl, waiting outside the room while Epstein and the governor had their meeting. "They came out and looked at us and they shook our hands," Bryant told me, "and went back into the room to have their meeting. And I don't know why he took me there."

Epstein's Manhattan mansion had a British feel to the décor, according to Bryant. Contrary to how it has previously been described, she claims that the New York townhouse was actually hollow in design, with a concealed open space in the middle. On the ground floor of this hollow space, she says, was a gold dome, which she assumed was the roof of Epstein's bedroom. Bryant knew this because, one evening when she was feeling particularly stressed, she climbed out of her bedroom window to have a cigarette. From here, she could see down into the hollow cavity with the golden dome at the bottom. The next day, Bryant was approached by one of Epstein's security personnel, who asked her if she had opened her window the previous night. The man then took her into the mansion's concealed room with its dozens of CCTV cameras and showed her how every inch of the property was under surveillance.

Bryant also visited Epstein's Paris apartment, which she said had "girls in all the rooms." His Palm Beach property is where she says Epstein did most of his 'work,' which mostly seemed to involve talking to people on the phone. Bryant says Epstein spoke to Bill Clinton a lot. She also heard him speaking to George W Bush who, at that time, would have been the US president. She says she heard the name 'Andy' spoken a lot, which she now realises probably referred to Prince Andrew. She even claims Epstein told her that Michael Jackson had expressed an interest in visiting the Palm Beach property. On another occasion, she heard him doing a deal to buy some helicopters for $20 million. This raises the question – was Epstein still arms dealing at this point? For more information about Epstein's arms dealing activities in the eighties, see my first Epstein book, *Who Killed Epstein? Prince Andrew or Bill Clinton*.

In all the travelling around, Bryant was struck by the lack of red tape when it came to Epstein and his entourage. "When we used to fly around, they never checked any of our luggage," Bryant told me. "They never checked any of our passports. Nothing got checked. We just used to walk right through."

After two years with Epstein, Bryant says she started to unwind psychologically. She was putting on weight and wouldn't give up smoking, both of which were not to Epstein's taste. This, coupled with the fact that Bryant wouldn't recruit other girls, made her less and less useful to him. "He's like a chess board with all the pieces," Bryant told me. "If you're not a useful piece, he just tosses you out."

The crunch came when Bryant asked to accompany one of Epstein's assistants on a night out in New York. Drinking, partying and especially drugs were forbidden to all of Epstein's girls, so Bryant had never had a night out in New York, despite the many times she had stayed there. This time, Bryant begged Epstein and he finally agreed. Bryant got her night out but began to feel unwell so decided to go home. Epstein's assistant, who Bryant says was called Deborah, had the keys to the Manhattan townhouse and didn't want to go back yet, so Bryant climbed into a taxi and returned alone. Without keys, she was forced to knock on the door, waking Epstein up in the early hours of the morning. The next day, Epstein confronted her. "He said I was irresponsible and unreliable," Bryant told me, "and within four hours, I was on a plane."

Bryant was finally out, but not before a final chilling warning. "He told me he worked for the CIA," she said, "and he had my family's name on a list. He told me that a girl who accused him of rape, he planted drugs in her apartment and had her put in prison for six months."

But escaping Epstein wasn't the end of Bryant's ordeal. For years, she suffered terrible nightmares and panic attacks, some so severe that she was hospitalised several times. Epstein would email her periodically and, for years, Bryant would get the uncomfortable feeling he was somehow watching her through her computer's camera. In 2011, just after Epstein's Florida jail sentence, she received a strange email from one of his assistants. The message contained a naked picture of Bryant, which the assistant said Epstein had asked her to send. According to Bryant, Epstein had allegedly got Sarah Kellen to take naked pictures of her when she was in his employ. But Bryant was so shy and embarrassed during the shoots that Epstein wasn't happy with the pictures. One day, when Bryant was getting changed in her room, Epstein had barged in with his camera and taken a snapshot of her naked. This picture had been framed and hung in the bathroom of his Paris apartment. It was this photo that his assistant emailed to Bryant in 2011, in what seems to have been a crude attempt at blackmailing her into silence.

In 2016, Bryant received another email, this time from Epstein himself, asking if she knew Sarah Ransome, another survivor, who was taking Epstein to court. Bryant herself never took action or even spoke about Epstein until after his death, because she was so scared of him. Bryant says she felt like she had been a kind of human experiment for Epstein on how to psychologically control people.

Bryant was at a birthday party when she found out about Epstein's death. "I was just utterly shocked and freaked out," she told me, "because I didn't think anyone like that could die, because he was so powerful and in control of everything." When she heard of Maxwell's subsequent arrest, Bryant says she felt "huge relief." Bryant has finally found enough relief from her fear to speak openly about her time with Epstein and Maxwell, but some of the things she underwent she says are still too painful and horrifying to speak about.

Bryant has become friends with several other Epstein survivors, including Virginia Giuffre, with whom she shares a strangely coincidental symbol. Bryant kept a diary in 2002 when she was still with Epstein. On the cover was a blue butterfly. She also created a painting in 2002, which featured a blue butterfly and a reptile. Virginia Giuffre uses the symbol of a blue butterfly for the logo of her charity organisation helping sex trafficking victims, Victims Refuse Silence. And, according to Bryant, Sarah Ransome has a blue butterfly tattooed on her wrist. It's hard to think of a better symbol to represent the metamorphosis and transformation that Epstein survivors like Bryant and Giuffre have gone through to get where they are now. And yet the choice of the same image by the three women was purely coincidental, according to Bryant.

For herself, Bryant feels that Epstein's hold over her has finally lapsed. She no longer experiences the weird sensation that he is watching her through her computer. She now has a family of her own and is writing a book about her story, entitled *Epstein's Butterflies: a Survivor's Story of True Horror*. She wants the book to offer hope to other survivors of sexual abuse, and to help shed further light on Epstein and Maxwell's crimes.

"That's why I wanted to do the book," Bryant told me, "because there's so many intelligent people out there who will help go through the information and see. And hopefully we can all together come to some conclusion, and try and make the world a better place."

CHAPTER 8
GHISLAINE MAXWELL'S TRIAL

After four nights in Merrimack County Jail, Maxwell was transferred to the Metropolitan Detention Center in Brooklyn. After the debacle of Epstein's death, there was no way the authorities were taking any chances with his former associate. Maxwell was put immediately on suicide watch, held in an eight-foot by ten-foot cell with just a mattress, blanket and pillow. She was allowed out of the cramped space for only one hour a day, to exercise in a caged outside space.

As her stay went on, Maxwell was moved from cell to cell to keep her safe from possible attacks from other inmates. She was forced to wear a paper-thin orange jumpsuit and prison-issue slippers. Unsurprisingly, her usual impeccably groomed appearance soon began to slip. Her coutured hair began to look unkempt. The woman Maria Farmer had once described as looking like something off the cover of a fashion magazine now seemed like a character in a gritty prison drama.

In terms of the conditions, Brooklyn's MDC may have been even worse than Manhattan's MCC, where Epstein spent his last days. Condemned by investigators as one of the worst jails in the US and compared to similar institutions in developing countries, it had recently been the subject of controversy, early in 2019, when inmates had been locked in unlit, unheated cells for over a week during the coldest period of the year, after an electrical fire caused a power cut. A federal magistrate who visited the prison found a hundred and sixty-one female inmates locked in two large windowless rooms, twenty-four hours a day, seven days a week.

On top of all this, there was Covid, which had been raging through US prisons since earlier in the year. Inmates at MDC were forced to go without hand sanitiser, gloves or disinfectant wipes and were restricted to their beds, only allowed to get up to use the toilet or shower. Maxwell probably counted herself lucky to be kept in isolation during this period, as it prevented her from being infected.

On her arrest, Maxwell had been charged with six offences, including sex trafficking, enticement of minors and two counts of perjury. The sex trafficking charges covered the period between 1994 and 1997, the years that Maria Farmer had described her time with Epstein and Maxwell. Indeed, Maria's younger sister, Annie Farmer, would be one of the prosecution's key witnesses. According to the indictment, Maxwell had "assisted, facilitated, and contributed" to Epstein's abuse of minors, despite knowing that one of the victims in the prosecution's case had been just fourteen years old at the time.

Maxwell's arraignment and bail hearing came a couple of weeks after her arrest, on 14th July 2020. Due to Covid restrictions, the hearing was held by video link. Press and public were given access by live audio link, which was available for up to a thousand interested spectators. Although no one could see Maxwell, a court drawing showed a rather dishevelled-looking woman, with her hair worn in a simple bun. Maxwell also appeared to have put on weight. Whether this was a ploy by Maxwell and her lawyers to gain sympathy or whether the 58-year-old had really let herself go is hard to tell. Perhaps it was a bit of both.

Maxwell pleaded not guilty to all charges and her lawyer put forward their client's case for bail. They offered a $5 million bond, secured by an anonymous group of six "financially responsible people" with strong ties to Maxwell. One of these was almost certainly her husband, Scott Borgeson, to whom, it was later discovered, she had transferred $28.5 million of her own fortune for protection.

One of the bombshells of the hearing was the news that

Maxwell was indeed married, as this information had not yet hit the public. One of my regular guests, Kirby Sommers, was one of the people who had live access to the hearing. She described the moment when state prosecutors revealed Maxwell's marital status as coinciding with a failure in the audio link so that almost no one heard it. But although Maxwell was married, according to the prosecution, she declined to provide her husband's identity or any information about his finances.

Maxwell was equally vague about the whereabouts of her money, saying she had less than $1 million in Swiss bank accounts. The prosecutors argued that this didn't fit with her lifestyle. Maxwell also claimed that the Tuckedaway mansion didn't belong to her and had only been on loan. This, despite the fact that a real estate agent had identified Maxwell as the mysterious 'Jen Marshall,' who had bought the house.

Maxwell offered to provide her London town house, valued at $3.75 million, as part of her bail security. If granted bail, Maxwell's lawyers suggested she be allowed to stay in a luxury hotel in New York in the run up to and during the trial. Maxwell's lawyers also played the Covid card, claiming that further incarceration during the pandemic would put Maxwell's health at risk and seriously limit access to her legal team, thus hindering her chance for a fair trial.

Arguing against bail, the prosecution said Maxwell posed a considerable flight risk, as evidenced by her year spent hiding from the authorities, following Epstein's arrest. Furthermore, she was a citizen of three countries, one of which – France – had no extradition treaty with the US. As part of their case, the prosecution included statements from Epstein and Maxwell's victims, including Annie Farmer, who delivered her message by phone. Farmer told the hearing, "I met Ghislaine Maxwell when I was sixteen years old. She is a sexual predator, who groomed and abused me and countless other children and young women. She has never shown any remorse for her heinous crimes or the devastating lasting effects her actions caused." She went on to say that Maxwell "has associates across the globe, some of great means, and is a significant flight risk." And she concluded, "We may never know how many people were victimised by Ghislaine Maxwell but those of us who survived implore this court to detain her until she is forced to stand trial and answer for her crimes."

After weighing up both sides of the case, Judge Alison Nathan decided that Maxwell was a significant flight risk and denied her bail. In her ruling, Judge Nathan said, "Not only does that defendant have significant financial resources, but she has demonstrated sophistication in hiding those resources and herself. The court finds by a preponderance of evidence that no combination of conditions could reasonably assure her presence at court."

Judge Nathan set the trial date for July 12th, 2021. Whatever would happen to Maxwell in the future, one thing now looked certain – she would spend the next year behind bars.

More bad news for Maxwell was soon to follow. On 30th July, the court ruled to release more documents from the Giuffre defamation case. This included over seven hours of interviews, a deposition by Giuffre, and details of emails between Maxwell and Epstein, some from 2015. This last was particularly damaging because a large part of Maxwell's case depended on her having had no significant dealings with Epstein for several years. The 2015 emails contradicted that claim. One email in particular was illuminating. On January 25th, 2015, Epstein had written to Maxwell, "You have done nothing wrong and I would urge you to start acting like it. Go outside, head high, not as an escaping convict. Go to parties. Deal with it."

Later in 2020, Epstein researchers and victims had even more cause for celebration. On 16th December, Jean-Luc Brunel was arrested. Brunel ran the MC2 modelling agency, which supplied Epstein with countless underage victims. Like Epstein, Brunel had been accused numerous times of rape and sexual assault. I go into detail about Brunel's history and his association with Epstein in my first Epstein book. Like Epstein, Brunel had always managed to slip through the net when it came to the many allegations of sexual misconduct, mostly against models working for the various agencies he ran over his long career. That was, until now. With Epstein and Maxwell's arrests, and with French authorities conducting their own investigation, the net had been closing around Brunel for some time.

Brunel was arrested at Paris's Charles de Gaulle airport, attempting to flee to Dakar in Senegal. He was stopped by airport authorities when an immigration system flagged him as being wanted for questioning by French police. He was charged with rape and sexual harassment of several minors over the age of fifteen by French magistrates. Prosecutors said in a statement that Brunel "is suspected of having committed acts of rape, sexual assault and sexual harassment on various minor or major victims and of having in particular organized the transport and accommodation of young girls or young women on behalf of Jeffrey Epstein."

With Brunel behind bars, attention switched back to Maxwell as her team of lawyers submitted a second bail attempt on 18th December. In addition to the original $5 million bond package, Maxwell and her husband Borgeson offered to put up $22.5 million of their own money – presumably taken from the $28.5 million that Maxwell had transferred to his name, prior to her arrest. This was supplemented by a $1 million pledge from a security firm that offered to hand over the money if they allowed Maxwell to escape. Maxwell, her lawyers said, would live with a friend in New York, under twenty-four-hour surveillance. The judge declined and Maxwell saw the new year in behind bars.

Not to be discouraged, Maxwell's legal team tried again in February 2021. This time, they offered to put the bulk of her $22.5 million estate into a special account overseen by an asset manager – a former federal judge and US attorney from Georgia. This, the lawyers hoped, would allay any fears of Maxwell accessing her funds to flee the country. On top of this, Maxwell would renounce her British and French citizenship. Judge Alison Nathan was still unmoved and bail was once again denied.

To add salt to the wound, in March, two new charges were added to Maxwell's case, bringing the total to eight (including two charges of perjury relating to the Giuffre defamation case in 2016). The previous four sex trafficking charges had related to the years 1994 to 1997. The two new charges related to the years 2001 to 2004 and concerned a fourth, unnamed, victim, whom prosecutors said Maxwell had recruited for Epstein in Palm Beach. The two new charges meant Maxwell could now face up to seventy years in jail for the sex trafficking charges alone (the two perjury charges were to be dealt with in a separate case). Judge Nathan moved the date of the sex trafficking case from July to November, to allow Maxwell's defence team time to work on the new allegations.

During the pre-trial period, Maxwell's lawyers made numerous complaints about the conditions in the prison. These included having a torch shone in her face every fifteen minutes to check against suicide attempts, and not being allowed a sleep mask. In a statement, her legal team said, "There's no evidence she's suicidal. They're doing it because Jeffrey Epstein died on their watch." In one particularly colourful statement, Maxwell's lead attorney, Bobbi Sternheim, compared her client's situation to that of Hannibal Lector, saying, "Maxwell's conditions of detention for the past sixteen months continue to be reprehensible and utterly inappropriate for [a] woman on the cusp of turning sixty with no criminal record or history of violence. It is unwarranted, unrelenting, and utterly inappropriate."

But Maxwell's conditions weren't as harsh as her lawyers were making out. For instance, she had access to her laptop thirteen hours a day during weekdays, in order to help prepare her defence. When she made a request to have access to the device on weekends and holidays as well, this was granted. It was reported that she was using her computer to learn Russian, as well as to peruse the numerous court documents required for her case.

As the trial date of November 29th approached, the process of selecting twelve jurors from a pool of a hundred and thirty-two began. At the beginning of November, Maxwell's team made a final desperate bail request, this time using a dubious comparison to other high-profile sex offenders. Maxwell's lead lawyer reiterated complaints about Maxwell's harsh prison conditions and claimed her lack of bail was unfair, as Bill Cosby and Harvey Weinstein had received bail before their trials. Unsurprisingly, Judge Nathan denied bail for the fourth and final time. Everything was now set for the trial.

As the day of 29th November began, the legal teams, officials and jurors – five men and seven women – shuffled into the Thurgood Marshal US Federal District Courthouse in Lower Manhattan, just a stone's throw away from the Metropolitan Correctional Center, where Epstein had spent his last days. It was cold and New York was in the grip of the Omicron variant of Covid-19.

Maxwell faced six charges: conspiracy to entice a minor to travel to engage in illegal sex acts; conspiracy to transport a minor with the intent to engage in criminal sexual activity; transporting a minor with the intent to engage in criminal sexual activity; conspiracy to commit sex trafficking of minors; sex trafficking of minors; and enticing a minor to travel to engage in illegal sex acts. The charges related to four women, who were all witnesses at the trial. Three were anonymous, testifying under the pseudonyms Jane, Kate and Carolyn. The fourth was Annie Farmer, the younger sister of Maria Farmer, whom Epstein had sexually assaulted at his New Mexico ranch. Maxwell could face up to seventy years in prison, if found guilty.

The Judge presiding was Hon Alison J Nathan, a rising star in the court system, who had once served Barack Obama as White House Counsel and Special Assistant to the President. After graduating from Cornell University in 2000, Nathan served as a law clerk before going into private practice for a law firm based in Washington and New York. She then moved into state and federal government practice as Special Counsel to the Solicitor General of New York, and in Obama's White House Counsel's

Office. In 2011, President Obama appointed Nathan as District Court Judge for the Southern District of New York. In her ten years as a district judge, Nathan presided over many notable cases but none which came close to the worldwide attention surrounding Maxwell's trial. Just prior to the trial, Nathan was nominated for promotion to become an appeal court judge but stated that she would preside over Maxwell's trial before taking up the new position.

Maxwell's defence team was made up of four top-flight lawyers, two of whom – Jeffrey S Pagliuca and Laura Menninger – had represented her for several years. Another of the team, Christian Everdell, had previously been a prosecutor in the US Attorney's Office in Manhattan, the same office that was now prosecuting Maxwell. Everdell's ten years' service as a federal prosecutor included successful prosecutions of high-ranking Mexican drug cartel members, including the notorious 'El Chapo.' His experience would no doubt have provided crucial insights into how the prosecution would build their case against Maxwell. Maxwell's lead attorney was Bobbi Sternheim, a high-flying defence lawyer who had represented several high-profile clients, including Khaled al-Fawaz, one of Osama bin Laden's closest henchmen. Sternheim had often represented defendants in organised crime and racketeering cases and, on several occasions, had defended clients facing the death penalty. Together, this formidable team would have commanded a serious price tag. It's unclear exactly how much Maxwell was paying her lawyers, but it is known from her bail requests that she had put aside $7 million to cover legal fees.

On the prosecution team representing the US Attorney's office of the Southern District of New York was Lara Pomerantz. A member of the office's Public Corruption Unit, Pomerantz had been involved in numerous sex-crime prosecutions since 2015, including one against a UN official charged with drugging and sexually assaulting several women. Alongside Pomerantz was Maurene Comey, daughter of former FBI director, James Comey.

Comey had been due to prosecute Epstein before his death in 2019. Making up the rest of the four-person team were Alison Moe and Andrew Rohrback. Moe had been one of the team that prosecuted Donald Trump's advisor, Steve Bannon. Rohrback, a graduate of Harvard Law School, was the junior member of the team, having served at the office since 2019. Together, they represented a State Attorney's office that was one of the most prestigious in the US, having successfully prosecuted such high-profile historical cases as the 1993 World Trade Center bombers, Richard Nixon's Attorney General during Watergate, and injury and loss of life claims from the sinking of the Titanic.

However, the SDNY team were at a severe disadvantage when it came to experience. Lead prosecutor, Lara Pomerantz, was the eldest at thirty-seven years of age. Alison Moe and Andrew Rohrback were both thirty-four and Maurene Comey was thirty-three. On the other side, Bobbi Sternheim was sixty-eight, Jeffrey Pagliuca sixty-four, Laura Menninger fifty-three, and Christian Everdell forty-seven. This gave the defence team a staggering ninety-four years more experience than the prosecution, leading some spectators to predict that the state attorney's team were going to be trampled by their ultra-high earning adversaries. With everyone in court and the battle lines drawn up, we were about to find out.

Opening statements began with the prosecution. From behind the protection of a plastic barrier in the middle of the courtroom, lead prosecutor, Lara Pomerantz, addressed the jury. Pomerantz pointed to Maxwell, sitting at the corner of two long tables, flanked by her lawyers, as she painted a picture of the defendant as a sexual predator. Maxwell was Epstein's partner, according to Pomerantz, a kind of madam who procured young girls and "served them up to be sexually abused." In her twenty-five minute statement, Pomerantz mentioned Maxwell's name in conjunction with Epstein more than a dozen times, making it clear that the prosecution's case would centre on associating the two as partners in crime.

Bobbi Sternheim's opening statement attacked this association, pointing out repeatedly that Maxwell was not Epstein and that, ever since her arrest the previous year, the public's view of Maxwell had been biased by Epstein's crimes. Sternheim's opening gambit was full of rhetoric and biblical allusions. She pointed out that, ever since the story of Adam and Eve, women have been blamed for men's crimes. She also portrayed Epstein as a kind of real-life James Bond figure, whose mysterious lifestyle had created a negative mystique that had tainted those around him, especially Maxwell.

In her statement, Pomerantz had offered to tell the tale of a young woman called Jane, one of the anonymous victims who would appear as witnesses. Sternheim attacked the credibility of Jane, pointing out that she was a professional actress, who had played many varied roles in movies, soap operas and reality TV shows. Sternheim pointed out that Jane – and the other three witnesses – had changed their stories several times over the years, mostly in the hope, she claimed, of obtaining pay-outs from the Epstein victims' fund. Sternheim listed the pay-outs the four women had received, ranging from $1.5 million to $5 million.

Sternheim's address lasted fifty-nine minutes and was far more detailed and precise than Pomerantz's, leading to pessimism amongst some spectators that predictions about the defence team's superiority were coming true.

After the opening statements, it was the prosecution's chance to call its witnesses. The SDNY team kicked off with Epstein's long-term pilot, Larry Visoski. As day two of the trial began, the jury heard Visoski recount how he had known Epstein for twenty-five years, flying the billionaire and his guests around the world, first in his Gulfstream G550 jet, then later in his Boeing 727, nicknamed the Lolita Express. Visoski also piloted the helicopter that took Epstein and his guests from the main island of St Thomas to his private island, Little St James. Visoski described all of Epstein's five main properties in detail, saying he had stayed in all of them and also installed home entertainment systems and movie theatres in each. Visoski said he had flown Jane and remembered her as having "piercing, powder blue eyes." The pilot denied ever witnessing or knowing about any sexual misconduct, saying he had two young daughters who had met and spent time with Epstein and that he would have quit his job immediately if he had known about the sexual abuse of minors.

The defence's cross-examination of Visoski concentrated mostly on his flight records and the many famous names who flew with Epstein. Bill Clinton, Leslie Wexner, Prince Andrew, Donald Trump, Kevin Spacey and Chris Tucker were all name-dropped, in what appeared to be an attempt to establish a kind of respectability by proxy, as if the defence were suggesting that, with these kinds of high-profile names on board, nothing nefarious could possibly happen.

The defence's second witness was Jane, the actor who Pomerantz had introduced in her opening statement. Jane told the jury how, as a 14-year-old, she had first met Epstein and Maxwell at a summer camp in Michigan. Jane said she was hanging out with some friends eating ice cream when a "tall thin woman" with "a cute little Yorkie" walked by. The woman was Maxwell. She stopped at the bench where the girls were sitting and they asked if they could stroke the dog. Jane's friends left but Jane stayed and Maxwell was soon joined by a man.

The summer camp was a school for talented teenagers, based at the Interlochen Center for the Arts, and the man was Epstein. Epstein, it turns out, funded a building at the Interlochen Center called the 'Jeffrey Epstein Scholarship Lodge,' where he and Maxwell would often stay. Clearly, the summer camp was a prime grooming ground. Epstein got talking to Jane and asked her about her favourite subjects at school. He told her he was someone who liked to help people and asked for her phone number.

It so happened that Jane lived in Palm Beach. She was going through a rough time. Her father had recently died and her family had been forced to sue for bankruptcy and move into a friend's pool house. Jane felt her mother was "unavailable" emotionally and had begun seeing a counsellor, but when the counsellor called her mother, Jane said she responded by shouting at her and slapping her, so she never saw the counsellor again.

Several weeks after the chance meeting in Michigan, when Jane received an invitation to have tea at Epstein's Palm Beach mansion, she jumped at the chance. The El Brillo Way house impressed Jane, as did Epstein and Maxwell's talk of the famous people they knew, giving the impression that they were "well connected and affluent." Jane began visiting Epstein's house once every one or two weeks. On one occasion, Epstein handed her a cheque saying, "This is for your mother. I know she's having a hard time." Jane began to regard Maxwell as a kind of older sister figure, "odd," in Jane's words, "but nice."

However, after a few weeks, Maxwell began talking to her about sex. Then Maxwell and Epstein took her shopping to Victoria's Secret, where they bought her a pair of white cotton briefs. Jane remembered the first time she went poolside at the El Brillo Way house. "I walked out there and there was these four women and Ghislaine, all topless and some of them were naked," she recalled. "I was just shocked because I hadn't seen that before."

The grooming culminated one day when Epstein was talking about introducing her to talent agents. Suddenly, he cut short the conversation, stood up and said, "Follow me." Epstein took her by the hand and led her into one of the mansion's pool houses. Inside, he led her to a couch and took off his pants. He pulled her on top of him and began masturbating. "I was frozen in fear," Jane told the jury. "I had never seen a penis before." When he was done, Jane said, Epstein went into the bathroom to clean up and acted "like nothing had happened."

Jane said she didn't tell anyone about what had happened because she was "terrified and felt gross and felt ashamed." The abuse became regular, with Epstein touching her breasts and vagina and encouraging her to touch his penis, nipples and feet. Maxwell was sometimes involved in the abuse, Jane said, and acted like it was "no big deal." Maxwell, she said, gave her instructions on how to give erotic massages and sometimes joined in, touching Jane's breasts. Sometimes, the abuse involved groups of people, often including Maxwell. These orgies would include "kissing, oral sex on each other, oral sex on Jeffrey, full on intercourse." Jane recalled occasions where a group of people would be socialising when they would suddenly be "summoned" into Epstein's bedroom or a massage room. Epstein would lie down and Maxwell and the others would take off their clothes and the whole thing would turn into "this orgy."

All this happened when Jane was fourteen years old and the abuse continued for years. She told the court that, even though she was a well-known actress, she wanted to remain anonymous because victim-shaming was still prevalent in the entertainment industry. She said she had remained silent for so many years because she had feared being turned down for work, if people knew she had accused Epstein and Maxwell of sexual abuse.

On day three, it was the defence's turn to cross-examine the witness. Laura Menninger led the questioning, seeking to cast doubt on Jane's memory of events, on her acting, and on her financial motivations.

Menninger began by challenging Jane's testimony that her family had been struggling financially before her first meeting with Epstein. Menninger pointed out that both Jane and her two brothers had attended the Interlochen Center for the Arts summer camp three years in a row, at the cost of $4,000 per child per year.

Menninger also tried to cast doubt on Jane's recollection of Maxwell's involvement in her abuse. The lawyer implied that Jane had not mentioned Maxwell to federal investigators in 2019 and 2020. She asked whether Jane could remember mentioning Maxwell in the investigation, to which Jane replied she couldn't. Menninger also said Jane had told federal investigators that Epstein always called to invite her to the house. This conflicted with her testimony in court that Maxwell arranged appointments.

"Two years later, now you remember that Ghislaine called your home to make appointments?" Menninger asked.

"Right," Jane replied.

"That memory has come back to you in the past two years?" Menninger continued.

"Memory is not linear," Jane replied.

The prosecution also tried to cast doubt on Jane's recollection of her first meeting with Maxwell and Epstein. In her testimony, Jane had claimed it was Maxwell who had approached her first, followed by Epstein. Menninger said that Jane had earlier told her brothers that it was only Epstein who had approached her at Interlochen.

"True, you told your brother Brian you had been approached by Epstein?" Ms. Menninger asked. "Told your brother nothing about Maxwell being there?"

"I don't recall," Jane responded.

Bizarrely, much of the debate revolved around a Disney movie. Menninger said Jane had told federal investigators that Epstein flew her to New York in 1994 to see the film, The Lion King.

"The Lion King did not come out until 1997," said Menninger and continued to fire questions at Jane, concerning her memory of the trip. Jane admitted that she must have been "incorrect in my timeline."

Menninger fired several questions about Jane's acting career, attempting to suggest that her testimony was another performance. She asked if Jane was "someone who plays the role of a fictional character" and "someone who takes lines borrowed from a writer."

Menninger also pointed out the wide range of roles Jane had adopted in her career, including a protective mother, a prostitute, a car-crash victim, and someone stalked by serial killers, the implication being that Jane would find it easy to adopt the role of sexual abuse victim for the trial.

Finally, Menninger sought to cast doubt on Jane's motives, pointing out that she had filed civil lawsuits against both Maxwell and Epstein and had received $5 million from the Epstein Victims' Compensation Fund.

The defence again seemed intent on pointing out Epstein's connections with famous people, quizzing Jane about a 1994 trip to Mar-a Lago, where she said she met Donald Trump. Jane also said Prince Andrew had flown on Epstein's private jet while she was on board.

Jane kept her cool throughout most of Menninger's questioning but broke down during the prosecution's follow-up questions, often having to pause to cry into some tissues.

When SDNY attorney, Alison Moe, asked her what it had meant to be awarded the $5 million, she responded tearfully, "I wish I would have never received that money in the first place. Hopefully, this just puts it to an end and I can move on with my life."

Regarding the difference between Jane's current testimony and what she had told the federal investigation in 2019/20, Moe asked why Jane hadn't mentioned Maxwell to the investigators. "I was sitting in a room full of strangers," Jane replied, "and telling them the most shameful, deepest secrets I had been carrying around with me everywhere. It was too difficult, too difficult emotionally, too difficult on every level."

Seeking to clear up the defence's accusations about Jane acting in court, the prosecution lawyer asked her if she understood the difference between acting and testifying in court. Jane insisted she was not acting. "Acting on television is not real and testifying in court is real and is the truth," she said.

By the end of day three, it was clear that the gloves were off. No quarter would be given to the victims and Maxwell's defence team would pull no punches. How would the other three witnesses stand up under the intense psychological pressure of the defence's scrutiny? We would soon see.

Day four saw a break from victim testimony. Instead, proceedings began with a clinical psychologist, Dr Lisa Rocchio, taking the stand. Dr Rocchio, an expert in child sexual abuse cases, described how abusers groom their victims. Grooming, Dr Rocchio said, typically involves a five-step process. First the abuser selects the victim; then obtains access to and isolates the victim; thirdly, the abuser uses lies, deception and manipulation to build trust and attachment; then desensitises the victim to physical and sexual touching; and finally maintains their control over the victim, coercing them into further abuse.

This was important because it established Maxwell's role in grooming Epstein's victims. It fitted with their testimony of her befriending them, taking them on shopping trips, and expressing concern and sympathy with their situations, before gradually introducing the subject of sex into conversations. Dr Rocchio's testimony coincided exactly with the way Pomerantz had described Maxwell in her opening statement:

"The defendant took these girls on shopping trips, asked them about their lives, their schools, their families. She won their trust. She discussed sexual topics with them. She helped normalize abusive sexual conduct. She put them at ease and made them feel safe, all so that they could be molested by a middle-aged man."

After the expert testimony came the insider's eye view of day-to-day life at an Epstein property. Epstein's Palm Beach house manager, Juan Alessi, was called to the stand.

From the start, Alessi made it clear that, as soon as Maxwell arrived on the scene, she was the one in charge. Alessi worked at the El Brillo Way property from 1990 to 2002. He said that he had enjoyed a "cordial" relationship with Epstein, until Maxwell turned up in the early nineties. Once Maxwell was in charge, Alessi told the jury, she instructed him to never look Epstein in the eyes when speaking to him. Maxwell seemed to have a penchant for micromanaging, according to Alessi's testimony. So much so that she created a fifty-eight-page instruction manual for all house staff to follow. Instructions included the placement of telephone directories (always to the right of the telephone), to patching up holes in the fence to prevent her Yorkshire terrier, Max, from escaping. There was a "tremendous amount of instructions" Alessi told the court, including how to "anticipate the needs of Mr Epstein, Ms Maxwell and their guests."

A more sinister rule was that staff should: "Remember that you see nothing, hear nothing, say nothing, except to answer a question direct to you. Respect their privacy." Alessi said he interpreted this instruction as a warning. "I was supposed to be blind and dumb," he told the court, "to say nothing of their lives."

Alessi also testified to seeing "many, many, many females" arrive at the house, most of whom he estimated to be in their twenties. Of the hundreds of times Alessi saw women bathing by the pool, he estimated eighty percent of them were topless. But he said he never witnessed or knew of any sexual abuse of minors occurring during his twelve years' service at the Palm Beach mansion. Alessi said he only remembered two girls visiting the property who looked underage, both of whom appeared to be around fourteen or fifteen years old.

Alessi confirmed that one of these was 'Jane,' the witness who had testified on days two and three of the trial. Alessi described jane as a "strikingly beautiful girl, beautiful eyes, long hair, long brunette hair, tall, very pleasant." Alessi said he remembered the first time Jane visited the house with her mother in 1994. He also remembered being instructed to pick her up from either school or home. This corroborated Jane's testimony that she remembered being driven to the Palm Beach house by a Latin American man – Alessi is from Ecuador.

Alessi told the court how each of Epstein's cars had to be stocked with hundred-dollar bills, adding weight to the testimony of various Epstein survivors that Maxwell would cruise around in Epstein's vehicles, looking for attractive young girls. Alessi said that Epstein originally received one massage a day but was soon receiving three massages a day, one in the morning, one in the afternoon, and one in the evening. The former house manager said he would often find sex toys lying around after Epstein's massages and would wash them before replacing them in a basket that also contained pornographic videos and a black leather costume.

Day five began with the defence cross-examining Alessi. Maxwell's lawyer, Jeffrey Pagliuca, quizzed him about an order from Epstein to remove pictures of Maxwell before hosting other female guests. Pagliuca suggested this order had been hidden from Maxwell and was a "secret" between him and Epstein.

The implication seemed to agitate Alessi. He responded, "It was not a secret, it was a mandate." Adding that Epstein "never shared any of his personal life with me … He never suggested, implied anything."

Pagliuca asked why he thought Epstein would want the pictures taken down, to which Alessi replied, "I have no idea." The argument Maxwell's team were trying to establish, it seemed, was that Maxwell was in a romantic relationship with Epstein and that she would be jealous if she knew her pictures were being removed when Epstein entertained other female guests. The defence seemed to imply that someone so susceptible to feelings of jealousy towards Epstein's other women would hardly be complicit in obtaining and grooming them for him.

Pagliuca tried to pick holes in Alessi's testimony by comparing it with statements he had made in previous civil cases. Pagliuca pointed out that, in a sworn deposition given in 2016, Alessi had testified that he first met Jane much later than 1994. Alessi countered that he had confused her with another young girl.

Pagliuca then took Alessi to task about an admission he had made of once stealing money from Epstein. Pagliuca pointed out that he previously admitted to stealing money twice from Epstein. Alessi denied the accusation angrily but Pagliuca produced the record of his previous statement, to which Alessi admitted, "I guess I did."

In the afternoon, the prosecution introduced another witness, retired Palm Beach police officer, Gregory Parkinson. Parkinson was one of the officers who raided Epstein's El Brillo Way mansion in 2005. Parkinson had taken a video of the property, which was shown to jurors but kept hidden from other members of the court. A green massage table was also brought into the courtroom and unfolded in front of the jury. Parkinson was asked to identify the massage table as the same one shown in the video, which he did. This corroborated Jane's and Alessi's testimony about massage tables being used as the scene of sexual abuse.

Alessi's claims about sex toys were also corroborated with the last prosecution witness of the day, Sergeant Michael Dawson. Dawson spoke about finding a large double-headed sex toy called the 'Twin Torpedo' – the same kind that Alessi had specifically mentioned – and the jury were shown a picture of the sex toy, taken from the 2005 search. Dawson also mentioned seeing lots of pictures of naked girls around the property, including inside closets, and that some of the computers did not have accompanying hard drives.

Dawson's testimony marked the end of week one of the trial. Week two of the trial would begin with testimony from another Epstein survivor and the defence would double-down on their aggressive approach.

On Monday 6th December - day six of the trial – the prosecution called 'Kate' to the stand. Kate was a British former model, who said she had first met Maxwell in 1994, when she was seventeen, during a trip to Paris. Kate told the jury that Maxwell seemed "sophisticated and elegant" and was interested in her, asking lots of questions about her life. A few weeks later, Maxwell invited Kate to her Belgravia house for tea. Kate said that she felt like she had made a new friend.

"I felt that I had found a new connection that could be really meaningful to me," she told the jury. "I was really happy that we had connected and she seemed as excited as I was to have a new friend."

She told the jury that, although Maxwell was significantly older – in her thirties, compared to Kate's seventeen – Maxwell was "almost like a schoolgirl". "Everything seemed to be a fun, silly joke," she said.

Kate and Maxwell stayed in regular contact and Maxwell told Kate about her boyfriend, a philanthropist who helped young people. A few weeks later, Maxwell invited Kate back to her Belgravia mews house. When she entered, Epstein was sitting in the lounge wearing sweatpants, Kate said. Maxwell suggested that Kate give Epstein's foot a squeeze to show how strong she was and Epstein said, "Oh, you can go ahead and do my shoulders."

Soon after this first meeting, Maxwell called Kate with an urgent request – Epstein's masseuse had cancelled, could Kate come over and fill in? Kate went to Maxwell's house and the older woman led her up the stairs to a dimly-lit room with towels and a massage table, where Epstein was waiting. Epstein slipped off his robe and stood naked facing the door as Kate entered. Maxwell handed her a bottle of massage oil and closed the door, leaving her alone in the room with the older man. Kate began to massage Epstein. He initiated sexual contact, she testified, and they engaged in a sex act.

After the encounter, Kate said Maxwell asked her how it went and if she'd had fun. "She seemed very excited and was happy," she told the jury. A few weeks later, Kate was called to Maxwell's house to give Epstein another sexualised massage. Afterwards, Maxwell said, "Did you have fun? You are such a good girl. He obviously likes you a lot." "She sounded really pleased," Kate told the court, "and I was pleased that she was pleased."

Kate began visiting Epstein regularly, flying to his Palm Beach, New York and Little St James properties. On one visit to the Palm Beach mansion, Kate found a schoolgirl outfit laid out on her bed. She asked Maxwell what the costume was for and Maxwell said, "I thought it would be fun for you to take Jeffrey his tea in this outfit." Kate put on the costume, Maxwell gave her a tray, and she found Epstein waiting by the pool. Epstein then initiated a sex act with her, she told the court.

Prosecution lawyer, Lara Pomerantz, asked Kate why she had put on the outfit and Kate replied, "I didn't know how to say no. I had never been to Palm Beach or Florida before. I had no idea where the house was. And I wasn't sure if I said no if I would have to leave, or what the consequence would be for not doing it."

Kate told the court that her relationship with Maxwell and Epstein continued sporadically until her early thirties and ended after she had her first baby.

Bobbi Sternheim conducted the defence team's cross-examination of the witness. Once again, she sought to cast doubt on Kate's motives, pointing out previous statements in which Kate had described herself as "fiercely ambitious." She pointed out that Kate had claimed $3 million from the Epstein Victims' Fund and that she was seeking to obtain a special kind of US visa that was open to victims of crimes like sexual abuse if they helped in government investigations or prosecutions.

Kate denied that she was seeking this kind of Visa but did admit that, at one time, she had been interested.

As with other witnesses, Sternheim then attacked Kate's memory of events, pointing out that she'd had an alcohol, cocaine and sleeping pill habit for a decade, during which she was seeing Epstein and Maxwell. Kate responded that she had never been allowed to use alcohol or drugs around Epstein and Maxwell, so her memory of those events remained unclouded.

Day seven saw a third accuser, Carolyn, take the stand. Carolyn was the witness added to the case earlier in the year, extending the period of accusations to 2001 and 2004. Carolyn told the court how she had experienced a troubled childhood in Palm Beach. Her mother was an alcoholic and she was sexually abused by her grandfather from age four. She had dropped out of middle school, Carolyn told the jury, and become addicted to cocaine and pain killers.

At age fourteen, Carolyn said she was introduced to Epstein by a friend of hers, Virginia Roberts (now Giuffre). Carolyn said that Roberts had told her she could earn money by giving massages to her friend, an older man who lived on Palm Beach Island.

On her first visit to the El Brillo Way mansion, Carolyn said she was accompanied by Roberts, who had dressed her "provocatively" and driven her to the property. The two girls were met at the door by Maxwell, who told them to go upstairs. Roberts got fully undressed, according to Carolyn, while she asked to keep her bra and underwear on. Then Epstein entered the room and lay on the massage table. Roberts instructed her on how to prepare the massage table and oils, then showed her how Epstein liked to be massaged. Roberts massaged him for forty-five minutes before Epstein turned over, then Roberts climbed on top of him and they had sex, while Carolyn watched from a nearby couch. Carolyn was paid $300 in hundred-dollar bills and went home, after giving her number to Maxwell.

The next time, Maxwell called to ask Carolyn to come on her own and she engaged in a sex act with Epstein during a massage. After that, Maxwell would arrange her appointments with Epstein, either by calling her, her boyfriend or her mother. Carolyn estimated she visited the Palm Beach property more than a hundred times over a four-year period. She would massage Epstein on his back, often while talking about her troubled upbringing, before he would turn over and touch her sexually, sometimes with a sex toy. Usually, he masturbated, a couple of times he penetrated her, according to Carolyn. "Something sexual happened every single time," she told the jury.

Carolyn was paid $300 dollars for each massage and given gifts like Victoria's Secret lingerie, tickets to an Incubus concert, and a massage book 'for Dummies'. She was also paid $500-$600 for a series of naked photos, taken by Sarah Kellen. Epstein asked her if she knew any friends that were her age or younger. Carolyn brought one of her friends along to a massage and received $600, while the friend got $300. She said she usually spent the money on alcohol and drugs.

Carolyn claimed Maxwell and Epstein must have known about her age because, when Maxwell, tried to get her to visit Little St James, Carolyn told her she didn't have a passport and there was no way her mum would let her travel overseas. She said Maxwell saw her naked in the massage room three times and, on one occasion, groped her sexually. "She came in and felt my boobs, my hips and my buttocks, and said that ... I had a great body for Mr Epstein and his friends," Carolyn told the court.

Carolyn fell pregnant with her then-boyfriend's baby but continued to do massages for Epstein because she needed the money. She said the relationship ended when Epstein asked her if she had any younger friends. "And that's when I realised I was too old," she told the jury. She was eighteen at the time.

Maxwell's team's cross-examination routine was becoming predictable and, at times, increasingly desperate. Pagliuca sought to discredit Carolyn's testimony by comparing it with earlier statements to the FBI. He compared her description of Maxwell having a "foreign" accent with an earlier statement in which she'd described Maxwell's accent as "unknown." "At that point in your life, you knew what a British accent was?" quizzed Pagliuca, as if her knowledge of British accents at age fourteen had any bearing on the credibility of her testimony.

At another time, Pagliuca tried to contradict her statement about Maxwell arranging the massages by pointing out that sometimes she had called Epstein using a number she had found in the phone book. "The telephone book you're talking about," Carolyn responded coolly, "was my personal book."

Pagliuca then tried to discredit the statement that she had twice been penetrated by Epstein. He pointed out that, in an earlier statement, when asked if she'd ever had sex with Epstein, she had answered "no." But Pagliuca didn't get the chance to finish his question. Carolyn interrupted, saying, "I replied 'no' because I was not a willing participant. He had intercourse with me, and I stopped it."

Carolyn kept up her strong façade against Pagliuca but, like Jane before her, she broke down in tears during the prosecution's rebuttal. Crying on the stand, Carolyn said she was only a young teenager when she met Epstein and had agreed to testify at the trial for no other motive than that she knew what Maxwell had done "was wrong."

Day eight saw another of Epstein's pilots, David Rodgers, take the stand. Rodgers testified that he had flown Epstein on thousands of flights between 1991 and 2019 and that Maxwell had been present on hundreds of those flights. As Epstein's chief pilot, Rodgers had been there for Epstein's first ever flight as a private jet owner, flying from Wilmington, Delaware, to Teterboro Airport in New Jersey, and had worked for Epstein right up until his arrest.

Rodgers described Maxwell as Epstein's "number two" and said she managed all Epstein's pilots, overseeing their vacations and expenses. Rodgers confirmed what many other witnesses have said – that Epstein and Maxwell were at first romantically involved but, after a few years, the relationship changed to a purely business one, with Maxwell becoming his property manager.

Rodgers said he knew the first witness, Jane, and had met her for the first time in 1996, which he knew from flight logs. Rodgers also confirmed that he had flown Epstein to Interlochen several times, the summer school where Jane said she was first picked up by Epstein and Maxwell. The pilot also said he had flown Virginia Giuffre on Epstein's jets on more than thirty occasions.

Day nine saw Annie Farmer's testimony, the only witness to testify under her own name. Farmer's sister, Maria Farmer, had worked for Epstein in New York after graduating from art school in the city. Maria, who was also sexually assaulted by Epstein and Maxwell, had told them about her younger sister, Annie, who she described as beautiful and intelligent, and Epstein had arranged to meet her. I go into great detail about Maria Farmer's experiences with Epstein and Maxwell in my first book on Epstein.

Farmer told the jury how she had flown to New York in 1995 to meet Epstein, when she was sixteen years old. Epstein had paid for the flight, and she visited him at his Manhattan townhouse, along with her sister. Farmer wanted to study medicine and Epstein said he was interested in helping her financially. The billionaire showered her with gifts, Farmer told the court, including a pair of cowboy boots and tickets to see The Phantom of the Opera on Broadway.

Farmer said she initially liked Epstein and was impressed at how "down to Earth" he was. But everything changed during a visit to the movies. Epstein was sitting next to Farmer when he started touching her arms and rubbing her feet and legs. Farmer wrote in her diary that she was confused about the encounter but decided to try to forget about it, not wanting to upset her sister.

In April of the next year, 1996, Epstein offered to fly Farmer to his Zorro ranch in New Mexico, saying he wanted to pay her college fees and future overseas travel. Epstein had assured Farmer – and even told her mother on the telephone – that she would be one of two dozen students attending the event at the ranch, and that his "wife," Maxwell, would be there to chaperone them. But during the flight, Farmer began to feel uncomfortable when Maxwell showed her how to massage Epstein's feet. Things got worse at the ranch. Maxwell persuaded Farmer to have a massage, she told the jury, and led her into a room with a massage table, telling her to remove her clothes.

Farmer lay on the table covered by a sheet, but was completely unprepared for what happened next. "She pulled the sheet down and exposed my breasts and started rubbing on my breasts," Farmer testified. "Once she pulled down the sheet, I felt kind of frozen. It didn't make sense to me that that would happen. I so badly wanted to get off the table and have the massage be done."

The next day, it was Epstein's turn. According to Farmer, he bounded into her room while she was still in bed and jumped in next to her, asking her if she wanted to "cuddle." Farmer said she felt "frozen" again and didn't know what to do. She got up, saying she needed to use the bathroom. She shut herself inside and waited until Epstein left. For the rest of that day, she said Maxwell no longer showed any interest in her studies.

During the cross-examination, Maxwell's defence lawyer, Laura Menninger, asked why Farmer hadn't recorded the New Mexico trip in her diary, as she had the incident at the cinema. Farmer said it was because she had felt "emotionally scarred" by the weekend at the New Mexico ranch.

In a more bizarre line of questioning, Menninger asked if Maxwell had touched Farmer's nipples during the naked massage, to which Farmer replied she hadn't. Menninger asked if Epstein had pressed his erect penis into Farmer's back when he cuddled her in bed, which Farmer also responded to in the negative.

When Farmer stepped down from the stand, the prosecution rested its case. It was Friday 10th December. The trial had so far been a no-holds-barred encounter with barely-concealed dislike between the two teams of lawyers, which at times broke out into open hostility. Defence attorney Laura Menninger and prosecution lawyer Alison Moe appeared to be particularly unfond of each other, with Moe repeatedly objecting to the way Menninger phrased her questions and the two engaging in a heated argument over photographic evidence. Judge Nathan had to repeatedly call for peace, telling everyone to "calm down." When the two teams finally managed to agree on a minor point of court protocol, Judge Nathan quipped sarcastically that it was a "magical moment."

There was a three-day break, while Judge Nathan travelled to Washington for the confirmation hearing for her upcoming promotion to the US Court of Appeals for the Second Circuit. The Maxwell trial restarted on Thursday 16th December. The day began with a ruling by Judge Nathan, stating that she had denied Maxwell's request to have three witnesses testify anonymously.

The defence then called three witnesses, one of whom was Cimberly Espinosa, Maxwell's assistant from 1996 until 2002. Espinosa told the court that Epstein had ordered her to buy flowers for his girlfriend, Celina Midelfart, a Norwegian businesswoman who had also dated Donald Trump. Espinosa told the court that she felt that Epstein and Midelfart were a couple, even though this could have been "concurrent for a little bit of time" with Epstein and Maxwell's relationship. Espinosa added that, although she was working for Maxwell, her boss was unaware of the flowers she had bought for Midelfart.

The defence was clearly building on the line of argument they had begun earlier in the trial, that Maxwell was unaware of Epstein's various infidelities and therefore unaware of any sexual abuse with minors.

Espinosa also said she had met prosecution witness, Jane, on several visits to Epstein's New York offices in the late nineties. She said Jane's mother had told staff at the offices that Jane was

Epstein's goddaughter and that she was treated with "utmost respect."

Day eleven saw Epstein's ex-girlfriend, Eva Andersson-Dubin, take the stand. Andersson-Dubin was a former Miss Sweden, who said she was in an on-off relationship with Epstein between 1983 and 1991. In her memoirs, Virginia Giuffre claimed that Epstein had sent her to massage Andersson-Dubin when she was pregnant. Giuffre said that, after massaging Andersson-Dubin, she gave a sexual massage to her husband, billionaire financier, Glenn Dubin, while his wife was sleeping in the other room. It was also widely reported that Epstein had said he wanted to marry the Dubins' eldest daughter, Celina, when she was still a teenager.

Andersson-Dubin told the court that Celina and her other two children – a daughter now aged 20 and a son aged 25 – all had close relationships with Epstein, whom they called "Uncle Jeff". Andersson-Dubin told defence attorney, Jeffrey Pagliuca, that she was comfortable with Epstein's relationship with her children and had never seen any inappropriate behaviour involving the older man.

Earlier in the trial, Jane had testified that she was once involved in a sexual massage with Epstein, in which a woman called Eva took part. Andersson-Dubin denied that this was her and, on being shown a photo of Jane, said that she couldn't recall ever meeting her.

The afternoon's proceedings began with a typically arrogant statement from Maxwell. Asked by the judge if she intended to testify, Maxwell said, "Your honour, the Government has not proven its case beyond a reasonable doubt, so there is no need for me to testify." Defence teams usually advise their clients not to testify, especially in high-profile criminal cases. But in Maxwell's case, they would have especial reason not to. Maxwell hadn't performed well under examination in previous civil cases. Her innate sense of entitlement tended to make itself shown when taking the stand, and she often failed to control her temper, on one occasion even banging her fist down on the table in front of her.

The defence rested its case shortly after Maxwell's statement on Friday afternoon. The defence's case had lasted just two days and had been marred by squabbles over how much time they had been given to prepare, and trouble locating witnesses. After suggesting in their opening statement that they would call as many as thirty-five witnesses, they had called just eight. After initial fears that the prosecution would botch the case, based on age, experience and salaries, it had turned out the other way round. The defence team's effort looked fairly shambolic, hardly worth the several million dollars Maxwell had forked out on them.

The examinations and cross-examinations were now over, the evidence all presented. The scene was set for closing statements on the following Monday.

As the last day of the trial dawned, Maxwell was joined in court by four of her siblings – Ian, Kevin, Christine and Isabel. The Maxwells sat in the front row behind their younger sister and spoke to each other in muted French as they listened to the closing arguments. These arguments followed much the same lines as the opening statements, with prosecution lawyer, Alison Moe, seeking to tie Epstein and Maxwell closely together, while defence lawyer, Laura Menninger, tried to separate them.

"Maxwell and Epstein were partners," Moe told the jury. "They were partners in crime, who sexually exploited young girls together." She rubbished the idea that Maxwell knew nothing of what was going on, saying, "Ladies and gentlemen, when you're with someone for eleven years, you know what they like. Jeffrey Epstein liked underage girls. He liked to touch underage girls. Maxwell knew it."

Moe also countered defence claims that the four witnesses had somehow misremembered what had happened to them, saying this was all a "distraction." "They're not all suffering from the same mass delusion," Moe said. "Being molested is not something you forget, ever. You remember an adult woman groping your breast. You remember a middle-aged man touching your vagina. You remember feeling scared and frozen and trapped and confused."

Moe concluded with a description of Maxwell as, "a grown woman who preyed on vulnerable kids."

She went on, "She targeted a girl whose father had just died. She targeted a girl whose mother was an alcoholic. She targeted a girl with a single mom who was struggling to raise her daughters. Maxwell was a sophisticated predator, who knew exactly what she was doing. She ran the same playbook again and again and again."

Laura Menninger summed up for the defence by once again trying to distance Maxwell from Epstein, saying, "He is not my client." She accused the prosecution of portraying their case like a sensational tabloid, showing countless pictures of tropical islands, multi-million-dollar homes and private jets. She once again attacked the accusers' motives, suggesting that they were driven by financial gain. She concluded with the words, "Ghislaine is being tried here for being with Jeffrey Epstein. Maybe it was the biggest mistake of her life, but it's not a crime. Acquit her."

Once the closing arguments were complete, Judge Nathan sent the jury away to begin deliberations immediately. The Omicron variant of Covid was sweeping through New York and the judge clearly wanted a result before the pandemic could interfere with proceedings. The jury continued deliberating for the next two days, before taking a four-day break for Christmas. They returned the following Monday, the 27th. Maxwell meanwhile spent Christmas – which was also her 60th birthday – behind bars.

During their deliberations, the jury asked several questions of the court, most of which involved requesting transcripts of witness testimonies. One question seemed to throw the court into confusion, when the jury asked if count four – transporting Jane to New Mexico – still counted if Maxwell aided in Jane's return flight but not her flight there. There was a lengthy debate between the prosecution and defence, much of it centering around the placement of a comma. The prosecution wanted the judge to point the jury to the relevant page of the jury's instructions, while the defence wanted her to simply say "no." In the end, Judge

Nathan agreed with the prosecution, sending a note to them to refer to page 28 of the instructions. At the defence table, Maxwell dropped her head into her hands.

Another request highlighted how detailed and complex the deliberations were becoming, when the jury asked for a delivery of office supplies, including coloured Post-It notes, a white board and highlighters. By the end of Monday 27th's proceedings, Judge Nathan told the jury they would have to stay late the next day if they hadn't reached a verdict. The jury didn't take kindly to this instruction, saying it smacked of a message to "hurry up." Come five o'clock on Tuesday, the jury sent a note, asking to finish at the normal time and resume at nine the next morning. Early on Wednesday morning, the jury sent another note, asking if they would have to stay over the weekend, if they hadn't reached a verdict. Judge Nathan responded that they would have to come in every single day, because of the threat posed by the Omicron variant.

Just hours later, the jury sent a note saying it had reached a verdict. Maxwell's hour of judgement had come.

The twelve men and women filed back into a hushed courtroom. Deathly silence fell as Judge Nathan read the verdict.

> **Count One:** Conspiracy to entice a minor to travel to engage in illegal sex acts (maximum sentence of five years).
>
> Guilty.
>
> **Count two:** Enticing a minor to travel to engage in illegal sex acts (maximum sentence of five years).
>
> Not guilty.
>
> **Count three:** Conspiracy to transport a minor with the intent to engage in criminal sexual activity (maximum sentence of five years).
>
> Guilty.

Count four: Transporting a minor with the intent to engage in criminal sexual activity (maximum sentence of ten years).

Guilty.

Count five: Conspiracy to commit sex trafficking of minors (maximum sentence of five years).

Guilty.

Count six: Sex trafficking of minors (maximum sentence of forty years).

Guilty.

Maxwell's face remained expressionless as Judge Nathan read the verdict. When the judge had finished, Maxwell poured herself a cup of water and took a drink. Judge Nathan then asked if the decision had been unanimous and a microphone was passed to each of the jurors, who confirmed that it was. Maxwell's long-term attorney, Jeffrey Pagliuca, patted her sympathetically on the back.

The jury was dismissed. Bobbi Sternheim asked if the judge could arrange for Maxwell to get a Covid-19 booster shot, and with that, the newly-turned sixty-year-old was led from the courtroom back to her jail cell, a cell where she is set to spend a significant part – perhaps the whole – of the rest of her life.

For Maxwell and Epstein's victims, it was the culmination of a long struggle for justice, which had taken over a decade to reach. Virginia Giuffre summed up the thoughts of all the survivors with her words:

"My soul yearned for justice for years and today the jury gave me just that. I will remember this day always. Having lived with the horrors of Maxwell's abuse, my heart goes out to the many other girls and young women who suffered at her hands and whose lives she destroyed."

Maxwell's defence team protested their client's innocence and announced they had already started working on the appeal. Their chance would come sooner than they could have hoped when, in January, it emerged that one of the jurors, a man identified as 'Juror 50' or Scotty David (his first and middle names) had failed to mention on his juror questionnaire that he had suffered sexual abuse as a child. Maxwell's lawyers argued that this had prejudiced his opinion and resulted in an unfair trial.

However, Judge Nathan held a hearing on the matter, in which she questioned the prospective juror and was satisfied that he had merely made a mistake when filling in the questionnaire and hadn't purposefully failed to mention his history of sexual abuse. Nathan was also satisfied that Juror 50 had been "fair and impartial", noting that the same court had previously included a juror in a murder trial who had suffered the murder of a family member. The call for a mistrial was denied.

In January, it also emerged that Scott Borgeson had informed Maxwell he was filing for divorce before the trial started. A close friend of Maxwell's told *The Daily Mail* that Borgeson had spoken to Maxwell by phone while she was in prison, to inform her that he was moving on with a "pretty young yoga instructor." The revelation made sense of the fact that Borgeson hadn't attended a single day of Maxwell's trial.

In the meantime, Judge Nathan set the date for Maxwell's sentencing as June 28th, 2022. Then, in February, more shocking Epstein-related news emerged – Jean-Luc Brunel had committed suicide in prison. In circumstances incredibly similar to Epstein's death, Brunel was found hanging by his bed sheets during a night check of his cell. Brunel's lawyer, Mathias Chichportich, told the Miami Herald that Brunel had attempted to take his life on several occasions previously. Yet, like Epstein, Brunel wasn't on suicide watch when he was found dead.

Had Brunel really killed himself, or was he suicided like Epstein? Ghislaine's brother, Ian Maxwell, seemed to imply the latter when he told the New York Post that he "feared for her safety." Maxwell was now on suicide watch herself, which Ian

Maxwell noted was "ironic," since neither Epstein nor Brunel had been on suicide watch when they died. For an in-depth look into Brunel's life and his role in Epstein's sex trafficking ring, see my first book on Epstein, *Who Killed Epstein?*

On the morning of Tuesday 28th June, Maxwell shuffled into court wearing ankle shackles and grey-blue prison scrubs, to hear her sentencing. Her defence team had pushed for a term of between four and a half to five and a half years. The prosecution wanted thirty to fifty-five years. Judge Nathan decided to follow the advice of federal probation officials. She sentenced Maxwell to twenty years behind bars.

On delivering the sentence, Judge Nathan said, "The damage done to these girls was incalculable." And added, "Whether you are rich or powerful, nobody is above the law". She also noted that Maxwell didn't appear to show remorse or accept responsibility for what she had done.

It was finally Maxwell's turn to have her say and address the court and the victims. Perhaps she would show the remorse that had been so obviously lacking up until now? Sadly, it wasn't to happen. Standing at the lectern in the centre of the courtroom, Maxwell followed the tired old line of blaming Epstein for her crimes. Addressing her accusers, she told the court, "Despite the many helpful and positive things I have done in my life and will continue to do ... I know that my association with Epstein and this case will forever and permanently stain me."

She said, "Jeffrey Epstein should have been here before all of you. He should have stood before you all those years ago. He should have stood before you in 2005, again in 2009, and again in 2019." She added, "It is the greatest regret of my life that I ever met Jeffrey Epstein."

Maxwell did finally manage an apology of sorts, saying, "I am sorry for the pain that you experienced."

But Epstein survivors weren't buying it. Annie Farmer responded that the apology sounded "hollow" and that she believed Maxwell had failed to take responsibility for her actions.

Farmer told the court, "Today, I can look at Ghislaine and tell her that I became what I am today, in spite of her and her efforts to make me feel powerless and insignificant, and I will cast that empowerment on my daughter."

Another Epstein survivor, who wasn't part of the case but was allowed to speak at the sentencing, was Sarah Ransome. Finally given the chance to confront the woman who had ensnared her into Epstein's orbit, Ransome gave a tearful account of the pain Maxwell had caused her. She told the court she had been treated as "nothing more than a sex toy" in Epstein and Maxwell's "upside-down, twisted world of rape, rape, rape." Ransome described how the sexual abuse had caused her to attempt suicide several times, as well as leading her into alcoholism. "Only by the grace of God do I continue to live," she told the court. Ransome said she was unable to trust people and had never got married, something which she had dreamed of as a child. Speaking directly to Maxwell, she said, "You broke me in unfathomable ways."

Virginia Giuffre was in Australia but spoke through a lawyer, who read her statement to the court. In her statement, Giuffre said, "I want to be clear about one thing: without question, Jeffrey Epstein was a terrible paedophile. But I never would have met Jeffrey Epstein if not for you. For me, and for so many others, you opened the door to hell."

Giuffre's statement ended, "You deserve to spend the rest of your life in a jail cell."

When Maxwell was led out of the courtroom, head bowed, feet shuffling in ankle chains, that prospect must have weighed heavily on her mind.

CHAPTER 9

JIMMY SAVILE'S ABUSE BEGINS

Kelly Gold was a 15-year-old dancer and actress, attending stage school in London. When she wasn't studying, she would audition for parts in adverts and films or for modelling and dancing roles. Kelly was a regular dancer for the BBC's most popular music show, Top of the Pops. It was the early seventies and, every week, the young people of the nation would gather round the TV to watch the likes of David Bowie, The Rolling Stones, Cliff Richard or T Rex perform their latest releases, while teenage girls bopped chaotically on the show's crowded dancefloor.

It was at one of these shows that Kelly met Claire McAlpine, another 15-year-old dancer. "She was a good dancer," Gold told me, "and she was very beautiful. That's one of the things that stood out about Claire, she was a very pretty girl, and she was funny. She also had quite a serious side. She kept a diary and she wrote down any of her experiences. Even at auditions, I would often see her writing, I don't know what, she always put it in the diary."

The two girls quickly became friends, seeing each other regularly at Top of the Pops and other auditions. They would chat between acts and share titbits about their private lives. Schoolgirls like Kelly and Claire would be driven to the TOTP studio at the BBC's Television Centre in Hammersmith, west London. There, they would change out of their school uniforms and into the hot pants, mini-skirts, short dresses and high heels they would wear for the show.

After the performances, some of the girls would go back to

the dressing rooms of the DJs who hosted the show, to continue the party. Floor managers would whisper invites in the girls' ears on the dancefloor and they would make their way to the appropriate dressing room after the show. "I only went there once to a dressing room and I can't remember which DJ's dressing room it was," Gold said, "but there were a few people in the dressing room at the time drinking, and slightly what I might consider inappropriate behaviour with the girls. I only had someone try it on with me once and I sort of smacked their hand down and I made excuses to go to the toilet. And that was the only time I ever went into a Top of the Pops dressing room. I knew that what might be happening in there isn't what I wanted to happen to me."

One day, Claire received an invite from one of the floor managers and disappeared even before the performances had finished. Claire told Kelly that she had been invited out for a drink by one of the stars performing on TOTP and asked if she could stay over at Kelly's house that night. Kelly agreed and waited at home for Claire to arrive, but her friend never turned up. When Kelly next saw Claire, her friend told her she had spent the night with the famous singer.

Similar invites now started coming Claire's way, thick and fast. As she recorded in her diary, she was now having trysts with a Radio One DJ and one of the TOTP presenters. Claire's mother, Vera McAlpine, subsequently told the press that the diary entries involving the TOTP presenter were "so shocking that I would rather not repeat them."

"I think she had found when she was turning up at some DJ's places that she had got herself in a bit deep, "Kelly Gold said, "and didn't really know how to get out of it. And I told her then, 'Just don't go there.' But I think she'd found that she was already on a spiral of being obliged to meet these people. And then a few weeks on, she was very worried… that she might be pregnant. Meanwhile, her mum had found her diary… and she was really upset that her mum now was taking matters further… she was going to go to the BBC."

A month after Claire's mother found her diary, Claire was found dead on her bedroom floor. Lying next to her were two empty bottles of sleeping pills and her red diary. The BBC did nothing about Vera McAlpine's complaints. Neither did the police, who kept Claire's diary as evidence, until it mysteriously disappeared. In the inquest into her death and the subsequent press reports, Claire was branded a fantasist. Top of the Pops, meanwhile, carried on as usual, except that a minimum age was introduced for the dancers.

Claire's half-brother, Mark Ufland, told the press that the DJ presenter named in Claire's diary was Jimmy Savile, TOTP's main host and one of the most well-known and popular celebrities in the country. On the day before the inquest into Claire's death, Savile was interviewed by the *Daily Express*. He told the newspaper, "Many a time, I have dated a good-looking girl I have met on the show. But what I say to them is, 'Ask your folks if I can come round for tea.' I much prefer being with a family, with a pretty girl in the centre, than a session in the back of my car. For one thing, you can't see how pretty the girl is in the back of my car."

This was 1971. Jimmy Savile already had a long career of sexual abuse, rape and paedophilia behind him, and an even longer one ahead.

Jimmy Savile was the darling of the British nation. Host of *Top of the Pops*, long-running disc jockey on Radio One, and the presenter of the immensely popular TV show, *Jim'll Fix It*, he was a household name, from the sixties until his death in 2011. Over his six-decade career, he raised over £40 million pounds for charities and charmed and bamboozled a nation with his eccentric dress sense, his quirky sense of humour, and his trademark Cuban cigar.

But beneath the glamorous exterior, Savile led another, hidden life, one that lasted as long, perhaps longer, than his celebrity one. Its scale rivalled the magnitude of his public success, its numbers were equally eye-popping, but its toll was counted not in pounds, but misery and the destruction of innocence.

Savile was a serial sexual abuser and paedophile on a scale

seldom seen before. Spanning six decades, Savile's career of abuse affected at least 500 victims. According to a 2014 NSPCC report, the victims were mostly in the 13-to-15-year-old age range, but the oldest was 75 and the youngest was just two years old. At least 72 of Savile's victims were at the BBC, of whom 34 were under 16, the UK's legal age of consent. Over 80 allegations came from the various hospitals Savile volunteered in, including Leeds General Infirmary, Stoke Mandeville Hospital, and Broadmoor, a high-security psychiatric hospital, holding some of the most dangerous criminals in the UK. Summing up Savile's career of abuse, the NSPCC report concluded, "There's no doubt that Savile is one of the most, if not the most, prolific sex offender that we at the NSPCC have ever come across."

Perhaps even more staggering than the scale of the abuse is the fact that Savile got away with it for so long. Right up until his death in 2011, the millionaire celebrity never faced a single criminal charge or a single exposé in the press. And all this despite constant rumours, as well as frequent and none-too-subtle hints from the man himself. Savile had access to some 40 hospitals across the nation and had his own offices, rooms and beds in at least three of them. At Broadmoor, he was given the keys to the entire high-security facility. And at Duncroft Approved School for girls with behavioural problems, he would often be seen taking the teenage girls out for rides in his Rolls Royce.

Savile's influence ranged from police to politicians to prime ministers and even the top echelons of the royal family. And all the while, he was abusing, molesting and raping underage girls and boys on a scale hitherto unknown.

The ultimate question, when faced with such a career of abuse, cover-up and manipulation has to be – how did he get away with it for so long?

What made Jimmy Savile untouchable? Untouchable is the name of my 4-hour Savile documentary available on my YouTube channel.

James Wilson Vincent Savile was born on Halloween, 1926.

He was the youngest of seven children, growing up in a working class family in Leeds. His father, Vince, worked as an illegal bookmaker, taking bets on horseraces off-course, an activity that was illegal until 1960. His mother, Agnes, was a supply teacher from the north east. She met Vince when he was working at a rural Yorkshire train station she passed each day on her way to work. The two got married in 1911 and moved in with Vince's parents in Leeds. They had their first baby a year later.

Jimmy Savile arrived five years after his next oldest sibling. In every way, he appeared the runt of the litter. As a young child, he was undernourished and sickly and almost didn't survive. "He was like a miracle child," said Boris Coster, an ex-employee at Broadmoor, and author of the book, *Broadmoor Sinister*, which details many of Savile's crimes. "It was about three months old… that he was actually being pushed in the buggy and he fell out of the buggy, causing substantial injuries, which resulted in Savile being placed into a hospital for three months. They actually thought they were going to lose him."

According to Savile's mother, Agnes, when baby Jimmy fell out of the pram, one of the muscles in his neck had been severed. The injury meant Savile could no longer sit up or close his eyes. He lay on his back, staring perpetually at the ceiling, suffering intermittent spams, in which his head would twist so far round, he would be staring over his back.

The hospital wanted to perform an operation but Agnes refused. She chose instead to pray for him at Leeds Catholic Cathedral. She had been praying unsuccessfully for six months when, in desperation, she tried an appeal to a little-known Scottish nun called Margaret Sinclair, who had been credited with several miraculous cures, according to a leaflet Agnes picked up at the cathedral. When Agnes got home later that day, little Jimmy's eyes were closed for the first time in six months. When he woke up, he was cured.

The miraculous healing became a central feature of Savile's personal mythology. He had somehow, he felt, been chosen. His life was to have a special purpose. "He was a sort of dream child," Coster told me. "Of all the brothers and all the sisters, he was the one that they all sort of rallied around. He was that type of special kid to them."

Contrasted with this feeling of specialness was a lonely childhood, in which Savile had little contact with other children. As the youngest child by five years, Jimmy didn't get to hang around with his older brothers and sisters much, instead spending most of his time with his parents. In an interview with journalist and Savile biographer, Dan Davies, Savile said that, as a young child spending so much time in the company of adults, he learned to watch and listen, taking everything in and filing it in his growing brain.

Starved of company, the young Savile spent much of his time across the road from the family house at St Joseph's Home for the Aged. He would chat with the elderly patients and smuggle in gifts for them. According to Davies, this is where Savile first developed his fascination with death, a morbid curiosity that would last his whole life and may have led to some of his darkest crimes. "They were always dying," Savile told Davies in an interview. "I'd ask, 'Where's Mrs so-and-so?' and one of the nuns would tell me that she'd died." Savile would say goodbye to the old people as they lay dead and would even ride along in their hearses.

As he got older, Savile's isolation only grew. At 14 years old, the Savile children were expected to fend for themselves. Savile would come home to an empty house and have to cook dinner for himself – usually a tin of baked beans and an egg. Savile's relationship with his father doesn't seem to have been particularly close and was something of a mystery. He hardly ever spoke about the man, who died when Savile was 26 years old. One thing we do know is that Vince Savile was a formative influence on one aspect of his son's life. Savile's father introduced him to cigars at the tender age of seven, by giving him a drag of his own cigar in the misguided hope that it would put the young Jimmy off smoking for life. Instead, it had the opposite effect. Cigars would be a lifelong passion and would become one of Savile's trademarks. When he was found dead at his flat in 2011, there was a half-smoked Cuban cigar in the ashtray.

In contrast to the distance between father and son, Jimmy's relationship with his mother couldn't have been closer. He was her miracle child and her favourite of the seven siblings. He called her 'the Duchess' and, later in life, kept a room in his Leeds flat dedicated to her memory, complete with a wardrobe full of her clothes.

Although there is no evidence, there are some suspicions that Savile's relationship with his mother was unnaturally close. "I think that we will never know what was going on in that relationship with his mum," said Mark Williams-Thomas, the investigator who first blew the lid on Savile in the ITV documentary, The Other Side of Jimmy Savile. "But I think it would be fair to say – and people will draw their own conclusions – that it was unhealthy at best."

There were certainly some odd hints that emerged later in Savile's life, several coming, characteristically, from his own lips. In interviews, Savile always maintained that his mother was the "only true love" of his life. Later in life, he and Agnes spent a lot of time together, often going on holidays and cruises with each other. In his autobiography, Savile said of time spent with his mother that she had "the energy of a teenager and could pleasure all night, as often as the opportunity arose."

When Agnes died, aged 85, Savile spent five days sitting alone with her corpse. This was a period he later described as "the best five days of my life." In another interview, he described the happiness he felt that "when she was dead, she was all mine, for me." Given the rumours about Savile's predilection for necrophilia, the image leaves a chilling feeling in the mind.

It also raises the question of sexual abuse in Savile's childhood. Many sexual abusers were themselves abused as children, so it would certainly make some sense of Savile's lifelong career of offending. "I don't know what else, of course, took place in his relationship," Williams-Thomas told me. "He's saying there was a possibility of incest. I leave that to people to make their own determination."

Savile was twelve years old when the Second World War broke out. As a big industrial city, Leeds was a potential target for the Luftwaffe, so Savile was initially evacuated to rural Lincolnshire. But his time in the countryside didn't last long. When his parents found out that the house he was staying in was next to several large gas storage tanks, Agnes decided to move him back home. Leeds wasn't badly bombed during the war but, during one rare heavy bombing raid, Savile and Agnes were caught out in the open. As bombs fell all around them, the pair had to take shelter in a doorway. When the raid was finished, Savile stepped outside to help with the damage and picked up a black leather glove, only to find it still had a hand inside.

At 14, Savile left school and got a job as an office boy for a company that manufactured military uniforms. In his spare time, he would accompany his parents to the local Mecca Locarno dancehall, where the adult couples would dance in pairs to the big band music. But as well as being a social hub, the dancehall was the centre of an underground culture of crime, prostitution and gangs. Savile once again applied his habit of silently watching, listening and learning, and received an informal education in all aspects of criminality. As an example of this parallel underworld, Savile recounted in his autobiography how, one day, he found the dead body of one of the dancehall's female clients chopped up and left in a ditch.

Savile was growing up fast, and he soon secured a job as a percussionist at the Mecca Locarno, accompanying a female pianist, who played in an all-girl band. It was the beginning of a dancehall career that would eventually lead him to the big time. Another part of growing up was accelerated by the shortage of older males, who were off fighting the war. In his autobiography, Savile recalled scoring his first date with a woman when he was just 12 years old. His partner was a 20-year-old woman from the dancehall box office. Jimmy took her to the cinema, where there was some inexpert fumbling in the dark. He lost his virginity sometime between the ages of 13 and 15 to a woman who, he said, picked him up at the dancehall. Savile accompanied her home on the train, where she attempted to have sex with him. The act was finally consummated in a bush at the back of her house. Savile described the process giving rise to feelings of "terror mixed with embarrassment."

Savile was training part-time with the Air Training Corps and hoped for a call-up to the RAF when he was old enough to begin his national service. However, when he turned 18 in 1944, he failed a sight test, which ruled him out of the air force. Instead, he was destined for a rather less glamourous role. His name was selected for conscription as a so-called 'Bevin Boy,' after the Minister of Labour, Ernest Bevin. Bevin Boys served down the pits, mining coal for the nation's energy supply. It was down the mines that Savile said he learned his first lesson in "the power of oddness."

Savile was working at South Kirkby Colliery, where he was given a job none of the other miners wanted. He was stationed on his own, down a tunnel that linked two of the larger chambers by rail. Savile's job was to lever back onto the tracks any coal trucks that became derailed. The eight-hour shifts alone in the darkness used to drive the other superstitious miners mad, imagining ghosts and potential disasters. But Savile thrived off it. He sewed a hidden pocket into his jacket and smuggled down books on science, languages and travel, which he would devour by the light of his single lantern.

One day, he arrived late for work, still dressed in his suit from the night before. With no time to change, he rushed into the pit cage, still wearing his suit and holding a newspaper. Ignoring the stares of his fellow miners, Savile walked blithely to his station down the lonely tunnel.

"I was a mile and a half away from the pit bottom and two miles from the coal face," Savile later recounted in a TV interview. "So what I did, I took all my clothes off, because it's very warm down the pit. I took all my clothes off and folded them in the newspaper and worked in the noddy, right. And I saved a little bit of water in the bottle. And just before it was knocking-off time, I cleaned my hands off and cleaned my face off, right. And I got back into the pit bottom immaculate. Now then, nobody but nobody ever did eight hours down a pit and came back as immaculate as they set off with white shirts. They were quite convinced that I was a witch. And I never said a word. And I suddenly realised that if you were different, and you didn't say anything about it, you'd see it had a tremendous effect on people. And that stayed with me."

By the end of the war, Savile had been transferred to Waterloo Main Colliery in Leeds. It was here that he claims he had the accident that ended his coal-mining career. Savile told biographer, Dan Davies, that he was assigned to shovelling dust off the conveyor belt and was lying on his side in a cramped, 18-inch-high space, when the tunnel was suddenly detonated. Half buried and concussed, Savile managed to call for help and the other miners dragged him out. Savile's back had been injured and, he claims, he was discharged from hospital with two walking sticks and the prognosis that he would never walk unaided again. Savile claimed he had spent seven years down the pits, followed by three years recovering from his injury. But this timeline, as well as the injury itself, are highly contentious.

As Davies points out in his book, *In Plain Sight: the Life and Lies of Jimmy Savile*, seven years in the mines would have timed Savile's release in 1951 or 1952, a period when he was already on record as taking part in long-distance cycling competitions, hardly the pastime of someone recovering from a major back injury. In another timeline, Savile reported that he had suffered the injury when he was 20 years old which, as Davies points out, would date the accident to 1946/47. But again, Savile is on record looking fit and healthy in 1948, appearing as a cyclist in the British film, 'A Boy, a Girl and a Bike'. So when did the accident happen? Or did it happen at all?

Davies has uncovered newspaper reports that cast significant doubts on Savile's story. In the 1980s, Savile gave an interview with *The Sun* which stated, "In 1948, Jimmy was finally allowed to leave the pits when a chest cold showed up on X-ray." And in a 1981 article in The People, Savile said, "When I was James Wilson, working down the pits for £2 a week for six shifts, it didn't matter to anyone." As Davies points out, James Wilson was the name of Savile's dead cousin. It seems plausible then that the accident was just another of those myths that Savile used to dine out on. It may even be possible that, for most of the time he was supposedly working down the mines, Savile was actually using a dead relative's identity to evade the work altogether.

"That was a very short period of his life," Savile researcher, Boris Coster, told me. "That wasn't something to brag about extensively. I mean literally a couple of months down the mines. He used that quite a lot with people. I mean, he played on the downtrodden bit."

The fit and healthy Jimmy Savile had, in fact, taken up cycling as a serious sport by the late forties, and by the early fifties, he was competing in some big races. Savile had received his first bike aged 11 and had done some long cycles to the east coast and to Scotland during the war. After the war, he joined a local cycling club under the name Oscar 'The Duke' Savile, a supposed company director, and soon he was competing in major races. In 1950, he came second in the annual Edinburgh-Newcastle race. Now he set his sights on the big one.

Modelled on the famous Tour de France, the first Tour of Britain was due to take place in 1951. Savile aimed to qualify as part of the four-man team representing Yorkshire. To do so, he had to prove himself in a seven-day series of races between Butlins holiday camps in the north.

Savile earned his place in the Tour of Britain by finishing third in the qualifiers. But perhaps more importantly, this is where he first established his knack of off-the-wall showmanship, which attracted publicity wherever he went. Rather than wearing the usual cycling kit, Savile would show up to races wearing a suit and tie and smoking one of his trademark Cuban cigars. His bizarre antics even landed him a front page on the *Daily Express*, the newspaper which sponsored the Tour.

When it came to the big race, Savile fared less well. More interested in gaining press attention and chatting up women he met along the route, he came last in some stages and missed the start of others. By the Morcombe-to-Glasgow stage, 'The Duke' had had enough, pulling out of the race after a gruelling climb to the top of Shap Fell Peak in the Lake District. But Savile had made such a name for himself as a character that the *Daily Express* asked him to stay on and act as a race commentator, entertaining live crowds of up to 50,000 people. Savile went on to commentate for next three Tour of Britains. It was his first introduction to broadcasting. It was also the start of a life-long trend of putting showmanship before sportsmanship, especially when it came to his later hobby of long-distance running. "I think he finished two marathons," Williams-Thomas told me. "All the other marathons, he got in the car and he got driven to the end. I mean, the man's just a complete liar."

Alongside his racing antics, Savile was experimenting with the other great passion of his early adulthood – DJing. While he was still using walking sticks, according to Savile's account, he was introduced to a new invention that would eventually revolutionise dancehalls – amplified music. Spotting the potential of the technology, Savile organised a 'Grand Record Dance' at a local Catholic social club in Leeds. Instead of dancing to a live band, for the first time, attendees would be bopping to records played on a gramophone and transmitted through speakers.

The night turned out to be a bit of a disaster. Only twelve people turned up and the revolutionary technology malfunctioned, causing a blackout in the hall and toasting the gramophone. But Savile was upbeat. He had got his first taste of the power of the DJ – the ability to control people's actions and emotions by the music he played.

Soon after, with an improved device, Savile and some friends put on a record dance for a girl's 21st birthday in the nearby town of Otley. The event was a roaring success and Savile picked up one of the girls to boot. It was the start of a trend that would continue throughout his life.

In 1953, Savile's father died of cancer. Savile was working in the scrap metal trade, earning a handsome £60 a week, while cycle racing and DJing on the side. But his dad's death spurred Savile to think more deeply about the direction of his life, and he quickly decided it went beyond selling scrap. What he really wanted was the big time.

The answer to his prayers came when he saw an advert for a job at the Mecca Locarno, the local dancehall where, as a boy, he had worked as a percussionist. Savile went for the interview and got the job, becoming the dancehall's assistant manager.

According to Coster, Savile's older brother, Vince, played a major part in his introduction to the dancehall scene. Vince had served in the navy during the war and was a 'face' in the Leeds underworld that centred around the dancehalls. "His brother Vincent got Jimmy into nightclubs, being a disc jockey," Coster told me. "His brother is a key to a lot of things. Not a lot of people know, but Vincent was a bit of a villain. He was well known in the underworld scene. He had money, he had power, which I think is what Jimmy Savile played on… Cigarette rackets, booze rackets, the nightclub game would have been one of them as well because you can hide a lot behind a nightclub."

With his new career underway, Savile soon moved out of the family house, first sleeping in the dancehall's cloakroom under a pile of coats, then moving onto a lifeboat moored on a canal near the city centre.

Savile became an instant success at Mecca, wearing colourful vibrant clothes instead of the usual staid suits and ties. He experimented with new music and record dances and began to draw in the crowds. His success soon earned him a promotion – taking over a struggling Mecca dancehall in Ilford, East London. At his new post, Savile immediately went about organising a regular record dance, like those he was famous for in Leeds. 'Off the Record' would be an eclectic night at which punters would be encouraged to bring their own records, for the simple reason that the club didn't have any of its own. The first night saw hundreds of young customers turn up, a huge improvement of the pitiful trickle before Savile took over.

High on his success but homesick for Leeds, Savile asked for a transfer back to the north. He was handed a gig managing The Plaza, a Mecca club in Manchester. At The Plaza, Savile applied the same Midas touch, launching a weekly talent contest and introducing the new craze for skiffle music. He also opened the club on weekday lunchtimes for record dances, which attracted hordes of local teenagers, many of whom got in trouble for returning late to school.

It was at The Plaza that Savile's two-sided nature really became apparent. As the flamboyant face of the club, he wore see-through shirts and carried a roll of (fake) twenty-pound notes in his breast pocket; he drove a Rolls Royce (faked using an old Bentley with a Rolls Royce radiator grill welded to the front); and smoked his trademark giant cigars. But on the less-public side of things, he was using his power in darker ways. By his own admission, Savile would tie up and gag troublemakers in the basement of the club and have them beaten up by the bouncers at the end of the night. Other unwanted guests were slung out, their heads used as battering rams to open doors on the way.

Savile was hanging around with local gangsters, such as the notorious Bill Benny. His underworld connections secured the safety of his club from extortion, racketeering and gang violence. And it seems that Savile too was dabbling in the murky world of underground crime. He even admitted to biographer, Dan Davies, that in Manchester, he hired three "Hungarian heavies," who had worked in the death camps in Europe, dispatching bodies for their Nazi overlords. Savile called them his 'Sonderkommandos' and used them to do his dirty work. "Well, these guys," Savile told Davies. "All I'd need to do was ask and they'd go and knock someone off, that was all there was to it." It was an astonishing admission, if true – that Savile was having his underworld enemies killed in 1950s Manchester.

If so, conspiracy to commit murder wasn't Savile's only crime. The vast hordes of teenagers flocking to The Plaza gave him the opportunity to develop his taste for underage girls. Savile explained the possibilities for picking up girls in typically cold fashion. "I would stand on the stage with a record player with a thousand people in the room for four or five hours," he told Davies. "Of the thousand people, 700 were girls. If half of them can't stand you, that leaves 350 who can stand you. If half of them are not too keen on you at all, then the other half is. That's 125 people. If half of them actually don't fancy you, that leaves around 65 girls that might want to go off with you. You don't have to be a brain surgeon to work out that you're never going to be short of ladies' company."

Of course, not all of these girls were over the age of consent. In the early 1950s, word was already getting round that Savile was more than just your average 'ladies' man'. One colleague told Davies he had joked with Jimmy that he "was either going to be a huge success or in prison for screwing 14-year-old girls". Another said, "He was a naughty man, a naughty man. He'd go with teenagers… I don't know how he got away with it." Savile was frequently seen disappearing into his car or his office with the young girls. Other witnesses told of wild parties at his flat in Leeds, where Savile and his friends would invite all the girls on his street, some as young as 13. Tony Calder, a young marketing executive in the music industry, described spending time at Savile's "shag pad" in Leeds, where there were three of four bedrooms with "people shagging in them all night long." Calder told Davies, "There were queues of girls outside waiting to get shagged. He'd share them out. They'd do as they were told."

That Savile's name was already familiar to the police is clear from further witness testimony. One of Savile's bouncers, Dennis

Lemmon, told Davies that, one day, Savile had come to work in a bad mood. When Lemmon quizzed colleagues about it, they told him Savile was due in court the following day for "messing about with a couple of girls." When Lemmon later enquired about the court case, he was told Savile had paid them off, and not for the first time.

It seems Savile was already a serial offender, and already protected from the consequences of his crimes. But how? Savile himself gave a clue in a typically brazen passage from his own autobiography. Recounting an episode where he took advantage of an attractive young girl, who had escaped from a remand home, Savile said he had been asked by a local policewoman to look out for the girl at his dancehall. He did so, found the girl, and persuaded her to give herself in. But only, of course, after spending the night with him. When he presented the girl to the shocked female police officer the next morning, he wrote in his memoir, "The officer was dissuaded from bringing charges against me by her colleagues, for it was well known that were I to go I would probably take half the station with me."

Calder, the young music executive, told Dan Davies about a time he went out with Savile to a jazz club in Leeds. Savile was paying for his guest's meal and drinks, which was highly unlike the notoriously tight DJ. When Calder asked Savile why he was paying, Savile explained that the man was the chief of police, and a "friend." Later, Calder remembers the high-ranking police officer telling Savile, "You've got to cut it out." Whatever it was he had to cut out, it was clear that Savile was paying to have himself protected.

Savile's meteoric rise through the ranks of Mecca continued. He became the regional manager for the north west in 1954. His flamboyant character and style were becoming so well known that, in 1959, he got the call up for his first TV appearance as a guest on Jukebox Jury, a panel show in which guests would predict whether new music singles would become a 'hit' or a 'miss'. Savile appeared on the show in his usual exuberant attire – a light-brown suit, pink shirt, green shoes and gold bowtie. At his home club of Mecca in Leeds, Savile was well-known as an outrageous showman, sometimes wearing suits that were half black, half white and hair that was similarly dyed down the middle. On other occasions, he would wear tartan clothes and have his hair dyed to match. He once turned up to an interview for Tyne-Tees Television sporting pink hair. All of this was in the fifties when such things were unheard of. It was around the same time that Savile made the switch in appearance which would remain a permanent trademark throughout the rest of his life – he had his hair bleached blonde.

The publicity of the Jukebox Jury appearance helped Savile's rising star, and he was soon offered the big break that would set him up for the rest of his career. Radio Luxembourg was a pirate commercial radio station, broadcasting into the UK from across the Channel. Compared to the stuffy BBC, it appealed to young people, offering light-hearted entertainment and, mostly importantly, the new Rock 'n' Roll music that was taking the world by storm. Savile was contacted by a representative from Decca Records, who wanted a DJ on Radio Luxembourg to showcase their new releases.

Savile turned up at the interview for Radio Luxembourg with tartan-coloured hair. Two days later, while on holiday in New York, he was summoned back to start working for the station immediately. Savile began his first ever radio show with what would become a trademark greeting, "Hi there, guys and gals…" With his non-received pronunciation, non-BBC accent and his quirky delivery, Savile was a breath of fresh air and an instant hit. He quadrupled his listeners in just one month and soon had five different shows running on the pirate station, including the Teen and Twenty Disc Club, which went on to become one of the station's most successful shows. To add to his success, Tyne-Tees Television commissioned him to co-present a weekly popular music show for teenagers.

Savile even got the chance to fly to the US to present Elvis

Presley with a gold disk on behalf of Decca. He had his photo taken with the King and distributed copies to the press, posting others outside the Mecca Locarno dancehall. Savile's name was duly featured in newspapers up and down the land, with headlines like "Jimmy and the King."

Savile also sold some of the pictures through his Radio Luxembourg shows, donating the proceeds to the National Playing Fields Association. His charitable work earned him the admiration of the charity's patron, the Duke of Edinburgh, and, according to Savile, launched the start of a lifelong friendship between the two.

The same period saw the beginning of another lifelong association, this time with Leeds General Infirmary, the city's main hospital. Chief porter, Charles Hullighan, invited Savile to help launch the hospital's new radio station and Jimmy agreed, throwing in several days' voluntary work as a porter. It was the beginning of a career of healthcare fundraising, which would provide convenient access to young vulnerable people.

As part of his continued rise, Savile was made an associate director at Mecca. He celebrated the promotion by purchasing a brand-new Rolls Royce, this one genuine. He also released a music single and followed it up with another the following year. He then went on tour around the country, accompanying the band, Johnny & The Hurricanes.

Bizarrely, despite his new-found wealth, Savile decided to move into a rented one-bedroom flat in Manchester in a derelict Victorian mansion. He painted the whole flat black and it came to be known as the 'Black Pad' – a suitable name for some of the activities that no doubt took place there. While hiding himself away in run-down properties, Savile chose to flaunt his wealth in other ways. Parked alongside his Rolls Royce, he had an E-Type Jaguar, and his neck, wrists and fingers were weighed down with gold. The ostentatious jewellery would become another Savile trademark, one that some say inspired the 'bling' style of future American rappers.

In Manchester, Savile set about opening a new club night at the New Elizabethan Ballroom in Belle Vue, an amusement park and zoo. Savile replaced a tired old dance night, held every Sunday, with a new rock and pop event that played all the latest hits, hosted by the UK's 'DJ of the Year,' Jimmy Savile himself. The Top Ten Club opened in May 1963 and was soon drawing crowds of around 2,000 every Sunday, with live acts that would include The Rolling Stones, Jimi Hendrix, Stevie Wonder and Ike and Tina Turner.

To top his success, Savile was given his own column at The People newspaper, where he was encouraged to share anecdotes about his colourful lifestyle, alongside prognostications about the music industry. Savile's People column would become a source of some almost unbelievably brazen admissions of the dark activities he was getting up to.

Bizarrely, 1963 also saw Savile get into wrestling. It started as a stunt to raise money at a benefit contest for a recently deceased wrestler. Savile was asked to referee the event but instead said he wanted to compete. He trained for six weeks before entering the ring with 'Gentleman' Jim Lewis, the undefeated welterweight champion of the world. Who knows how much of the contest was staged but Savile lasted until the seventh round and managed to score some points against Lewis before finally succumbing to defeat. Savile broke a toe but described it as "about the best experience of my life." He was hooked and began a wrestling career that would last several years.

His DJ and broadcasting career was also about to take a stellar turn. The BBC wanted to produce a new pop music show aimed at teenagers, to rival ITV's immensely popular Ready Steady Go. The BBC decided to mimic Ready Steady Go's format of bands miming in front of live teenage audiences. But, unlike Ready Steady Go, the Beeb decided to base its acts around current chart hits. The show now needed a charismatic frontman, and Jimmy Savile's name was quickly bandied about. However, there were already doubts about Savile amongst the BBC executives, with one or two saying they didn't want him on television. Savile's crowd-drawing appeal ultimately won the day and, on New Year's Day 1964, he presented the first episode of Top of the Pops from a converted church in Manchester. The show kicked off with The Rolling Stones' new single, 'I Want to Be your Man' and ended with The Beatle's number one hit, 'I want to Hold your Hand.'

Top of the Pops went on to be the most successful UK music show ever, spanning five decades. But for Savile, with its live audience of teenage girls, it was just another hunting ground, a hunting ground that would lead, seven years later, to the suicide of Claire McAlpine. Those few BBC executives were right to worry about Savile, it turned out. And no wonder. Despite his relatively unsullied public image that year in 1964, there were already lots of rumours and several allegations.

A 2013 Her Majesty's Inspectorate of Constabulary (HMIC) report into Savile found that, in 1963, a man had gone into a Cheshire police station to report a rape, naming Savile as the perpetrator. Incredibly, the man was told to go home and forget about it. In the same year, another man went to a Metropolitan Police station in Westminster to report that his girlfriend had been sexually abused by Savile at a BBC studio. According to Williams-Thomas, the man was told, "You know how serious it is to make allegations like that? You could get yourself arrested. Go away."

In 1964, the Metropolitan police received another tip-off about Savile. In 2012, an intelligence report by the Paedophile Unit of the Met police was discovered, dating back to 1964. It included details of a vice ring, centred on a house in Battersea Bridge Road in London. The house was used by teenage girls absconding from Duncroft Approved School for girls. The vice ring involved several Duncroft girls and a younger boy and was run by three "coloured" men, according to the report, who were arrested for living off the immoral earnings of their charges. One of the men was imprisoned for two years, the second was found not guilty, and the third failed to appear at court. In the file, it was stated that Jimmy Savile was a regular visitor to the house.

"Savile was connected at that address," said Williams-Thomas. "So, as a result of that, that intelligence went into the police system in 1964. But nothing happened with it. So, if you take it in its simplistic form, the very first time that people knew that Jimmy Savile was connected to the sexual abuse of children was 1964."

The allegations didn't just involve underage girls. In an interview with Dan Davies, Savile admitted that Leeds police officers had entered his dancehall in the 1950s to tell him he had been reported hanging around public toilets in Leeds. Savile dismissed the police officers in his usual offhand manner and the matter was dropped.

In October 1963, two boys appeared at Salford Juvenile Court for stealing a £152 watch from Savile's Manchester flat. One boy, aged 14, received two years' probation and the other, aged 11, a fine of £10. It was conveniently not mentioned what they were doing in Savile's flat. In another 1963 allegation, a 10-year-old boy said he had approached Savile for an autograph outside a hotel and had subsequently been "assaulted by penetration".

All in all, according to the 2014 NSPCC report into Savile's crimes, 13 separate allegations of sexual abuse had been made against Savile by the end of 1963. None of these allegations were followed up or shared with Savile's home force, West Yorkshire Police. All of them were quietly filed, the victims told to "go away," "move on," or "forget about it." Rumours about Savile already abounded in the club scene and at the BBC, yet the organisations he worked for continued to provide him access to more and more teenagers.

It was 1964. Jimmy Savile's career as a serial sex abuser had only just begun. Yet already, it seemed, he was untouchable.

CHAPTER 10

UNTOUCHABLE JIMMY SAVILE

It was 1977 and a 12-year-old girl was in Stoke Mandeville hospital in Buckinghamshire after having her tonsils removed. For some reason, she had been put in the geriatric ward. She was bored and wandered down to the day room to watch TV in her nightdress.

As she left the ward, the girl noticed a man wearing a long coat, brown tracksuit bottoms and lots of gold jewellery. He had shoulder-length blonde hair and was smoking a large cigar.

The man asked her where she was going and she told him the television room. "I'll show you," he replied, and walked her down the corridor. The man seemed very friendly and the girl felt comfortable.

The day room was empty and the girl sat in one of the chairs. The man asked her if she had a boyfriend. She didn't reply. The man then knelt down in front of the girl, positioning himself between her legs. She noticed that the man had pulled his tracksuit bottoms down to reveal his penis. The man then manoeuvred himself forward and penetrated the girl. After a short time, the man made a groaning sound and withdrew. His semen was all over the seat and the girl's thighs. He wiped the semen off with the front of his white coat and, without saying anything, left the room. The door had been open the whole time.

Confused and disoriented, the girl wandered around the corridors, trying to find her way back to the ward. On her way, she bumped into a nurse. She said, "Your porter hurt me." The nurse asked where, and the girl pointed to her vagina. The nurse said, "Don't say anything. I'll get into trouble."

The girl went back to her bed and thought over what had happened. She knew it was wrong and wanted to tell someone. She found a pencil and tore out two pages of her bedside Bible. On one of the pages she wrote, "To the doctor. Your porter hurt me. Please ring my dad," followed by the phone number and address of her father and her own signature. She posted the note in a box that said 'Letterbox' in the corridor outside the ward, thinking it would be read by the doctors.

Later that night in bed, the girl saw the same man come into her ward and head straight for her bed. She pulled the covers over her head but the man put his hand under the sheets and began rubbing her vagina, making sounds of pleasure as he did so. The contact lasted only 10 or 20 seconds, then the hand was withdrawn. The girl peeked her head out of the covers as the man walked away and watched as he jumped on top of an elderly patient, lying face down on top of her. A nurse suddenly appeared and shouted, "You shouldn't be in here, Jimmy." The man got off the woman and left the ward, without anything else being said.

Two years later, aged 14, the girl was watching TV at home when she saw the porter who had raped her. He was on television. She couldn't understand what the porter from Stoke Mandeville was doing on TV. "In time," she declared in her statement, made decades later to lawyers representing dozens of similar victims, "I came to know that the porter was Jimmy Savile."

This account marks a shift in Savile's offending in the 60s and 70s. As the famous DJ got older, his targets shifted from young party-goers at dancehalls or on Top of the Pops to even more vulnerable victims at hospitals, care homes, special schools and mental institutions around the country.

It started at Leeds General Infirmary, the hospital where he had already helped launch the radio station and done voluntary work as a porter. In the late 60s, Britain's economy was in such dire straits that the government endorsed a scheme called 'I'm Backing

Britain', whereby staff across the nation volunteered to work extra, non-paid shifts to help prevent businesses going under. Savile saw his opportunity and, in 1968, turned up at Leeds Infirmary in his Rolls Royce Silver Shadow, sporting a Union Jack waistcoat, to work nine shifts as a porter. From then on, Savile became a more or less permanent fixture at the hospital, and the hospital became his permanent hunting ground for victims.

One patient in the neurological ward, June Thornton, described watching in horror as Savile sexually molested a young girl in the bed opposite her. "Jimmy Savile come to a young lady sat in a chair," Thornton told a BBC report in 2012. "Unfortunately this lady, I think, had brain damage because she just sat there, and he kissed her. And I thought he was a visitor coming to see her. And he started rubbing his hands down her arms. And then, I don't know of a nice way to put it, but he molested her. He helped himself, and she just sat there and couldn't do anything about it." When Thornton told a nurse about the assault, the woman "merely shrugged her shoulders," she said.

Another patient undergoing spinal surgery recounted being touched inappropriately by Savile in a lift, but being too frightened to report it because "everyone thought he was a saint." Another 16-year-old girl named Beth told Savile biographer, Dan Davies, how she was assaulted by Savile after being admitted to Leeds hospital following a nervous breakdown. Her story shows the stunning complicity of the hospital staff in Savile's crimes.

Savile first groomed Beth by taking her to a newsagent outside the hospital and promising to buy her anything she wanted. The next day, a porter came to collect her and took her to a small office stationed off an underground corridor. Savile was waiting inside. He immediately began kissing Beth and stroking her thigh. He asked if she was on the pill and, when she said no, he forced her to masturbate him. When he was done, another man was waiting outside to take her back to the ward. Beth said she tried telling the nurses but, as soon as she mentioned Savile's name, they all laughed and walked away.

Savile, it seems, had all the porters at Leeds in his pocket, offering them free holidays at his various caravans around the country. The head porter, Charles Hullighan, the man who had originally invited Savile to launch the hospital radio, was made company secretary of one of Savile's firms, receiving a monthly salary and a share in directors' pay.

Incredibly, Savile also had access to the nurses' accommodation at Leeds and would let himself in when the women were dressing or showering, to "clean" their rooms. The staff complained to the hospital's board but nothing was done.

But Savile's access went even further and eventually led to rumours of necrophilia. Since his childhood experiences at the old people's home, Savile had nurtured a lifelong obsession with death. As a porter, he took particular delight in wheeling corpses to the mortuary, saying in his autobiography that he held it as a "great honour" to be with the bodies after their death. There is only anecdotal evidence of Savile's necrophilia but, as criminologist and author, Christopher Berry-Dee, explained, it definitely fitted with Savile's offending behaviour.

"We've got to remember that Savile was a control freak," Berry-Dee told me. "He was an extreme narcissist. He's a sexual predator. And so, if he thought a young girl's laying on a mortuary slab or a woman on a mortuary slab, it's like a sweet shop. The mortuaries became sweet shops for him."

Savile found a way into another institution in 1968, when he received a request from one of the patients to open a fete at Broadmoor, a high-security psychiatric hospital that housed some of the most dangerous criminals in the UK. As with Leeds Infirmary, Savile worked his way deeper inside the institution and was soon organising regular concerts and discos. He boasted that he had access to all the wings and would wander about, chatting to the patients. With the self-styled title 'Honorary Assistant Entertainments Officer,' Savile soon had two attic rooms inside Broadmoor for his personal use, plus his own set of keys. For the nation's highest-security hospital, it was an incredible level of access.

Boris Coster, author of *Broadmoor Sinister*, told me about Savile's behaviour inside the hospital, provided by a first-hand witness. "In those days, the female ward would have baths," Coster explained, "kind of like old dormitories in private schools. So the baths would be alongside each other. And she was taking a bath one day, and she remembers having this bath, Savile just stood in the background, just wandering around between the girls. And she talks about one occasion when he then took her into one of the rooms and indecently assaulted her."

Next came Stoke Mandeville hospital in Buckinghamshire. As with the other institutions, Savile worked his way inside with charity and fundraising events, then began volunteering until he was a regular fixture, and even had his own office and accommodation. In the early 70s, allegations were already being made about Savile's conduct at the hospital. A 13-year-old girl who was paralysed from the waist down described Savile approaching her in the corridor and ramming his tongue so far down her throat, it made her gag. He then walked off as if nothing had happened.

Another 11-year-old girl reported how Savile repeatedly assaulted her over a three-to-four-year period, during Catholic Mass at the hospital's chapel. Savile would stand in a separate room during the mass and, when the girl entered to collect the offering plate, Savile would grope her. All the while, the door would be open so that Savile could see the priest while he assaulted the 11-year-old.

Patients have subsequently talked about the air of resignation amongst the nurses, how there was sarcastic chatter about who would be the "lucky one" to be selected as his next victim, and that young girls were advised to pretend to be asleep whenever Savile was around. One of the nurses did complain to a Thames Valley Police officer, saying the nurses were concerned about the way Savile touched patients. Detective Constable John Lindsay passed the complaint on to a senior colleague, but the officer brushed it off, saying Savile "must be okay" because he was "a high-profile man."

Haut de la Garenne was another institution linked to Savile. The children's home in Jersey was the centre of a police investigation in 2007, after it emerged that children had been abused and possibly even murdered there. Savile had opened a fete at Haut de la Garenne in the early 70s and visited regularly throughout the rest of the decade. When the investigation surfaced in 2007, Savile at first denied ever having visited the children's home. But The Sun published a picture of him at the home, surrounded by children, and Savile was promptly forced to remember. No evidence has come out to link Savile with child abuse at the Jersey institution but Coster claims Savile was at the heart of allegations concerning children at Haut de Garenne being pimped out.

"Savile was what I'll call the kingpin," Coster told me. "He was the person that would be sitting at the top, and if I wanted a boy, let's go to Savile. He can supply a boy of whatever age or a girl of whatever age. And it is known that Savile pimped out youngsters."

Another institution where Savile preyed on vulnerable youths was Duncroft, an approved school for girls with emotional and behavioural problems. Savile was first invited to the school in the early 70s, he claimed, by the girls themselves in various fan letters. Never one to pass up such an invitation, Savile was soon found regularly visiting the school in his Rolls Royce. Following his usual modus operandi, he buttered up the school's headmistress, Margaret Jones, inviting her to take holidays in one of his homes on the south coast. Once established, Savile began taking the girls out for rides in his Rolls Royce, all with the sanction of Jones herself.

In 2008, one of Duncroft's former pupils, Keri, began writing a memoir, detailing what happened to her and other girls who accepted these rides. They were given sweets and cigarettes in return for being groped and fondled, and sometimes more. Keri said Savile was always pushing her for oral sex. One time, she succumbed on the promise of a trip to the BBC. Keri obliged but afterwards gagged. Savile leaned across to open the car door, shouting, "Not in the car!" Keri said several Duncroft girls obliged Savile in a similar manner, providing him with blowjobs, or what he called "Jimmy Specials."

After Savile was finally exposed, one Duncroft girl explained how Savile manipulated everyone to cover up his crimes. "You knew it was your word against his and your word would never be believed," she said. "He manipulated situations. We were vulnerable and in need of love and attention."

"Every time, it was brushed under the carpet," Coster explained to me, "because you bear in mind you've got someone at an approved school that's gone out and committed theft, then you've got Jimmy, who's a public figure, spins records for a living on telly. Who are you going to believe? Are you going to believe Savile is in the wrong, or are you going to believe Jimmy, who's buttered up to be some kind of demigod in the 1970s?"

However, Duncroft may have been a step too far for Savile, although he would never realise it in his lifetime. Allegations from some of the girls would be the first to trigger the exposé that finally nailed him, after his death in 2011. And the journalist who would investigate the claims would be Meirion Jones, the grandson of the headteacher, Margaret Jones. Jones had visited the school several times as a boy and been struck by Savile's odd behaviour.

But back at the time when Savile was insinuating himself into institutions like Duncroft, Savile's star was still on the rise and exposure was decades away. By the late 60s, Savile had added to his CV a job as a DJ on the BBC's new youth-oriented channel, Radio 1. As part of his new contract with the BBC, Savile demanded a new Rolls Royce every year. At the same time, he was proving his physical fitness in several long-distance charity runs, and he had even completed the Royal Marines Commando training course, becoming the first civilian to gain an honorary green beret. As part of his association with the marines, Savile also met its commandant general, Lord Louis Mountbatten, Prince Philip's uncle and Savile's ticket into the royal family.

Savile was also enjoying an ever-closer relationship with the police. In Manchester, Savile would invite local police to his flat, according to the memoirs of one ex-officer, where there would always be girls available. Some of the officers would disappear into other rooms with the girls, according to the ex-policeman, Stephen Hayes, while others would sit smoking cannabis with Savile.

Similar goings-on occurred in Leeds, where Savile groomed the West Yorkshire Police at his regular 'Friday Morning Club,' where they joined local businessmen and bigwigs at his penthouse flat for gatherings that would continue right up until his death in 2011. "Jimmy Savile had access to so many teenage girls who were kind of like groupie category back then," Coster told me, "that he was supplying these girls to the cops who were attending his lunches… Jimmy Savile had a few nephews and nieces, and one of his nephews turned up at Jimmy's house one day, and it was noted by him that there was other young boys and girls there of a minor age. And there were people in high power places that were actually there at the time. He managed somehow to be ushered out and he had said on camera that he knew back in the 50s and 60s that Jimmy was a sexual predator. He was grooming young girls and boys far back then with the police."

By the 70s, Savile appeared to have his hand in so many pies that he could fight potential fires before they turned into conflagrations. Such was the case with a newspaper investigation that could have been his first major exposé.

In 1967, The People launched a major investigation into Savile. The paper had conducted interviews with underage girls who were willing to come forward and speak about their abuse at the hands of Savile. The girls' statements had been read and rubber-stamped by the paper's lawyers and the story was ready to go. But it never made it to press. The reason – the same paper had recently hired Savile as a columnist, in a bid to appeal to younger readers. The People's editor, Sam Campbell, didn't want to ruin that relationship. The story was killed.

Perhaps emboldened by his lucky escape, Savile became even more brazen. One of the most incredible stories about his behaviour comes from later in the same year. Savile received an invitation to attend an annual civic ball in the rural town of Otley in the Yorkshire Dales. The town's mayor, Ronnie Duncan, wanted to make the annual event more attractive to young people, so decided to invite Jimmy Savile, a celebrity with local connections.

Savile responded to the mayor's letter, accepting the invitation on six conditions. These included – donating his fee to a local charity, a trip round Otley hospital, a framed picture of Otley, and some cigars. So far so reasonable. It was Savile's last two demands that must have raised eyebrows, to say the least – to spend the night in a tent on a hill above the town, and to be provided with, in his own words, "A guard of honour of six young ladies – in another tent of course – to keep me safe."

The mayor agreed to all six of Savile's demands but, at a subsequent meeting of the town council, it must have struck home how weird and creepy this request was, because half the councillors stormed out of the meeting in disgust. However, the decision was ratified and six girls were duly selected from over a hundred applicants. The girls were even kitted out in identical dresses, like so many sacrificial virgins.

On the day of the ball, Savile recounted in his autobiography, the girls looked "good enough to eat." Sadly for Savile, one of their number was lost when her father turned up and dragged her home, kicking and screaming. The other five girls made it through to the end and were driven, alongside Savile and a friend, up to the hillside overlooking the town.

In his autobiography, Savile claimed that the girls' tent blew down overnight, forcing the happy campers to share the same tent. It's an incredibly brazen admission in itself. But the truth, as tracked down by Dan Davies, is even worse. Davies spoke to one of the girls who was there that night. She told him that Savile and his friend plied the girls with vodka all evening then, in the early hours of the morning, he entered their tent and "tried it on" with each of the girls in turn. According to the girl, they were saved when some boys from the local rugby club appeared. She said that Savile got into a fight with the lads and that he was "violent, really nasty once he turned." This was a characteristic confirmed by another friend of Savile, who had been set upon by a bunch of youths while visiting him in London. Savile, said the man, joined in the fight and stuck his thumb into one of the men's eyes, causing "horrific" liquid to spurt out.

Incredibly, nothing was ever said about the night's events in Otley, and the mayor and the town councillors never suspected any foul play until the revelations about Savile surfaced, following his death.

Perhaps with the Otley tent 'disaster' still in mind, it was not long after that Savile purchased his first trademark motorhome. The custom-built Mercedes camper had a large double bed in the back and provided Savile with the mobility he craved. It also improved his ability to assault young girls at any location he chose. One girl who was abused in Savile's camper van was Dee Coles, a 14-year-old on holiday with her family in Jersey. Savile posed with Cole for photographs outside his van, then invited her and her friend inside. Once inside, Savile's friendly demeanour changed. He locked the door and thrust Cole's hands down his trousers, forcing her to masturbate him.

On another occasion, Savile himself boasted in his autobiography of having six girls in the caravan with him. He was given a rude awakening when one of the girls' parents knocked on the door in the morning, with the girls still naked. However, in typical Jimmy style, Savile brazened it out, inviting the parents inside and joking about how he'd been there for half an hour and still not been offered breakfast.

Savile's offending wasn't limited to females, and this was already true in the late 60s. Dan Davies interviewed one of Savile's many nephews, Guy Marsden, who said he accidentally bumped into Savile in an all-male paedophile scene in London. Marsden had run away from Leeds in his early teens and hitchhiked to London with three friends. The group were hanging around Euston train station, when they were approached by a man who offered to buy them food. Marsden and his friends followed the man to his flat, where they spent a few days.

On one of these days, Marsden's uncle, Jimmy Savile, unexpectedly turned up at the flat and took him and his friends to a nearby house, where he put them up. According to Marsden, Savile took the group of young teenagers to several parties over the next few weeks, held in houses around London. One of the houses had a large swimming pool and was owned by a famous pop music figure. All the parties featured only men, several of whom were famous celebrities, and boys aged between six and 10. The boys would occasionally disappear into rooms with the men and noises would be heard coming from behind the doors.

Marsden and his friends were eventually sent back to Leeds in disgrace, after they were caught stealing from one of the houses. Marsden told Davies he thought he and his friends were at the parties to make the younger boys feel more comfortable. He said he never saw his uncle go into a room with one of the young boys. But Savile was clearly heavily connected with this organised paedophile scene and, given his previous offending, it seems highly likely that he himself engaged with the young boys on some occasions.

Whatever went on behind closed doors, in the limelight, Savile was more popular than ever. In 1971, a two-hour BBC Christmas special was aired, telling the story of his life. And in 1972, he received an OBE for his charity work. But in the same year, tragedy struck. Savile's mother, Agnes, died suddenly at the age of 85. Savile arranged for a requiem mass to be held in Leeds Catholic cathedral and paid for a lavish marble tombstone with the words 'The Duchess' inscribed on it.

Meanwhile, Savile's TV presence was growing. He had been the face of a TV advert promoting seatbelts, called the 'Clunk Click' campaign. In 1973, he was given his own show on the BBC, also called Clunk Click, in which Savile would interview everyday people. The series aired for a year, until it gave way to something which would become much bigger, and see Jimmy Savile become one of the best-known household names in the country.

Jim'll Fix It featured a novel format – Savile, the nation's favourite uncle, would fix it for children's wishes to come true, in front of a live audience on national TV. Children from all around the country wrote letters to Savile, detailing their wishes and dreams, and a lucky few would be selected to feature on the show. Fix-its ranged from swimming with dolphins to flying with the Red Arrows to helping dig the Channel Tunnel. As the show grew in popularity, so too did the scope of the fixes, involving celebrities like Mohammed Ali, Dr Who and The Osmonds. With its feelgood vibe, the television series would soon capture the nation's hearts. It ran for 20 years and averaged 15 million viewers, receiving around 5,000 letters a day. But behind the scenes, not everything was so rosy. The series' producer, Roger Ordish, warned staff never to leave Savile alone with the children, many of whom found the presenter "scary" or "creepy."

One of these less-than-impressed audience members was a young Dan Davies, the journalist who interviewed Savile many times and went on to write a biography of him. Davies watched the show live in 1980 when he was nine years old and left with a feeling that would haunt him throughout his life – that there was something sinister lurking behind Savile's Santa Claus façade. "In his gruff manner, there seemed to be a suggestion of menace," Davies wrote in his Savile biography, In Plain Sight. "For someone we all felt we knew so well, there was something remote and cold and untouchable beyond the façade. I spent the car journey home in silence."

The Christmas special for *Jim'll Fix It*'s first year was due to feature a nine-year-old boy, who wanted to visit the place where Jesus was born. Being a 'good' Catholic, Savile decided to tag along, spending 10 days in the Holy Land and visiting some of the major religious sites. Savile spent what he later described as a particularly meaningful few hours on his own in the desert near the Dead Sea. But there were rumours – some started by Savile himself – that his trip had other, deeper motives. Savile hinted that he had been invited to Israel by its president, Ephraim Katzir, on some undisclosed diplomatic mission. A Jewish friend of Savile's from Manchester confirmed this, claiming Savile had been invited to set up a secret meeting between the Israeli prime minister, Menachim Begin, and the Egyptian president, Anwar Sadat, because of Savile's friendship with Sadat's mother-in-law, Gladys Cottrell.

How much of Savile's Israel trip was political and how much was just his own spin is open to debate, but the episode provides one of a few tantalising hints that something deeper was going on behind the scenes in Savile's career. Such undercover diplomatic missions might go some way to explaining Prince Charles' mysterious note to Savile on his 80th birthday, which read, "Nobody will ever know what you have done for this country, Jimmy."

Hobnobbing with politicians was soon to become another of Savile's hobbies back in England, where he became pally with future prime minister, Margaret Thatcher. Savile first met Thatcher in 1976 at a Young Conservatives conference in Scarborough, when she was leader of the opposition. The two felt an instant attraction, perhaps because of their working-class, outsider status, and went on to form a life-long friendship. Savile was soon using his influence with Thatcher to get her as a guest on his radio talk show, Speakeasy, and to feature on an episode of *Jim'll Fix It*.

Another influential friend was Prince Charles, whom Savile had met at several fundraising events. Already liked and respected by Charles' father, Prince Philip, Savile now became one of a trusted group of friends and informal advisors surrounding the heir to the throne, so much so that Princess Diana would later describe Savile as Charles' "mentor." It's thought that Charles and Philip were attracted to Savile because of his 'common touch,' a class of person they were not used to socialising with. It seems they also appreciated his eccentric and zany humour, which others found creepy. Some even suggested that Savile played up to the role of court jester when around the royals.

Whatever the case, Savile used his newfound political and royal friendships to promote his latest charity cause. The spinal injuries unit at Stoke Mandeville hospital faced closure, after a series of storms had wrecked the primitive Nissen huts in which unit was housed. With the NHS stretched to breaking point, there was no funding left to build a new unit, so Savile offered to step into the breach, with a fundraising campaign of incredible ambition, with a target of £6 to £10 million. The scheme would be government backed but privately funded, with every £5 donation paying for a brick, £50,000 for a bed, and £250,000 for a ward. Savile used his ties with royalty to help the fundraising, using Charles and Philip's influence to persuade big donors like the *Daily Express* to come on board.

But while Savile was publicly promoting such good works, behind the scenes, his behaviour was as bad as ever. He was kicked off a cruise on the SS Canberra after complaints from the parents of a 14-year-old girl, whom he had lured back to his cabin and inappropriately touched. The parents complained to the captain, who quizzed Savile and found his denials unconvincing. Savile was confined to his cabin and removed from the ship when it docked in Gibraltar, where he was left to find his own way home. Despite his strict stance, though, the captain apparently didn't see fit to report Savile's behaviour. Neither did the press, who got wind of the story.

Meanwhile, back in Britain, Savile's face had become even more ubiquitous as the force behind British Rail's new advertising campaign. Savile's grinning face adorned billboards and TV ads across the country, proclaiming, "This is the age of the train," for a fee of £80,000 a year. The adverts were stopped in 1984, it was revealed after Savile's death, because British Rail bosses had heard rumours that he was having sex with corpses at Stoke Mandeville's morgue.

Savile's public reputation seemed to be made of Teflon but he was a still a 'person of interest' to the police. This is illustrated by one remarkable story from the height of his popularity. In 1980, Savile was briefly treated as a suspect in the Yorkshire Ripper case. The Yorkshire Ripper was a serial killer called Peter Sutcliffe, who murdered 11 women in and around Leeds. Savile's name was supplied to police by an anonymous tip-off and he was called in to provide a cast of his teeth, which could be compared with bite marks found on a victim's corpse. Savile's teeth didn't match and he was cleared of suspicion, but the fact that he would even be considered a suspect speaks volumes about what West Yorkshire Police must have known about him.

Savile went on to meet Sutcliffe, first at Parkhurst Prison on the Isle of Wight, where he went for a run with the serial killer, and later at Broadmoor, where he described him as "ordinary" and "good as gold." Sutcliffe wasn't the only serial killer Savile defended. He once backed the infamous Moors Murderer, Ian Brady, against a woman who claimed that Brady's wife and fellow serial killer, Mira Hindley, had been innocent of the killings. Even more bizarrely, when Louis Theroux asked Savile about the Moors Murders and the Myra Hindley story as part of his documentary on Savile, the aging disc jockey replied, "I am the Myra Hindley story."

It's a measure of the incredible double nature of Savile's life that, just after he was a suspect in the Yorkshire Ripper case, he was presented with a papal knighthood. In October 1981, in a private ceremony in Wimbledon, Savile was made a Knight Commander of St Gregory for his charity work.

Savile got to meet the pope a year later at a papal mass at Westminster Cathedral. In typical Savile fashion, he claimed that he gave a blessing to Pope John Paul II, rather than the other way round, saying that his Holiness looked tired. In return the pope presented Savile with a rosary, which he kept in his briefcase for the rest of his life. Savile's photograph with the pope joined his collection of other celebrity pics – Savile with Elvis, Savile with the Beatles, Savile with the Rolling Stones, the list went on.

Savile was at the height of his powers in the early 80s, and he needed to be, because he was about to face his sternest examination from the press so far. In 1983, two girls, aged 10 and 11, claimed they had been invited into Savile's Leeds flat sometime in the mid-70s. One of the girls told her father, who promptly called the *News of the World*. The tabloid ran an investigation that saw photographers camped outside Savile's Leeds flat for several months. Savile later boasted that, despite all the newspaper's digging, it couldn't find anything that would stick. Interestingly, the same year, Savile sanctioned a string of articles in the News of the World's rival, *The Sun*, in which he 'confessed' to being a violent mob-style boss at his dancehalls. Savile had been known as 'the Godfather,' he admitted, and told stories about tying up and beating troublemakers in club basements. The timing of the self-promoted exposés was odd and, as Davies suggests in his biography, was probably calculated to head off any rival – and far more damaging – revelations from the News of the World.

Savile undoubtedly knew how to play the press. He had a good team of lawyers and would threaten to sue at the drop of a hat. "Editors have the final say," ex-journalist and author, Christian Wolmer, told me, "but you know, if the lawyers strongly counsel against doing something, you have to accept. With Jimmy Savile, he was litigious and so it's difficult to actually go right up against him. He was very famous. He was quite powerful… You have to devote quite a lot of resources to it… So some of it is just a lack of resources, but even then I do wonder just why nobody quite had the guts to do it."

Perhaps emboldened by his victory over the News of the World, Savile became more brazen than ever, even putting his name to a book called Stranger Danger, which warned children about the dangers of sexual predators. In 1983, he even had the temerity to share a story with *The Daily Star* about how he had lured a paralysed young girl back to his caravan. Savile told The Star that he had approached the depressed girl and said, "Listen, I've got to tell you that I fancy you and I'm here for the weekend.

If I can spring you off the ward, will you come and watch TV with me in my motor caravan? But I've got to warn you – the caravan only has a bed in it." Savile explained that the girl agreed. Savile bought her flowers and chocolates and they spent four hours "watching TV" in his motorhome.

Savile must have felt truly untouchable. That same year in August, Stoke Mandeville's gleaming new 120-bed spinal injuries unit was opened. Jimmy Savile took pride of place alongside Prince Charles and Princess Diana at the official opening ceremony. Meanwhile, his other friend, prime minister Margaret Thatcher, invited him to Chequers for New Year's Day drinks and lunch. She had already nominated Savile for a knighthood.

In 1987, Savile was dropped by Radio 1, after two decades working at the station. With his typical need to control every situation, Savile insisted that the BBC spin it that he had moved aside voluntarily to let younger blood in. But as one door closed, another opened. In 1988, Savile was appointed as part of a six-man taskforce to restructure the failing system at Broadmoor, the maximum security hospital, where he had already served 20 years as its unofficial entertainments officer. Savile quickly moved to have an old friend from Leeds hospital installed as Broadmoor's new general manager. Alan Franey had been an administrator at Leeds during Savile's long service at the hospital. "Savile took this taskforce role and they wanted a new general manager," Boris Coster told me. "And Franey, who had no experience in the mental health system, no experience in the prison system, he'd come from a hospital, and was simply a friend of Savile's."

Savile's role in the taskforce was typically ill-defined but, in customary fashion, he soon took it upon himself to be its de facto leader, seeing himself as a kind of bulldog 'fixer,' who occasionally played outside the rules. It turned out that playing outside the rules meant blackmailing staff into accepting his changes. Savile went into the staff's employment records and found that some had been paying themselves undue overtime to the tune of as much as £800 a week. Savile threatened to leak his findings to the press and succeeded in getting his changes pushed through. It also suggested a modus operandi that Savile used to cover up his crimes at Broadmoor and all the other institutions he worked for – any time someone threatened to expose him, he could counterattack with blackmail threats of his own.

At Broadmoor, Savile's power certainly reached new heights. "At Broadmoor, he had a free rein," Coster told me. "I mean, there was staff that called us who were there at the time who hated him, hated him with a vengeance because he effectively thought that he was the boss. He could come and go, he could do what he wanted. He ignored things. I mean, the keys, for example. You had to hang the keys up at the end of every shift. He didn't, he took the keys with him."

Edwina Currie was the politician who approved Savile's position on the taskforce. Currie was a junior health minister at the time and would go on to become another of Savile's friends in high places. "This is a lady who's helping run the country," said Coster, "and she's now put a lunatic in charge of an asylum. He's got a set of gold keys. He comes and goes as he pleases. He has a massive palatial caravan in the grounds. He gets his gold-plated Rolls Royce serviced by the mechanics there."

Part of Savile's reforms included moving 60 patients out of Broadmoor to other institutions, two of whom were murderers. This caused The News of the World to run with the headline, 'Jim Fixes it for 60 Psychos to Go Free'. Jim immediately fixed it for the newspaper to be sued, winning considerable damages.

By this time, Savile was approaching 60 but still running several marathons and half-marathons every year. He was granted life-long entry into the London Marathon, after writing to the queen to stop the race being rerouted away from Buckingham Palace. After the marathon, Savile dropped into the palace to shower and have tea with the queen.

He was also becoming friendly with Princess Diana, whom he had met through his friendship with Charles, and separately via her interest in Stoke Mandeville. He also steered Diana into participating in the Just Say No anti-drugs campaign with which he was heavily involved, persuading her to make an appearance on Drugwatch, a TV fundraising programme for the campaign.

Savile's influence with the Prince and Princess of Wales reached new heights when he was invited to fix it for the couple to get over their much-publicised marriage troubles. According to Charles' press secretary, Dicky Arbiter, Savile had free reign in Buckingham Palace and was allowed to "roll in and roll out again." Sources close to Diana said she was fond of Savile, but in her own words, she said she found him "creepy." Royal correspondent, Richard Kay, told an ITV documentary that Diana had "recoiled" on one occasion, when Savile licked her hand. Kay went on to say, "He would turn up, Diana told me, at Kensington Palace where she lived, uninvited, and would manage to persuade the police on the gate, who never let anyone in without an invitation, to walk in."

Not only did Savile have unparalleled access to royal palaces, Charles even put him in charge of hiring staff and inviting guests to royal events. And, according to Coster, Savile even had his own room in Clarence House, Charles' official residence in London. How did Savile get such access and, more importantly, how did the security services fail to do the necessary checks to discover the incriminating allegations from his past?

"I can tell you this," said Coster, "that if you try to get into a Category A prison today, you will have the most stringent security checks done and then you still might not get in. You're telling me that Prince Charles with the MI5 and MI6 and his own security staff, and you've got Princess Di, and she's got her entourage, and you've got the queen and all this mixing about, and not one single one of them had the brains and the wits to think, 'Let's do an in-depth security check on Mr Savile before we let him in here,' let alone within a hundred yards of the royal family. But no, they didn't."

Savile finally received a knighthood in 1990. Margaret Thatcher had first nominated him in 1981 and had done so every year following. Tellingly though, officials had always deferred due to Savile's self-confessed promiscuous lifestyle and background as a 'godfather' in the club scene. Like the British Rail officials, could they also have heard the darker rumours that surrounded Savile like flies? By 1990, however, they finally caved and Savile was invited to Buckingham Palace to collect the honour. In the television footage of the event, Savile looks proud as he flaunts the medal to the press, alongside his usual Cheshire grin and outsize cigar. But a remark he made in an interview with The Independent gave a hint at the deeper motives behind his pleasure. The status conferred by the knighthood, he told the newspaper, had let him "off the hook." He may have had a point. The 2013 NSPCC report showed that 19 allegations of sexual assault had been made against Savile in the years 1986 to 1990 alone.

In 1991, Savile received further proof of his value to the royals when the young Prince William was rushed into hospital with a fractured skull, after being accidentally hit by a golf club at school. Charles and Philip were both unable to present the annual Duke of Edinburgh awards at Buckingham Palace, so Charles asked if Savile would step in to perform the ceremony.

Meanwhile, in the same year, the public got a rare insight into how Savile really ticked, when he appeared on the BBC Radio 4 programme, 'In the Psychiatrist's Chair'. Savile's interview with the psychiatrist, Anthony Clare, was heated and revealing. Clare admitted to being shocked to find that Savile showed "a certain dislike for people." Clare concluded that Savile was a "calculating materialist" who could "cope with people needing him as long as they are satisfied with the things he is prepared and able to give them – in most instances material things, and in no instance himself." What Clare seemed to be saying, in polite terms, was that Savile was a psychopath.

Savile certainly fits the description of Robert Hare's psychopathy checklist – slippery charm; a mask to conceal true self; low cunning and willingness to manipulate; absence of normal human emotions; lack of empathy; sexual promiscuity; inability to admit mistakes; fear of commitment; and repeated attacks on the vulnerable.

In 1993, the last series of *Jim'll Fix It* was filmed. A new BBC controller, Alan Yentob, had been appointed to BBC1. It was unclear whether Savile, sensing the wind of change, decided to quit while he was at the top, or whether he'd been given the chance to fall on his sword. Savile himself, of course, claimed the former. He was now in his late sixties and ready to take it easy. His health, too, was declining. The same year, he was advised by a cardiologist that, without a heart bypass operation, he would be dead within days. Savile had been warned as early as 1970 that he had a congenital heart condition that meant the arteries around his heart were slowly closing, but he had chosen to ignore the issue. In 1993, despite the dire warning, he decided to do the same. It was only in 1997, after the death of his sister from the same condition, that he decided to undergo surgery.

The three-hour quadruple bypass operation was performed at Killingbeck Hospital in Leeds. Savile wore his Royal Marines green beret into the operating theatre and asked to have it placed back on his head after the surgery. The operation was a success and Savile woke up to find a nurse leaning over him to ask if he was alright. As if to provide evidence of the affirmative, he reached up and groped her breast. Business, clearly, was back to normal.

Savile had not only survived a brush with death but managed to fend off another attack by the press. Three years earlier, two Duncroft girls had gone to *The Sunday Mirror* with their stories of being sexually assaulted by Savile. Again, however, the story never made it to press. The girls insisted on remaining anonymous and the paper was short of resources. The editors feared a costly legal battle. The story was killed.

Not long after Savile's heart surgery, Princess Diana died in Paris. Savile was invited to the funeral but was too weak to attend. Instead, he told Davies off the record, he collected all the soft toys left by mourners outside the gates of Kensington Palace and had them stored inside his lock-up at Stoke Mandeville.

Savile's showbusiness career was winding down, as was

symbolised by his appearance on the last ever *Top of the Pops* episode in 2006. Savile was nearly 80 and, as the man who had introduced the first ever show in 1964, was invited back to host the final episode, alongside a gaggle of former presenters. It must have been an emotional occasion, and Savile celebrated it in typical fashion. According to Operation Yewtree, conducted after his death, Savile sexually assaulted a teenage girl from the audience in a gap between filming.

The year after the last *Top of the Pops*, when Savile was 80, he finally became the subject of a police investigation. Seeing Savile make a guest appearance on the 2006 show *Celebrity Big Brother*, brought back unpleasant memories for one viewer. The woman had been a student at Duncroft Approved School in the late 70s and had witnessed Savile sexually assaulting another girl, who was 14 at the time. She called the child protection charity, Childline, and they advised her to tell the police. She subsequently contacted Dorset Police, who forwarded the details to Surrey Police, the force responsible for Duncroft.

Surrey Police duly contacted the woman and visited her at her home to take a written statement. She said Savile made regular advances on her friend, so much so that they had arranged a code phrase for her friend to warn her when attacks were happening. She said that on the occasion in question, her friend said the code phrase and she looked over to see Savile grasping her hand over his crotch and squeezing it.

The allegations were logged and 'Operation Ornament' was underway. Surrey Police's Public Protection Investigation Unit managed to track down the woman whom Savile had assaulted. The woman was initially cautious and angry at having been pulled into a process she wanted no part of. She did confirm the other woman's story, however, saying that the incident had occurred at Duncroft in 1978 when she was 14 or 15, and that Savile had forced her hand onto his crotch and manipulated it until he got an erection. But she didn't want to be involved in the investigation, she told Surrey police officers, if it only focused on her.

Surrey Police duly started fishing around for other allegations. They contacted Savile's home force, West Yorkshire Police, to request a file on historic allegations against Savile. All they received back was a single case, when a girl had jokingly stolen a pair of his glasses at a hotel. It was the only crime report involving Savile that West Yorkshire Police claimed to have on file.

In the meantime, another woman had come forward. Jill from Worthing told Sussex Police how, in 1970, Savile had organised for his Rolls Royce to pick her up and drive her to his motorhome, which was parked in Worthing. Once inside the caravan, she said Savile pushed her onto the bed and forced her hand onto his crotch. Unfortunately, like the Duncroft victim, Jill was unwilling to go through with a formal complaint against Savile. Crucially, neither of them were told that other victims had come forward.

"Surrey Police were dealing with a tricky situation," said Mark Williams-Thomas, the man who first exposed Savile in an ITV documentary. "They knew [Savile] had expensive lawyers. They knew the backlash that would engulf them if things went wrong. Also the victims were aware of Savile's power and influence, and both women were reluctant to give any evidence. They didn't realise it at the time but by giving evidence other victims would have found the courage to come forward. We have seen this happen with similar cases involving powerful people like Harvey Weinstein or Bill Cosby. Multiple victims coming together would have made a stronger case. In Savile's case hundreds would have come forward. It was a massive mistake by Surrey Police not to realise that point."

However, more women were now coming forward. One contacted Surrey Police to say that she knew of another woman who had been assaulted by Savile at Stoke Mandeville. The Surrey team contacted the woman in question, who told them Savile had rammed his tongue into her mouth at Stoke Mandeville when she was 14. Meanwhile, Surrey Police had identified 14 other women who had been students at Duncroft during the late seventies. Another former Duncroft girl also came forward to state that

Savile had told her he could help her get a job as a nurse if she gave him oral sex.

It took two years before Savile himself was contacted as part of the investigation. What followed was highly irregular. Savile responded to Surrey Police's request with a phone call explaining that he had a friend at West Yorkshire Police, "who usually deals with this sort of thing." Five days later, this same inspector called Surrey Police, explaining that Savile was indeed a personal friend and mentioned casually that Savile got "so many of these types of complaints." While Surrey Police quizzed West Yorkshire Police about the comment and whether it meant they had further allegations against Savile on file, it took another three months to pin Savile down for an interview. Finally, arrangements were made to speak to the aging DJ at Stoke Mandeville on 24th September 2009. Notably, the conversation was taking place somewhere that was firmly Savile's territory, and this set the tone for the interview that followed.

Sitting down in Savile's private office in Stoke Mandeville, the two female police officers began by asking Savile if they could call him Jimmy. They then put the three allegations to him, one from Stoke Mandeville and two from Duncroft. Savile flatly denied the allegations and went on to regale the interviewers with tales of his various fundraising activities. He reminded them of his friend in West Yorkshire Police and talked about his Friday morning social club with West Yorkshire Police officers who, he said, he regularly gave his "weirdo letters" to. These letters weren't kept by West Yorkshire Police, Savile stated bluntly. Instead, he said, "They pass them round the office and everybody has a laugh." He also mentioned his high-powered legal team who, he said, could take a case all the way to the Old Bailey, if necessary. "And if we do," he threatened the two female police officers, "you ladies will finish up in the Old Bailey as well."

Savile, as was his wont, was completely in control of the interview from start to finish. But through his talkativeness, he could have shot himself in the foot. He even told the police about two separate, unrelated occasions when he had received allegations of sexual assault. Savile's anecdotes should have given several leads for further investigation. But shockingly, nothing that came out of the interview was followed up, and the following month, Operation Ornament was officially closed. No further action would be taken.

"Surrey Police did not advise Stoke Mandeville hospital of the allegations," said Williams-Thomas about the mistakes made in the investigation. "Three separate sexual abuse allegations against him. He was working at the hospital. He had access to the hospital, and he had access to vulnerable people, young children, at Stoke Mandeville. Yet he's been investigated for his sexual assaults on three people and they didn't bother telling Stoke Mandeville. Total failure. They didn't tell Thames Valley Police, whose force area it was, didn't tell them that. And the interview itself provided vital information that, had the police officers bothered to follow up on, would have shown Savile to be lying. But they just simply took what he told them as being true, dismissed everything else, the allegations against him, and did no investigations."

In 2010, it came to the BBC's attention that Savile was ill and that an obituary might be necessary. In an email, senior executive Nick Vaughan-Barratt, told the BBC Controller of Knowledge Commissioning, George Entwistle, why he thought an obituary show about Savile wouldn't be a good idea. "My first job in TV was on a JS show," Vaughan-Barratt wrote. "I know him well and saw the complex and sometimes conflicting nature of the man at first hand." Vaughan-Barratt finished the email by saying, "I'd feel very queasy about an obit. I saw the real truth!" The email begs the question, if he knew the real truth, why didn't Vaughan-Barratt do anything about it?

In September 2011, Savile went on a cruise around Britain on the Queen Elizabeth. He was taken ill and disembarked when the ship docked at Liverpool. It was confirmed that he had pneumonia and that several of his organs were failing. A week before his death, Savile checked himself out of hospital and returned to his Leeds flat. Lying in bed but still smoking his famous Cuban cigars, he gave his final interview to the Yorkshire Evening Post, in which he looked back on his life and even expressed regret at not having had kids or grandchildren.

Alan Franey, Savile's long-term friend from Leeds Infirmary and Broadmoor, called him the same week and later told the BBC Savile had told him he was "coming to the end of the tunnel." On the 29th of October, after Savile had failed to respond to several phone calls, the caretaker of his building called round to check on him. The man found Savile lying dead in his bed. Savile's fingers were crossed and he had a smile on his face. In the ashtray was a half-smoked cigar.

Carrying on his mother's faith, Savile had been a lifelong Catholic. He also had a lifelong obsession with death. Savile had often talked about his own death and his hopes of entering heaven. He seemed to genuinely believe that there would be a totting up of his good deeds against his crimes and that his 'credit' side – mainly his charity fundraising – would outweigh his 'debit' side, which he left enigmatically unstated.

In a TV interview, Savile put it in his own inimitable way. "When I stand in front of the pearly gates and St Peter's there and he says, 'You are not coming in.' And I'll say, 'Well, why not?' He'll say, 'Because you're a villain.' And he'll show me the debit side. And I'll say, 'Hang about.' And I'll show him the credit side. 'Does that mean anything?' And if he says, 'That means nothing,' then I'll threaten to break his fingers."

Despite all his charity work and his psychopathic lack of guilt, it seems clear that Savile knew his entry into heaven would be a touch and go affair. No wonder he had his fingers crossed.

Savile's funeral was held in Leeds Catholic Cathedral with an honour guard of Royal Marines commandos, a fleet of black limousines and a gold-enamelled coffin. Savile's body was dressed in its customary garb – a tracksuit and running gear. He was accompanied by his Royal Marines green beret, a Cuban cigar and a half bottle of whisky. The service was conducted by the Bishop of Leeds, the Right Reverend Arthur Roche, and attended by 700 people, with a large crowd gathered outside. The coffin was then taken to Scarborough, where a plot had been prepared at Woodlands cemetery, overlooking the town. Savile's coffin was placed into the plot at a 45-degree angle, in line with his wishes, so that he could look out to sea. On his gravestone were inscribed the words "It was good while it lasted" – perhaps, in typical Savile style, a cheeky reference to everything he had managed to get away with.

He wouldn't get away with it much longer. Just three weeks after Savile's death, BBC's *Newsnight* programme began investigating reports from former Duncroft girls about Savile's behaviour at the school. The investigation was led by Meirion Jones, the grandson of the school's headteacher, Margaret Jones, who had been in charge during Savile's reign of terror. Jones had visited the school several times as a youngster and been shocked by Savile's level of access to the girls. Jones had read the web memoir written by Keri, documenting her abuse by Savile at Duncroft, and he was following comments on the school's Friends Reunited page, where other girls were talking openly about the abuse at Duncroft.

In November 2011, Jones and fellow *Newsnight* reporter, Liz MacKean, were given the go-ahead by *Newsnight's* editor, Peter Rippon, to research the story for a potential report. Jones contacted Keri, who was initially sceptical, but she eventually agreed to be interviewed. Meanwhile, MacKean emailed the 60 ex-Duncroft girls from the Friends Reunited website. Jones began hearing rumours that Surrey Police had recently investigated Savile in relation to Duncroft. He contacted Mark Williams-Thomas to join the investigation as a consultant.

Williams-Thomas had previously worked for Surrey Police as a child protection officer and then in a specialist paedophile unit. Looking for new challenges, Williams-Thomas had left the police and set up his own child protection consultancy. He started getting media work and acted as a consultant on several TV crime dramas, as well as presenting his own ITV series on catching paedophiles. Williams-Thomas' connection to Surrey Police was invaluable to the *Newsnight* investigation, and Jones had worked with him before, so he was the natural choice to get on board.

"I was going to Interpol around 2011," Williams-Thomas told me, "probably to do a piece for BBC *Newsnight* on images of child abuse… and it was on the way there where my producer said to me, 'Have you ever heard anything about Savile being a paedophile?' And I went, 'No.' I said, 'He's a weirdo.' I said, 'I wouldn't want to spend any time with the bloke, but no, I've never heard that.' He said, 'Well, that's really interesting because a police force, either Surrey or Sussex, did investigate him for child abuse, and we're unsure what happened with that or where it went.' And I said, 'That's really strange.' I said, 'I've not heard that… but I'll make some enquiries and see what I can find out.' … So I then made some enquiries and established that actually Surrey Police had investigated him."

Meanwhile, five of the ex-Duncroft girls that MacKean had contacted had come back with stories of being sexually abused by Savile at the school, and three of them talked about abuse happening on trips to the BBC to watch Savile filming. The *Newsnight* team also interviewed Keri, the author of the online blog. But just as the investigation seemed to be gaining traction, it started to hit rough ground.

The team had been told the Crown Prosecution Service had decided not to press charges in 2009 because Savile was too old and infirm. Supposedly, one of the Duncroft victims had a letter from Surrey Police, which confirmed this. *Newsnight's* editor, Peter Rippon, now demanded that this letter be found, to confirm the CPS's reasons for shutting the case before the programme could go ahead. However, the ex-Duncroft girl may have been mistaken or lying about the letter because it never materialised. Another problem was a planned Christmas tribute show about Savile, which was due to be hosted by Shane Richie. Senior executives at the BBC were, it seemed, leaning on Rippon to pull the *Newsnight* story. Whether it was because they didn't want to undermine the Christmas special, or for deeper, darker reasons, has never become clear.

Whatever the reasons, the *Newsnight* story was cancelled. The BBC had missed the chance to be the first organisation to uncover Savile, and would later face the consequences. Fortunately for Savile's victims, however, Mark Williams-Thomas was on hand to run with the story.

"[Merion Jones'] editor basically said to him, 'Well that doesn't look to me like it's a story,'" Williams-Thomas told me. "So the story they were after was incompetence by police who failed to do an investigation, or failed to follow it up… I said, 'I think you're missing the point. The story is surely that he's been interviewed in relation to child abuse and that therefore there's an allegation in relation to child sexual offences against such a status of an individual.' … And I said, "Well if you're happy, let me run with it.' I said, 'You know I'm on a different network. You're on BBC, my relationship is with ITV, let me run with it and see what I can do.'"

Williams-Thomas realised from the outset that, to strengthen the *Newsnight* story, he would need to find victims outside of Duncroft. Fortunately, a lead wasn't long in coming. *The Mirror* had recently run a story about the BBC axing an investigation into Savile and alleged sexual abuse. After reading the article, an ex-BBC newsroom assistant, Sue Thompson, contacted *Newsnight*, telling Jones that she had worked with Savile on a regional West Yorkshire TV programme in the 70s. Thompson said she had once walked into Savile's dressing room and seen Savile molesting a young girl of around 13 or 14 years old. Jones forwarded the information to Williams-Thomas and Thompson became a key witness in the ITV investigation.

Williams-Thomas' investigation took a year. He managed to speak with 20 victims but not all were willing to go on record. He discovered that, even though Savile was dead, there was still a huge amount of fear among his victims about coming forward publicly. However, five of the women were willing to be interviewed for the ITV Exposure documentary; two from Duncroft, one from Stoke Mandeville and two from *Top of the Pops*. One of the TOTP victims said Savile had raped her in his motorhome outside the BBC studio, another said she'd had sex with Savile in his dressing room several times, and was aged 15 at the time.

Finally, on 3rd October 2012, ITV's Exposure documentary, 'The Other Side of Jimmy Savile', went to air. It had been a long and difficult road, to say the least. "Making that programme and getting it to air was the hardest thing that I've ever done and will ever do, I'm sure, in the rest of my life," Williams-Thomas told me. However, things were about to change, as the genie was finally let out of the bottle. As soon as the Exposure show was aired, more Savile victims started coming forward and the story escalated into an ongoing saga, both at home and abroad. "That story then ran on the front pages for a consecutive 41 days," said Williams-Thomas.

But the BBC still wasn't taking any blame for pulling the *Newsnight* investigation. It maintained its official line that the *Newsnight* programme had been about the Surrey Police's failed investigation. But the ball was rolling too fast to stop now. Liz MacKean, who had worked so hard on the *Newsnight* investigation, quit the BBC in fury. She later told The Observer, "There is a small group of powerful people at the BBC who think it would have been better if the truth about Savile had never come out, and they aim to punish the reporters who revealed it. When the Savile story broke, the BBC tried to smear my reputation. They said they had banned the film because Meirion and I had produced shoddy journalism. I stayed to fight them but I knew they would make me leave in the end."

Williams-Thomas experienced similar animosity within the media, he says, for exposing the Savile story. "I have identified 72 BBC victims of Savile, of whom 34 were under the age of 16," he told me. "His youngest victim was aged eight. His abuse included eight cases of rape, the youngest victim being only 10 years old. There are still people in the BBC, there's still people in television worldwide and in the media, who hate me for what I've done, who dislike me because I've exposed Jimmy Savile and subsequently exposed Max Clifford, Rolf Harris and other people."

Heads would roll at the BBC, with the director general, George Entwistle, announcing his resignation on 10th October 2012, just 54 days after accepting the job. However, the BBC's own investigation into Savile's abuse at the corporation failed to hold anyone to account. It stated that, although many staff had been aware of Savile's behaviour, they had failed to report it to senior levels of management because of a continuing culture of fear. It sounded like a convenient way of exculpating the top levels of the BBC hierarchy.

In fact, there is plenty of evidence to suggest that Savile's behaviour was known about, and ignored, by top BBC executives for five decades. In 1978, John Lydon, the lead singer of The Sex Pistols, said in an interview for the BBC, "I want to kill Jimmy Savile – he's a hypocrite. I bet he's into all kinds of seediness that we all know about but aren't allowed to talk about. I know some rumours." The punk frontman added, "I bet none of this will be allowed out."

He was right. The BBC refused to air the interview. What's even more astonishing is that, in 2015, Lydon claimed he had been banned from the BBC after the interview, because someone high up in the corporation wanted to stifle any rumours about Savile. In 1999, Sir Roger Jones, Chairman of the charity Children in Need and governor of BBC Wales, said he refused to let Savile "anywhere near" the appeal, televised live on the BBC, after hearing rumours from BBC colleagues in London. Then there was the decision, taken at the top levels, not to air an obituary programme on Savile's life because it made executives feel "queasy."

It seems clear that knowledge of Savile's abusive behaviour was rife throughout every level of the national broadcaster yet, astonishingly, no one has been held responsible for colluding with his crimes. "We're the taxpayers, We're the license payers," Christopher Berry-Dee told me, "and for years, we've been conned and snowed by the BBC. We have sexual cover-ups from top to bottom. How disgusting is that? And the BBC knew about it, and they condoned it, and not one person has been held responsible. In fact, they've been promoted, they're given pensions."

The BBC was not the only organisation that investigated itself in the wake of the Savile revelations. West Yorkshire Police, who had failed to record a single shred of evidence against Savile in his lifetime, launched Operation Newgreen in 2013, to discover what had gone wrong. The investigation took four months and, unsurprisingly, it mostly exonerated itself. The ensuing report was what Dan Davies called, "A study in defensive self-justification and the redirection of blame." All this, despite one of the Metropolitan police officers involved in the report claiming that it was common knowledge amongst West Yorkshire Police that Savile was abusing young children.

One of the pieces of intelligence that WYP had failed to log, the report found, was an anonymous letter forwarded by the Vice Squad at Scotland Yard. The letter claimed that Savile had been involved with a young "rent boy," who had subsequently tried to blackmail Savile by threatening to expose his paedophilia to the press. Savile had changed his Leeds telephone number at the time, the letter claimed, to avoid further blackmail attempts. "He thinks he is untouchable because of the people he mixes with," the letter claimed. It ended ominously, "When JIMMY SAVILE falls, and sooner or later he will, a lot of well-known personalities and past politicians will fall with him."

Operation Newgreen claimed to have spoken to every officer who'd had dealings with Savile, but it evidently hadn't contacted one former WYP officer, who spoke to *The Mirror* in 2013 under a hidden identity. "There wasn't a copper in Leeds who didn't know Savile was a pervert," the former police officer told the paper. The man went on to recount how, in 1965, he had come across Savile and a young girl late at night in a car in a secluded lay-by. Asking what Savile was up to, the local celebrity told the officer he was waiting for the girl to turn 16, which would be in

15 minutes, on the stroke of midnight. When the officer asked the girl if she was okay, Savile told him to "piss off," adding, "If you want to keep your job, I suggest you get on your bike and fuck off." When the young policeman relayed the incident to his sergeant, the senior officer warned him off. "He's got friends in high places," the sergeant said. "If you know what's good for you, you'll leave it there."

A year after Savile's death, prime minister Theresa May, commissioned an investigation into sexual abuse by Savile and others, called 'Operation Yewtree.' The investigation found only five allegations of sexual assault against Savile on record across the entire country, between 1955 and 2009. Despite its intention to get to the bottom of Savile's crimes, the report only managed to uncover three new pieces of intelligence held on Savile – one was the anonymous letter about the "rent boy" and the blackmail attempt; another was the house in Battersea where Duncroft girls lived and which Savile frequently visited; the third was a 2003 crime report from the Met police, regarding a woman who claimed she had been sexually assaulted by Savile on Top of the Pops in 1973. Needless to say, West Yorkshire Police, who should have held records for all files relating to Savile, reported that they knew nothing of any of these vital pieces of information.

When Savile's career of abuse was finally exposed, hundreds more allegations began to surface and it soon became clear that the scale of his operation was something never quite seen before. A joint investigation by the NSPCC and Met Police found at least 500 allegations of sexual abuse against the celebrity, spanning more than 50 years. Roughly four-fifths of the victims were female, mostly between the ages of 13 and 16, and a fifth were young men and boys. There were 31 rape allegations, more than half of which were committed against minors.

The British nation was plunged into a kind of post-traumatic shock that one of its most well-known and best-loved celebrities had lived such a heinous double life. The gravestone, which had so respectfully been erected in the cemetery above Scarborough, was hastily removed. The many honours and honorary awards were quickly withdrawn. The awful sadness was encapsulated by the fate of Savile's nephew, Vivian, who hero-worshipped his uncle. The 69-year-old died of a broken heart, two weeks after the revelations appeared. The mood of shock and horrified introspection was perhaps best summed up by Met Police Commander, Peter Spindler, who said, "Jimmy Savile groomed a nation."

But after all the questions, interviews, allegations, reports and inquiries, one question still remains unanswered – how did he get away with it? How did Jimmy Savile remain untouchable over six decades of continuous offending?

One explanation, the mainstream one, is that the culture was different back then. Allegations from children tended not to be taken seriously, and a culture of inappropriate touching and comments, especially towards females, was more widely acceptable. Savile chose his victims carefully – those whose testimonies would hold least weight, and he ingratiated himself with the top echelons of society, to provide a protective barrier of respect and power. His unstinting charity work provided another layer of protection, as did his hair-trigger litigiousness. All these points are true, of course, but one still can't help thinking there must have been something more going on.

One person who thinks he knows the answer is the researcher and author, David Icke. And the clue, he thinks, is in Savile's earnings, especially towards the end of his life.

"It turns out that, although he had no obvious income stream after he dropped out of being a so-called entertainer," Icke told me, "he had houses all over the place. He had loads of cars… Where's all the money coming from?"

The reason for Savile's continued wealth, according to Icke, is the same reason he was untouchable. "What is lost in the revelations about Jimmy Savile," Icke told me, "is the reason he got away with it – he was a procurer of children to the rich and famous. That's how he got away with it. They had to watch his back to watch their own."

One of the key figures in this high-level paedophile ring, according to Icke, was Lord Mountbatten. Mountbatten, as we have seen in a previous chapter, was a known paedophile. He was also the man who, in the 1960s, introduced Savile into the inner circles of the royal family, where he made close friendships with Prince Philip and Prince Charles. Icke says he was informed by a friend of Princess Diana's about Savile's offending, including his necrophilia, and that Diana herself had told the friend about it.

Icke claims that not only the royals but the whole state machinery surrounding them knew about Savile, rubbishing the idea that the security forces knew nothing about his offending. "You can't cough anywhere near the queen without the security forces and Special Branch knowing about it," Icke said, "The police knew, because they interviewed him a number of times, that Jimmy Savile was a paedophile. And he's allowed into the inner circle of the British royal family and Special Branch and MI5 are not screaming, 'What's going on?'"

Savile had relationships with other high-level suspected paedophiles, according to Icke, one of whom he alleged was the former prime minister Edward Heath. Heath was investigated in 2014 by Wiltshire Police, after a former Wiltshire police officer claimed that a criminal investigation into Heath had been cut short to prevent a defendant testifying that they had been involved in the supply of young boys to the former prime minister. Subsequent investigations turned up seven witnesses, from over 1,000 separate lines of enquiry, whom Wiltshire Police stated were credible enough to have brought Heath in for questioning if he were still alive. Some of the allegations against Heath involved satanic ritual abuse, others said much of the abuse occurred aboard his yachts.

Icke alleged that most of Heath's victims were murdered after the abuse, usually by being thrown off one of his yachts. He also alleged that Wiltshire Police were confident of Heath's guilt because of a uniquely weird and horrific detail that all of the witnesses corroborated – during the abuse, Heath would allegedly use a fake hand to touch his victims, because, according to Icke, he didn't want to touch them with his own hands.

Could Savile have been procuring these victims for Heath? Icke alleges he was. We know that Savile and Heath had a relationship and that Savile was pictured with Heath. One famous photograph shows Savile, his head craning forward, cigar in mouth, saying something to Heath, which makes the former prime minister crease up with laughter.

Savile also had a close relationship with prime minister Margaret Thatcher, whose government was at the centre of allegations of a Westminster paedophile ring. Senior members of Thatcher's government, such as former home secretary, Leon Brittan, and Thatcher's chief advisor, Lord McAlpine, were targets for several allegations of paedophilia and sexual abuse. One of Thatcher's other close political friends and her private parliamentary secretary, Peter Morrison, was allegedly a known paedophile within Thatcher's inner circle. Morrison, according to an MI5 insider, had a known "penchant for small boys" which was covered up in the "interests of national security". The chairman of the Conservative party had asked Morrison about the paedophile rumours, according to Edwina Currie's published diaries, and Morrison had assured the chairman he would be "discreet."

Currie, of course, was herself a friend of Savile, rubber-stamping his role on the Broadmoor taskforce. In the same diary, Currie admits to having known that Morrison was a paedophile and having been concerned that Thatcher had made a political mistake by appointing him as her private parliamentary secretary. Yet Currie made no effort to report Morrison to the police or the press. Her collusion in the sexual abuse of children is something that appears to have pervaded Thatcher's government.

"This record-breaking paedophile and procurer of children, Savile, is an associate of Thatcher," Icke said. "... At the same time, she's overseeing a cabinet that is at the centre of this Westminster paedophile ring, and her two big aides were both paedophiles... I mean, what?"

If what Icke claims is true, we have an incredible situation – that Savile was untouchable because he was allegedly providing children for paedophiles within the royal family and the highest levels of government. And not only was this known, it was allegedly sanctioned and enabled by the government, the police, the security forces, and the royal family itself.

It's quite an allegation and one we will probably never be able to substantiate, as it runs so deep within the system. It also can't help but remind one of Epstein and Maxwell – two other well-connected people who, for most of their lives, were untouchable, and who were also supplying underage victims to the rich and powerful.

We may never know just how deep Jimmy Savile's influence went but, as ever, some of the best clues may have come from his own mouth. Speaking about his relationship with the royal family, Savile once told Davies, "I am the man what knows everything but says nothing. I get things done but I work deep cover."

In the 2000 Louis Theroux documentary, 'When Louis met Jimmy', Theroux brought up the subject of the rumours that always surrounded him. Savile's response was telling. He replied, "They can say whatever they want about me. If they say any more, I'll bring them all down." Throughout his life, Savile made several quotes about his ability to bring everyone down. What was he talking about? It is certainly not a difficult step to connect it to what David Icke alleges – that Savile was supplying children to the elites.

If we take Icke's allegations and Savile's own hints seriously, we are left with one overwhelming question – where are all these people he could have taken down? Where are all these "well-known personalities and past politicians" that the 1994 Met police blackmail letter mentioned?

For all the investigations, reports and inquiries, and despite how clear it has become just how many people knew about Savile's offending within the police, the NHS, the education systems, the BBC, the press, the government and even the royal family, it remains an astonishing fact that no one has been held responsible for being complicit in Savile's crimes.

"I think the biggest problem about Savile," said Mark Williams-Thomas, the first person to expose Savile, "is that we know about Savile's offending, we know about his impact on society, but what has been lost is those people that could have stopped it from happening, or those people who had knowledge about it. So out of those 44 reviews, not a single person has been held to account. Everybody has managed to evade any level of real responsibility, and I don't think that's right."

It seems that Savile was just one head of the hydra. With his exposure, that head has been cut off. Other heads have popped up and they too have been cut off – Jeffrey Epstein, Ghislaine Maxwell and Lord Mountbatten, to name just a few. But no matter how many heads we cut off, there are hundreds, perhaps thousands, more that we will never even know about. Until we find and expose the body that connects all these heads, we are fighting a war against an invisible enemy.

But that is a different story, and the subject, perhaps, of another book.

WHO KILLED EPSTEIN? PRINCE ANDREW OR BILL CLINTON

CHAPTER 1

On July 6, 2019, Jeffrey Epstein was arrested at New York's Teterboro Airport, following a trip to France. During a raid on his mansion, the FBI found nude photos, including images of teenage girls. Charged with sex trafficking and conspiracy to traffic minors for sex, he offered to pay a $600 million bail bond, which the judge denied because he was a flight risk, an acute danger to the community and a threat to the witnesses.

With his case under scrutiny, his former protectors – including Prince Andrew and Bill Clinton, whom he had attempted to compromise in a honeytrap scheme – began to pull away. Facing a life sentence, he hoped to win a double-jeopardy motion or to cut a deal with the prosecutor, which would have required naming his accomplices. As his legal difficulties multiplied, so did the risk to his powerful co-conspirators. If their activity was documented in court, certain government agencies would be forced to act. Epstein had to be eliminated.

On August 3, 2019, I posted a video on YouTube: Has Bill Clinton Scheduled Jeffrey Epstein For Prison Death To Cover Up Lolita Scandal? I stated that Epstein would be killed and that it would probably be made to look like a suicide. On August 10, 2019, the news reported that he had died.

Just ten days before his death, on July 23, an incident happened that suggested his time was limited: in the Metropolitan Correctional Center, he was found unconscious with injuries to his neck. He had been assigned a cellmate called Nicholas Tartaglione, a musclebound ex-cop turned gangster accused of killing four men in his brother's bar after a drug deal soured. Facing the death penalty, Tartaglione had access to the outside world through an illegal cell phone. Under normal circumstances, sex offenders would never be housed with murderers and gangsters, because the convict code dictates that they should be killed on sight (KOS). Epstein complained to one of his lawyers that he had been attacked by Tartaglione. Naturally, when questioned by investigators, his cellmate denied having had anything to do with the injuries.

Whatever had prevented the first attempt on his life, Epstein was placed on suicide watch. On July 29, he was removed from suicide watch and put in a special housing unit with another cellmate. Every thirty minutes, a guard was supposed to check on him. The night before his murder, August 9, his cellmate was conveniently removed. The cameras monitoring the area malfunctioned and the guards on duty had supposedly fallen asleep or been so engrossed in online shopping that they were oblivious to the man dying a short distance from the guard station. The two guards, Tova Noel, thirty-one, and Michael Thomas, forty-one, would later be charged with falsifying records and conspiracy because for eight hours – from 10.30 p.m. on August 9 to 6.30 a.m. on August 10 – they had not gone to his cell door.

The indictment against the guards stated: They sat at their desks, browsed online and moved about the common area for a substantial portion of their shift instead of completing the required checks. Noel and Thomas allegedly appeared to be asleep at their desks for about two hours. Noel used her computer to search for furniture sales and benefit websites during her shift. Thomas allegedly searched online for motorcycle sales and sports news briefly at 1 a.m., 4 a.m. and 6 a.m. The pair were only 15 feet away from Epstein when he died. They found him dead when they went to serve him breakfast at 6.30 a.m. The last time they had checked on him was at 10.30 p.m. the night before.

Noel allegedly told a supervisor: "We did not complete the 3 a.m. and 5 a.m. rounds."

Thomas added "We messed up" and "I messed up, she's not to blame, we didn't do any rounds."

According to Nick Tartaglione's lawyer, "Nobody heard anything. It was a silent act."

The autopsy revealed that various neck bones had been fractured, including the hyoid, which most medical experts commenting on the case have stated is more common in homicide than suicide. Life is cheap in prison. A small amount of heroin is enough to get somebody killed. To get away with a professional hit, the victim would have to die in a way that would look like suicide.

Out of the methods that prisoners use to commit suicide or to die accidentally, a professional would probably go with hanging or a hotshot. Guards who have killed prisoners have been known to rope somebody up. Gang members often employ the hotshot because a prisoner found overdosed on heroin appears to be just another dead addict, which requires no further investigation.

In 2008, teenager Ronnie White, who was charged with killing a cop, was found dead in a Washington jail. After the medical examiner found a broken hyoid, the cause of death was changed from suicide to homicide. The examiners suspected that he had been strangled with a sheet, towel or the crux of an elbow. The guard who had moved his body was found guilty of obstruction, but no charges were filed for his murder. In 2013, a federal judge declared the cause of death a mystery.

One of the lawyers representing victims of Epstein, Spencer Kuvin, spoke to a staff member at the jail and told the media:

"I received a call from a supervisor at the MCC, which is the jail that Mr Epstein was held in. The first words out of his mouth to be honest were: 'Don't believe what you are hearing in regards to Epstein's death.' I had a lengthy conversation with him about the issue of security within MCC and he gave me a fairly detailed description of the interior of the jail, which led me to believe that he was credible. He told me how the SHU (Special Housing Unit) where Mr Epstein was kept was basically designed to be a jail within the jail. And then there was a separate, even more secure unit, inside the SHU, where the highest value targets were kept. He said every square inch of that place is covered by cameras. It was designed that way because of super-high-value targets that are kept there such as terrorists, drug dealers and other extremely high-value targets or suspects like Mr Epstein.

"If reports that there is no CCTV are true, it would mean that they'd either shut the cameras off or they were not functioning in some way. He says there's no way that they would not have been able to see what was going on. What my source found very suspicious was that his cellmate was pulled the day before. The purpose of a cellmate for someone who either was on suicide watch or is on suicide watch is to notify guards if something is happening. So, the fact that they pulled the cellmate is not only one level above negligent, it also appears intentional. Really, he should have been on suicide watch. Not only was he not on suicide watch, they pulled the one person that could have notified guards if something untoward was about to occur. It was almost as though they did it so that no one could see what was going to happen the following day.

"I met [Epstein] on three separate occasions and he never seemed to me to be a remorseful individual. He always seemed highly intelligent, arrogant, self-assured, confident; never thought he did anything wrong, even in light of all the evidence against him. He basically just blamed the victims and had an incredible ego about himself, and someone with that type of ego just never struck me as someone that could possibly commit suicide. I didn't think he was that brave to be perfectly honest. He always hid behind lawyers upon lawyers upon lawyers in his civil and criminal cases. I mean, you can't even count the number of people he hired to protect him from any allegations, both civil and criminal. This type of an act requires a certain amount of resolve, and he just never struck me as someone that could do that.

"I think the most likely scenario if it's not suicide is that somebody on the inside of the prison was paid essentially to make it look like a suicide, and the guards were paid to disappear and not be there, and his cellmate was taken away on Friday, so there'd be no witness. So, someone went in there in the early morning hours, tied him around the neck with a bed sheet, tied the bed sheet to the bed and pushed him down effectively and held him down until he choked to death.

"For something like this, you would expect to see some type of bruising or whatever around his shoulders if he was being held down against his will. So that would be the most likely scenario to make it appear as though he had done the act himself. With the fracture of the bone in his neck it suggests a high amount of force pushing down on him. I think the most likely scenario if it is not suicide is that there were too many people that were afraid that he would talk about what he may have done with them and others. They just paid off someone to go into the jail and take care of him."

Even with the most baffling assassinations, those responsible sometimes reveal themselves during the cover-up. The person assigned to investigate Epstein's death was Attorney General William Barr, whose headmaster father had hired Epstein in 1974 to teach teenagers mathematics and physics at the exclusive Dalton School on the Upper East Side of Manhattan. From 1973 to 1977, Barr worked for the CIA, starting out as an analyst and then becoming the assistant legislative counsel. From 1991 to 1993, he was the Attorney General for George H. W. Bush. According to the journalist Whitney Webb, while Barr was in the CIA's Office of Legislative Counsel, he stonewalled the Church and Pike committees, which were investigating the wrongdoing of the CIA, including sexual blackmail operations carried out in the 1970s. While working for the Bush administration, he pardoned several controversial Iran-Contra figures, including people linked to sexual blackmail operations involving children. Barr worked for Kirkland & Ellis, a law firm that defended Epstein. Stating that he didn't specifically work on the Epstein case, Barr refused to recuse himself from the investigation. His history of covering things up for the CIA suggests that the agency may have been used to coordinate the assassination.

If those responsible for Epstein's death were able to order an intelligence agency to perform the hit, then the suspect list must be comprised of people far more powerful and wealthier than the deceased. The next question that must be asked is: who had the most to gain from silencing Epstein? Which could be rephrased: who had the most to lose if Epstein remained alive?

OTHER BOOKS BY GADFLY PRESS

By William Rodríguez Abadía:
Son of the Cali Cartel: The Narcos Who Wiped Out Pablo Escobar and the Medellín Cartel

By Chet Sandhu:
Self-Made, Dues Paid: An Asian Kid Who Became an International Drug-Smuggling Gangster

By Kaz B:
Confessions of a Dominatrix: My Secret BDSM Life

By Peter McAleese:
Killing Escobar and Soldier Stories

By Joe Egan:
Big Joe Egan: The Toughest White Man on the Planet

By Anthony Valentine:
Britain's No. 1 Art Forger Max Brandrett: The Life of a Cheeky Faker

By Barbara Attwood:
Blue Plastic Cow: One Woman's Search for Her Birth Mother

By Johnnyboy Steele:
Scotland's Johnnyboy: The Bird That Never Flew

By Ian 'Blink' MacDonald:
Scotland's Wildest Bank Robber: Guns, Bombs and Mayhem in Glasgow's Gangland

By Michael Sheridan:
The Murder of Sophie: How I Hunted and Haunted the West Cork Killer

By Steve Wraith:
The Krays' Final Years: My Time with London's Most Iconic Gangsters

By Natalie Welsh:
Escape from Venezuela's Deadliest Prison

By Shaun Attwood:
English Shaun Trilogy
Party Time
Hard Time
Prison Time

War on Drugs Series
Pablo Escobar: Beyond Narcos
American Made: Who Killed Barry Seal? Pablo Escobar or George HW Bush
The Cali Cartel: Beyond Narcos
Clinton Bush and CIA Conspiracies: From the Boys on the Tracks to Jeffrey Epstein
Who Killed Epstein? Prince Andrew or Bill Clinton

Un-Making a Murderer: The Framing of Steven Avery and Brendan Dassey
The Mafia Philosopher: Two Tonys
Life Lessons

Pablo Escobar's Story (4-book series)

By Johnnyboy Steele:

Scotland's Johnnyboy: The Bird That Never Flew

"A cross between *Shawshank Redemption* and *Escape from Alcatraz*!" – Shaun Attwood, YouTuber and Author

All his life, 'Johnnyboy' Steele has been running. Firstly, from an abusive father, then from the rigours of an approved school and a young offenders jail, and, finally, from the harshness of adult prison. This book details how the Steele brothers staged the most daring breakout that Glasgow's Barlinnie prison had ever seen and recounts what happened when their younger brother, Joseph, was falsely accused of the greatest mass murder in Scottish legal history.

If Johnnyboy had wings, he would have flown to help his family, but he would have to wait for freedom to use his expertise to publicise young Joe's miscarriage of justice.

This is a compelling, often shocking and uncompromisingly honest account of how the human spirit can survive against almost crushing odds. It is a story of family love, friendship and, ultimately, a desire for justice.

By Ian 'Blink' Macdonald:

Scotland's Wildest Bank Robber: Guns, Bombs and Mayhem in Glasgow's Gangland

As a young man in Glasgow's underworld, Ian 'Blink' Macdonald earned a reputation for fighting and stabbing his enemies. After refusing to work for Arthur "The Godfather" Thompson, he attempted to steal £6 million in a high-risk armed bank robbery. While serving 16 years, Blink met the torture-gang boss Eddie Richardson, the serial killer Archie Hall, notorious lifer Charles Bronson and members of the Krays.

After his release, his drug-fuelled violent lifestyle created conflict with the police and rival gangsters. Rearrested several times, he was the target of a gruesome assassination attempt. During filming for Danny Dyer's Deadliest Men, a bomb was discovered under Blink's car and the terrified camera crew members fled from Scotland.

In *Scotland's Wildest Bank Robber*, Blink provides an eye-opening account of how he survived gangland warfare, prisons, stabbings and bombs.

By Michael Sheridan:

The Murder of Sophie: How I Hunted and Haunted the West Cork Killer

Just before Christmas, 1996, a beautiful French woman – the wife of a movie mogul – was brutally murdered outside of her holiday home in a remote region of West Cork, Ireland. The crime was reported by a local journalist, Ian Bailey, who was at the forefront of the case until he became the prime murder suspect. Arrested twice, he was released without charge.

This was the start of a saga lasting decades with twists and turns and a battle for justice in two countries, which culminated in the 2019 conviction of Bailey – in his absence – by the French

Criminal court in Paris. But it was up to the Irish courts to decide whether he would be extradited to serve a 25-year prison sentence.

With the unrivalled co-operation of major investigation sources and the backing of the victim's family, the author unravels the shocking facts of a unique murder case.

By Steve Wraith:

The Krays' Final Years: My Time with London's Most Iconic Gangsters

Britain's most notorious twins – Ron and Reg Kray – ascended the underworld to become the most feared and legendary gangsters in London. Their escalating mayhem culminated in murder, for which they received life sentences in 1969.

While incarcerated, they received letters from a schoolboy from Tyneside, Steve Wraith, who was mesmerised by their story. Eventually, Steve visited them in prison and a friendship formed. The Twins hired Steve as an unofficial advisor, which brought him into contact with other members of their crime family. At Ron's funeral, Steve was Charlie Kray's right-hand man.

Steve documents Ron's time in Broadmoor – a high-security psychiatric hospital – where he was battling insanity and heavily medicated. Steve details visiting Reg, who served almost 30 years in a variety of prisons, where the gangster was treated with the utmost respect by the staff and the inmates.

By Natalie Welsh:

Escape from Venezuela's Deadliest Prison

After getting arrested at a Venezuelan airport with a suitcase of cocaine, Natalie was clueless about the danger she was facing. Sentenced to 10 years, she arrived at a prison with armed men on the roof, whom she mistakenly believed were the guards, only to find out they were homicidal gang members. Immediately, she was plunged into a world of unimaginable horror and escalating violence, where murder, rape and all-out gang warfare were carried out with the complicity of corrupt guards. Male prisoners often entered the women's housing area, bringing gunfire with them and leaving corpses behind. After 4.5 years, Natalie risked everything to escape and flee through Colombia, with the help of a guard who had fallen deeply in love with her.

By Shaun Attwood:

Pablo Escobar: Beyond Narcos

War on Drugs Series Book 1

The mind-blowing true story of Pablo Escobar and the Medellín Cartel, beyond their portrayal on Netflix.

Colombian drug lord Pablo Escobar was a devoted family man and a psychopathic killer; a terrible enemy, yet a wonderful friend. While donating millions to the poor, he bombed and tortured his enemies – some had their eyeballs removed with hot spoons. Through ruthless cunning and America's insatiable appetite for cocaine, he became a multi-billionaire, who lived in a $100-million house with its own zoo.

Pablo Escobar: Beyond Narcos demolishes the standard good versus evil telling of his story. The authorities were not hunting Pablo down to stop his cocaine business. They were taking it over.

American Made: Who Killed Barry Seal?
Pablo Escobar or George HW Bush

War on Drugs Series Book 2

Set in a world where crime and government coexist, *American Made* is the jaw-dropping true story of CIA pilot Barry Seal that the Hollywood movie starring Tom Cruise is afraid to tell.

Barry Seal flew cocaine and weapons worth billions of dollars into and out of America in the 1980s. After he became a government informant, Pablo Escobar's Medellin Cartel offered a million for him alive and half a million dead. But his real trouble began after he threatened to expose the dirty dealings of George HW Bush.

American Made rips the roof off Bush and Clinton's complicity in cocaine trafficking in Mena, Arkansas.

"A conspiracy of the grandest magnitude." Congressman Bill Alexander on the Mena affair.

The Cali Cartel: Beyond Narcos

War on Drugs Series Book 3

An electrifying account of the Cali Cartel, beyond its portrayal on Netflix.

From the ashes of Pablo Escobar's empire rose an even bigger and more malevolent cartel. A new breed of sophisticated mobsters became the kings of cocaine. Their leader was Gilberto Rodríguez Orejuela – known as the Chess Player, due to his foresight and calculated cunning.

Gilberto and his terrifying brother, Miguel, ran a multi-billion-dollar drug empire like a corporation. They employed a politically astute brand of thuggery and spent $10 million to put a president in power. Although the godfathers from Cali preferred bribery over violence, their many loyal torturers and hitmen were never idle.

Clinton, Bush and CIA Conspiracies: From the Boys on the Tracks to Jeffrey Epstein

War on Drugs Series Book 4

In the 1980s, George HW Bush imported cocaine to finance an illegal war in Nicaragua. Governor Bill Clinton's Arkansas state police provided security for the drug drops. For assisting the CIA, the Clinton Crime Family was awarded the White House. The #clintonbodycount continues to this day, with the deceased including Jeffrey Epstein.

This book features harrowing true stories that reveal the insanity of the drug war. A mother receives the worst news about her son. A journalist gets a tip that endangers his life. An unemployed man becomes California's biggest crack dealer. A DEA agent in Mexico is sacrificed for going after the big players.

The lives of Linda Ives, Gary Webb, Freeway Rick Ross and Kiki Camarena are shattered by brutal experiences. Not all of them will survive.

Pablo Escobar's Story (4-book series)

"Finally, the definitive book about Escobar, original and up-to-date." – UNILAD

"The most comprehensive account ever written." – True Geordie

Pablo Escobar was a mama's boy, who cherished his family and sang in the shower, yet he bombed a passenger plane and formed a death squad that used genital electrocution.

Most Escobar biographies only provide a few pieces of the puzzle, but this action-packed 1000-page book reveals everything about the king of cocaine.

Mostly translated from Spanish, Part 1 contains stories untold in the English-speaking world, including:

The tragic death of his youngest brother, Fernando.

The fate of his pregnant mistress.

The shocking details of his affair with a TV celebrity.

The presidential candidate who encouraged him to eliminate their rivals.

The Mafia Philosopher

"A fast-paced true-crime memoir with all of the action of Goodfellas." – UNILAD

"Sopranos v Sons of Anarchy with an Alaskan-snow backdrop." – True Geordie Podcast

Breaking bones, burying bodies and planting bombs became second nature to Two Tonys, while working for the Bonanno Crime Family, whose exploits inspired The Godfather.

After a dispute with an outlaw motorcycle club, Two Tonys left a trail of corpses from Arizona to Alaska. On the run, he was pursued by bikers and a neo-Nazi gang, blood-thirsty for revenge, while a homicide detective launched a nationwide manhunt.

As the mist from his smoking gun fades, readers are left with an unexpected portrait of a stoic philosopher with a wealth of charm, a glorious turn of phrase and a fanatical devotion to his daughter.

Party Time

An action-packed roller-coaster account of a life spiralling out of control, featuring wild women, gangsters and a mountain of drugs.

Shaun Attwood arrived in Phoenix, Arizona, a penniless business graduate from a small industrial town in England. Within a decade, he became a stock-market millionaire. But he was leading a double life.

After taking his first ecstasy pill at a rave in Manchester as a shy student, Shaun became intoxicated by the party lifestyle that would change his fortune. Years later, in the Arizona desert, he became submerged in a criminal underworld, throwing parties for thousands of ravers and running an ecstasy ring in competition with the Mafia mass murderer, Sammy 'The Bull' Gravano.

As greed and excess tore through his life, Shaun had eye-watering encounters with Mafia hitmen and crystal-meth addicts, enjoyed extravagant debauchery with superstar DJs and glitter girls, and ingested enough drugs to kill a herd of elephants. This is his story.

Hard Time

"Makes the Shawshank Redemption look like a holiday camp."
– NOTW

After a SWAT team smashed down stock-market millionaire Shaun Attwood's door, he found himself inside Arizona's deadliest jail and locked into a brutal struggle for survival.

Shaun's hope of living the American Dream turned into a nightmare of violence and chaos, when he had a run-in with Sammy "the Bull" Gravano, an Italian Mafia mass murderer.

In jail, Shaun was forced to endure cockroaches crawling in his ears at night, dead rats in the food and the sound of skulls getting cracked against toilets. He meticulously documented the conditions and smuggled out his message.

Join Shaun on a harrowing voyage into the darkest recesses of human existence.

Hard Time provides a revealing glimpse into the tragedy, brutality, dark comedy and eccentricity of prison life.

Featured worldwide on Nat Geo Channel's Locked-Up/Banged-Up Abroad Raving Arizona.

Prison Time

Sentenced to 9½ years in Arizona's state prison for distributing ecstasy, Shaun finds himself living among gang members, sexual predators and drug-crazed psychopaths. After being attacked by a Californian biker, in for stabbing a girlfriend, Shaun writes about the prisoners who befriend, protect and inspire him. They include T-Bone, a massive African American ex-Marine, who risks his life saving vulnerable inmates from rape, and Two Tonys, an old-school Mafia murderer, who left the corpses of his rivals from Arizona to Alaska. They teach Shaun how to turn incarceration to his advantage, and to learn from his mistakes.

Shaun is no stranger to love and lust in the heterosexual world, but the tables are turned on him inside. Sexual advances come at him from all directions, some cleverly disguised, others more sinister – making Shaun question his sexual identity.

Resigned to living alongside violent, mentally ill and drug-addicted inmates, Shaun immerses himself in psychology and philosophy, to try to make sense of his past behaviour, and begins applying what he learns, as he adapts to prison life. Encouraged by Two Tonys to explore fiction as well, Shaun reads over 1000 books which, with support from a brilliant psychotherapist, Dr Owen, speed along his personal development. As his ability to deflect daily threats improves, Shaun begins to look forward to his release with optimism and a new love waiting for him. Yet the words of Aristotle from one of Shaun's books will prove prophetic: "We cannot learn without pain."

Un-Making a Murderer: The Framing of Steven Avery and Brendan Dassey

Innocent people do go to jail. Sometimes mistakes are made. But even more terrifying is when the authorities conspire to frame them. That's what happened to Steven Avery and Brendan Dassey, who were convicted of murder and are serving life sentences.

Un-Making a Murderer is an explosive book, which uncovers the illegal, devious and covert tactics used by Wisconsin officials, including:

- Concealing Other Suspects

- Paying Expert Witnesses to Lie

- Planting Evidence

- Jury Tampering

The art of framing innocent people has been in practice for centuries and will continue until the perpetrators are held accountable. Turning conventional assumptions and beliefs in the justice system upside down, *Un-Making a Murderer* takes you on that journey.

HARD TIME BY SHAUN ATTWOOD

CHAPTER 1

Sleep deprived and scanning for danger, I enter a dark cell on the second floor of the maximum-security Madison Street jail in Phoenix, Arizona, where guards and gang members are murdering prisoners. Behind me, the metal door slams heavily. Light slants into the cell through oblong gaps in the door, illuminating a prisoner cocooned in a white sheet, snoring lightly on the top bunk about two thirds of the way up the back wall. Relieved there is no immediate threat, I place my mattress on the grimy floor. Desperate to rest, I notice movement on the cement-block walls. *Am I hallucinating?* I blink several times. The walls appear to ripple. Stepping closer, I see the walls are alive with insects. I flinch. So many are swarming, I wonder if they're a colony of ants on the move. To get a better look, I put my eyes right up to them. They are mostly the size of almonds and have antennae. American cockroaches. I've seen them in the holding cells downstairs in smaller numbers, but nothing like this. A chill spread over my body. I back away.

Something alive falls from the ceiling and bounces off the base of my neck. I jump. With my night vision improving, I spot cockroaches weaving in and out of the base of the fluorescent strip light. Every so often one drops onto the concrete and resumes crawling. Examining the bottom bunk, I realise why my cellmate is sleeping at a higher elevation: cockroaches are pouring from gaps in the decrepit wall at the level of my bunk. The area is thick with them. Placing my mattress on the bottom bunk scatters them. I walk towards the toilet, crunching a few under my shower sandals. I urinate and grab the toilet roll. A cockroach darts from the centre of the roll onto my hand, tickling my fingers. My arm jerks as if it has a mind of its own, losing the cockroach and the toilet roll. Using a towel, I wipe the bulk of them off the bottom bunk, stopping only to shake the odd one off my hand. I unroll my mattress. They begin to regroup and inhabit my mattress. My adrenaline is pumping so much, I lose my fatigue.

Nauseated, I sit on a tiny metal stool bolted to the wall. *How will I sleep? How's my cellmate sleeping through the infestation and my arrival?* Copying his technique, I cocoon myself in a sheet and lie down, crushing more cockroaches. The only way they can access me now is through the breathing hole I've left in the sheet by the lower half of my face. Inhaling their strange musty odour, I close my eyes. I can't sleep. I feel them crawling on the sheet around my feet. *Am I imagining things?* Frightened of them infiltrating my breathing hole, I keep opening my eyes. Cramps cause me to rotate onto my other side. Facing the wall, I'm repulsed by so many of them just inches away. I return to my original side.

The sheet traps the heat of the Sonoran Desert to my body, soaking me in sweat. Sweat tickles my body, tricking my mind into thinking the cockroaches are infiltrating and crawling on me. The trapped heat aggravates my bleeding skin infections and bedsores. I want to scratch myself, but I know better. The outer layers of my skin have turned soggy from sweating constantly in this concrete oven. Squirming on the bunk fails to stop the relentless itchiness of my skin. Eventually, I scratch myself. Clumps of moist skin detach under my nails. Every now and then I become so uncomfortable, I must open my cocoon to waft the heat out, which allows the cockroaches in. It takes hours to drift to sleep. I only manage a few hours. I awake stuck to the soaked sheet, disgusted by the cockroach carcasses compressed against the mattress.

The cockroaches plague my new home until dawn appears at the dots in the metal grid over a begrimed strip of four-inch-thick bullet-proof glass at the top of the back wall – the cell's only source of outdoor light. They disappear into the cracks in the walls, like vampire mist retreating from sunlight. But not all of them. There were so many on the night shift that even their vastly reduced number is too many to dispose of. And they act like they know it. They roam around my feet with attitude, as if to make it clear that I'm trespassing on their turf.

My next set of challenges will arise not from the insect world, but from my neighbours. I'm the new arrival, subject to scrutiny about my charges just like when I'd run into the Aryan Brotherhood prison gang on my first day at the medium-security Towers jail a year ago. I wish my cellmate would wake up, brief me on the mood of the locals and introduce me to the head of the white gang. No such luck. Chow is announced over a speaker system in a crackly robotic voice, but he doesn't stir.

I emerge into the day room for breakfast. Prisoners in black-and-white bee-striped uniforms gather under the metal-grid stairs and tip dead cockroaches into a trash bin from plastic peanut-butter containers they'd set as traps during the night. All eyes are on me in the chow line. Watching who sits where, I hold my head up, put on a solid stare and pretend to be as at home in this environment as the cockroaches. It's all an act. I'm lonely and afraid. I loathe having to explain myself to the head of the white race, who I assume is the toughest murderer. I've been in jail long enough to know that taking my breakfast to my cell will imply that I have something to hide.

The gang punishes criminals with certain charges. The most serious are sex offenders, who are KOS: Kill On Sight. Other charges are punishable by SOS – Smash On Sight – such as drive-by shootings because women and kids sometimes get killed. It's called convict justice. Gang members are constantly looking for people to beat up because that's how they earn their reputations and tattoos. The most serious acts of violence earn the highest-ranking tattoos. To be a full gang member requires murder. I've observed the body language and techniques inmates trying to integrate employ. An inmate with a spring in his step and an air of confidence is likely to be accepted. A person who avoids eye contact and fails to introduce himself to the gang is likely to be preyed on. Some of the failed attempts I saw ended up with heads getting cracked against toilets, a sound I've grown familiar with. I've seen prisoners being extracted on stretchers who looked dead – one had yellow fluid leaking from his head. The constant violence gives me nightmares, but the reality is that I put myself in here, so I force myself to accept it as a part of my punishment.

It's time to apply my knowledge. With a self-assured stride, I take my breakfast bag to the table of white inmates covered in neo-Nazi tattoos, allowing them to question me.

"Mind if I sit with you guys?" I ask, glad exhaustion has deepened my voice.

"These seats are taken. But you can stand at the corner of the table."

The man who answered is probably the head of the gang. I size him up. Cropped brown hair. A dangerous glint in Nordic-blue eyes. Tiny pupils that suggest he's on heroin. Weightlifter-type veins bulging from a sturdy neck. Political ink on arms crisscrossed with scars. About the same age as me, thirty-three.

"Thanks. I'm Shaun from England." I volunteer my origin to show I'm different from them but not in a way that might get me smashed.

"I'm Bullet, the head of the whites." He offers me his fist to bump. "Where you roll in from, wood?"

Addressing me as wood is a good sign. It's what white gang members on a friendly basis call each other.

"Towers jail. They increased my bond and re-classified me to maximum security."

"What's your bond at?"

"I've got two $750,000 bonds," I say in a monotone. This is no place to brag about bonds.

"How many people you kill, brother?" His eyes drill into mine, checking whether my body language supports my story. My body language so far is spot on.

"None. I threw rave parties. They got us talking about drugs on wiretaps." Discussing drugs on the phone does not warrant a $1.5 million bond. I know and beat him to his next question. "Here's my charges." I show him my charge sheet, which includes conspiracy and leading a crime syndicate – both from running an Ecstasy ring.

Bullet snatches the paper and scrutinises it. Attempting to pre-empt his verdict, the other whites study his face. On edge, I wait for him to respond. Whatever he says next will determine whether I'll be accepted or victimised.

"Are you some kind of jailhouse attorney?" Bullet asks. "I want someone to read through my case paperwork." During our few minutes of conversation, Bullet has seen through my act and concluded that I'm educated – a possible resource to him.

I appreciate that he'll accept me if I take the time to read his case. "I'm no jailhouse attorney, but I'll look through it and help you however I can."

"Good. I'll stop by your cell later on, wood."

After breakfast, I seal as many of the cracks in the walls as I can with toothpaste. The cell smells minty, but the cockroaches still find their way in. Their day shift appears to be collecting information on the brown paper bags under my bunk, containing a few items of food that I purchased from the commissary; bags that I tied off with rubber bands in the hope of keeping the cockroaches out. Relentlessly, the cockroaches explore the bags for entry points, pausing over and probing the most worn and vulnerable regions. *Will the nightly swarm eat right through the paper?* I read all morning, wondering whether my cellmate has died in his cocoon, his occasional breathing sounds reassuring me.

Bullet stops by late afternoon and drops his case paperwork off. He's been charged with Class 3 felonies and less, not serious crimes, but is facing a double-digit sentence because of his prior convictions and Security Threat Group status in the prison system. The proposed sentencing range seems disproportionate. I'll advise him to reject the plea bargain – on the assumption he already knows to do so, but is just seeking the comfort of a second opinion, like many un-sentenced inmates. When he returns for his paperwork, our conversation disturbs my cellmate – the cocoon shuffles – so we go upstairs to his cell. I tell Bullet what I think. He is excitable, a different man from earlier, his pupils almost non-existent.

"This case ain't shit. But my prosecutor knows I done other shit, all kinds of heavy shit, but can't prove it. I'd do anything to get that sorry bitch off my fucking ass. She's asking for something bad to happen to her. Man, if I ever get bonded out, I'm gonna chop that bitch into pieces. Kill her slowly though. Like to work her over with a blowtorch."

Such talk can get us both charged with conspiring to murder a prosecutor, so I try to steer him elsewhere. "It's crazy how they can catch you doing one thing, yet try to sentence you for all of the things they think you've ever done."

"Done plenty. Shot some dude in the stomach once. Rolled him up in a blanket and threw him in a dumpster."

Discussing past murders is as unsettling as future ones. "So, what's all your tattoos mean, Bullet? Like that eagle on your chest?"

"Why you wanna know?" Bullet's eyes probe mine.

My eyes hold their ground. "Just curious."

"It's a war bird. The AB patch."

"AB patch?"

"What the Aryan Brotherhood gives you when you've put enough work in."

"How long does it take to earn a patch?"

"Depends how quickly you put your work in. You have to earn your lightning bolts first."

"Why you got red and black lightning bolts?"

"You get SS bolts for beating someone down or for being an enforcer for the family. Red lightning bolts for killing someone.

I was sent down as a youngster. They gave me steel and told me who to handle and I handled it. You don't ask questions. You just get blood on your steel. Dudes who get these tats without putting work in are told to cover them up or leave the yard."

"What if they refuse?"

"They're held down and we carve the ink off them."

Imagining them carving a chunk of flesh to remove a tattoo, I cringe. He's really enjoying telling me this now. His volatile nature is clear and frightening. *He's accepted me too much. He's trying to impress me before making demands.*

At night, I'm unable to sleep. Cocooned in heat, surrounded by cockroaches, I hear the swamp-cooler vent – a metal grid at the top of a wall – hissing out tepid air. Giving up on sleep, I put my earphones on and tune into National Public Radio. Listening to a Vivaldi violin concerto, I close my eyes and press my tailbone down to straighten my back as if I'm doing a yogic relaxation. The playful allegro thrills me, lifting my spirits, but the wistful adagio provokes sad emotions and tears. I open my eyes and gaze into the gloom. Due to lack of sleep, I start hallucinating and hearing voices over the music whispering threats. I'm at breaking point. Although I have accepted that I committed crimes and deserve to be punished, no one should have to live like this. I'm furious at myself for making the series of reckless decisions that put me in here and for losing absolutely everything. As violins crescendo in my ears, I remember what my life used to be like.

PRISON TIME BY SHAUN ATTWOOD

CHAPTER 1

"I've got a padlock in a sock. I can smash your brains in while you're asleep. I can kill you whenever I want." My new cellmate sizes me up with no trace of human feeling in his eyes. Muscular and pot-bellied, he's caked in prison ink, including six snakes on his skull, slithering side by side. The top of his right ear is missing in a semi-circle.

The waves of fear are overwhelming. After being in transportation all day, I can feel my bladder hurting. "I'm not looking to cause any trouble. I'm the quietest cellmate you'll ever have. All I do is read and write."

Scowling, he shakes his head. "Why've they put a fish in with me?" He swaggers close enough for me to smell his cigarette breath. "Us convicts don't get along with fresh fish."

"Should I ask to move then?" I say, hoping he'll agree if he hates new prisoners so much.

"No! They'll think I threatened you!"

In the eight by twelve feet slab of space, I swerve around him and place my property box on the top bunk.

He pushes me aside and grabs the box. "You just put that on my artwork! I ought to fucking smash you, fish!"

"Sorry, I didn't see it."

"You need to be more aware of your fucking surroundings! What you in for anyway, fish?"

I explain my charges, Ecstasy dealing and how I spent twenty-six months fighting my case.

"How come the cops were so hard-core after you?" he asks, squinting.

"It was a big case, a multi-million-dollar investigation. They raided over a hundred people and didn't find any drugs. They were pretty pissed off. I'd stopped dealing by the time they caught up with me, but I'd done plenty over the years, so I accept my punishment."

"Throwing raves," he says, staring at the ceiling as if remembering something. "Were you partying with underage girls?" he asks, his voice slow, coaxing.

Being called a sex offender is the worst insult in prison. Into my third year of incarceration, I'm conditioned to react. "What you trying to say?" I yell angrily, brow clenched.

"Were you fucking underage girls?" Flexing his body, he shakes both fists as if about to punch me.

"Hey, I'm no child molester, and I'd prefer you didn't say shit like that!"

"My buddy next door is doing twenty-five to life for murdering a child molester. How do I know Ecstasy dealing ain't your cover story?" He inhales loudly, nostrils flaring.

"You want to see my fucking paperwork?"

A stocky prisoner walks in. Short hair. Dark eyes. Powerful neck. On one arm: a tattoo of a man in handcuffs above the word OMERTA – the Mafia code of silence towards law enforcement. "What the fuck's going on in here, Bud?" asks Junior Bull – the son of "Sammy the Bull" Gravano, the Mafia mass murderer who was my biggest competitor in the Ecstasy market.

Relieved to see a familiar face, I say, "How're you doing?"

Shaking my hand, he says in a New York Italian accent, "I'm doing alright. I read that shit in the newspaper about you starting a blog in Sheriff Joe Arpaio's jail."

"The blog's been bringing media heat on the conditions."

"You know him?" Bud asks.

"Yeah, from Towers jail. He's a good dude. He's in for dealing Ecstasy like me."

"It's a good job you said that 'cause I was about to smash his ass," Bud says.

"It's a good job Wild Man ain't here 'cause you'd a got your ass thrown off the balcony," Junior Bull says.

I laugh. The presence of my best friend, Wild Man, was partly the reason I never took a beating at the county jail, but with Wild Man in a different prison, I feel vulnerable. When Bud casts a death stare on me, my smile fades.

"What the fuck you guys on about?" Bud asks.

"Let's go talk downstairs." Junior Bull leads Bud out.

I rush to a stainless-steel sink/toilet bolted to a cement-block wall by the front of the cell, unbutton my orange jumpsuit and crane my neck to watch the upper-tier walkway in case Bud returns. I bask in relief as my bladder deflates. After flushing, I take stock of my new home, grateful for the slight improvement in the conditions versus what I'd grown accustomed to in Sheriff Joe Arpaio's jail. No cockroaches. No blood stains. A working swamp cooler. Something I've never seen in a cell before: shelves. The steel table bolted to the wall is slightly larger, too. *But how will I concentrate on writing with Bud around?* There's a mixture of smells in the room. Cleaning chemicals. Aftershave. Tobacco. A vinegar-like odour. The slit of a window at the back overlooks gravel in a no-man's-land before the next building with gleaming curls of razor wire around its roof.

From the doorway upstairs, I'm facing two storeys of cells overlooking a day room with shower cubicles at the end of both tiers. At two white plastic circular tables, prisoners are playing dominoes, cards, chess and Scrabble, some concentrating, others yelling obscenities, contributing to a brain-scraping din that I hope to block out by purchasing a Walkman. In a raised box-shaped Plexiglas control tower, two guards are monitoring the prisoners.

Bud returns. My pulse jumps. Not wanting to feel like I'm stuck in a kennel with a rabid dog, I grab a notepad and pen and head for the day room.

Focussed on my body language, not wanting to signal any weakness, I'm striding along the upper tier, head and chest elevated, when two hands appear from a doorway and grab me. I drop the pad. The pen clinks against grid-metal and tumbles to the day room as I'm pulled into a cell reeking of backside sweat and masturbation, a cheese-tinted funk.

"I'm Booga. Let's fuck," says a squat man in urine-stained boxers, with WHITE TRASH tattooed on his torso below a mobile home, and an arm sleeved with the Virgin Mary.

Shocked, I brace to flee or fight to preserve my anal virginity. I can't believe my eyes when he drops his boxers and waggles his penis.

Dancing to music playing through a speaker he has rigged up, Booga smiles in a sexy way. "Come on," he says in a husky voice. "Drop your pants. Let's fuck." He pulls pornography faces. I question his sanity. He moves closer. "If I let you fart in my mouth, can I fart in yours?"

"You can fuck off," I say, springing towards the doorway.

He grabs me. We scuffle. Every time I make progress towards the doorway, he clings to my clothes, dragging me back in. When I feel his penis rub against my leg, my adrenalin kicks in so forcefully I experience a burst of strength and wriggle free. I bolt out as fast as my shower sandals will allow and snatch my pad. Looking over my shoulder, I see him stood calmly in the doorway, smiling. He points at me. "You have to walk past my door every day. We're gonna get together. I'll lick your ass and you can fart in my mouth." Booga blows a kiss and disappears.

I rush downstairs. With my back to a wall, I pause to steady my thoughts and breathing. In survival mode, I think, *What's going to come at me next?* In the hope of reducing my tension, I borrow a pen to do what helps me stay sane: writing. With the details fresh in my mind, I document my journey to the prison for my blog readers, keeping an eye out in case anyone else wants to test the new prisoner. The more I write, the more I fill with a sense of purpose. Jon's Jail Journal is a connection to the outside world that I cherish.

Someone yells, "One time!" The din lowers. A door rumbles open. A guard does a security walk, his every move scrutinised by dozens of scornful eyes staring from cells. When he exits, the din resumes, and the prisoners return to injecting drugs to escape from reality, including the length of their sentences. This continues all day with "Two times!" signifying two approaching guards, and "Three times!" three and so on. Every now and then an announcement by a guard over the speakers briefly lowers the din.

Before lockdown, I join the line for a shower, holding bars of soap in a towel that I aim to swing at the head of the next person to try me. With boisterous inmates a few feet away, yelling at the men in the showers to "Stop jerking off," and "Hurry the fuck up," I get in a cubicle that reeks of bleach and mildew. With every nerve strained, I undress and rinse fast.

At night, despite the desert heat, I cocoon myself in a blanket from head to toe and turn towards the wall, making my face more difficult to strike. I leave a hole for air, but the warm cement block inches from my mouth returns each exhalation to my face as if it's breathing on me, creating a feeling of suffocation. For hours, my heart drums so hard against the thin mattress I feel as if I'm moving even though I'm still. I try to sleep, but my eyes keep springing open and my head turning towards the cell as I try to penetrate the darkness, searching for Bud swinging a padlock in a sock at my head.

ABOUT THE AUTHOR

Shaun Attwood is a former stock-market millionaire and Ecstasy trafficker turned YouTuber, public speaker, author and activist, who is banned from America for life. His story was featured worldwide on National Geographic Channel as an episode of Locked Up/Banged Up Abroad called Raving Arizona.

Shaun's writing – smuggled out of the jail with the highest death rate in America run by Sheriff Joe Arpaio – attracted international media attention to the human rights violations: murders by guards and gang members, dead rats in the food, cockroach infestations…

While incarcerated, Shaun was forced to reappraise his life. He read over 1,000 books in just under six years. By studying original texts in psychology and philosophy, he sought to better understand himself and his past behaviour. He credits books as being the lifeblood of his rehabilitation.

Shaun tells his story to schools to dissuade young people from drugs and crime. He campaigns against injustice via his books and blog, Jon's Jail Journal. He has appeared on the BBC, Sky News and TV worldwide to talk about issues affecting prisoners' rights.

As a best-selling true-crime author, Shaun has written a series of action-packed books exposing the War on Drugs, which feature the CIA, Pablo Escobar and the cocaine Mafia. He has also written the longest ever Escobar biography: *Pablo Escobar's Story*, a 3-book series with over 1,000 pages. On his true-crime podcast on YouTube, Shaun interviews people with hard-hitting crime stories and harrowing prison experiences.

www.ingramcontent.com/pod-product-compliance
Lightning Source LLC
Chambersburg PA
CBHW030254100526
44590CB00012B/399